Hands-On C+ Game Animation Programming

Learn modern animation techniques from theory to implementation with C++ and OpenGL

Gabor Szauer

BIRMINGHAM—MUMBAI

Hands-On C++ Game Animation Programming

Commissioning Editor: Pavan Ramchandani
Acquisition Editor: Ashwin Nair
Senior Editor: Hayden Edwards
Content Development Editor: Akhil Nair, Aamir Ahmed
Technical Editor: Deepesh Patel
Copy Editor: Safis Editing
Project Coordinator: Kinjal Bari
Proofreader: Safis Editing
Indexer: Pratik Shirodkar
Production Designer: Jyoti Chauhan

First published: June 2020
Production reference: 1110620

Published by Packt Publishing Ltd.
Livery Place
35 Livery Street
Birmingham
B3 2PB, UK.

ISBN 978-1-80020-808-7

www.packt.com

Packt.com

Subscribe to our online digital library for full access to over 7,000 books and videos, as well as industry leading tools to help you plan your personal development and advance your career. For more information, please visit our website.

Why subscribe?

- Spend less time learning and more time coding with practical eBooks and Videos from over 4,000 industry professionals

- Improve your learning with Skill Plans built especially for you

- Get a free eBook or video every month

- Fully searchable for easy access to vital information

- Copy and paste, print, and bookmark content

Did you know that Packt offers eBook versions of every book published, with PDF and ePub files available? You can upgrade to the eBook version at packt.com and as a print book customer, you are entitled to a discount on the eBook copy. Get in touch with us at customercare@packtpub.com for more details.

At www.packt.com, you can also read a collection of free technical articles, sign up for a range of free newsletters, and receive exclusive discounts and offers on Packt books and eBooks.

Contributors

About the author

Gabor Szauer has been making games since 2010. He graduated from Full Sail University in 2010 with a bachelor's degree in game development. Gabor maintains an active Twitter presence, @gszauer, and maintains a programming-oriented game development blog: gabormakesgames.com. Gabor's previously published books are *Game Physics Programming Cookbook* and *Lua Quick Start Guide*, both published by Packt.

About the reviewer

Pedro Sousa is your typical software engineer by day, but at night he goes by the name SketchPunk as he develops various open source projects – basically whatever tickles his fancy at any given moment. Being self-taught in many areas of software development and having a pure love of art has given him a good amount of success in his career since he's able to balance writing good software with splashing a beautiful coat of paint over it.

In the last 3 years, Pedro has spent a great deal of time developing a game engine from scratch and, along the way, creating YouTube tutorials of all the nuts and bolts so that others can learn and follow in his footsteps. He has a strong belief that knowledge should be free and shared with all who want to learn.

Packt is searching for authors like you

If you're interested in becoming an author for Packt, please visit `authors.packtpub.com` and apply today. We have worked with thousands of developers and tech professionals, just like you, to help them share their insight with the global tech community. You can make a general application, apply for a specific hot topic that we are recruiting an author for, or submit your own idea.

Table of Contents

3
Implementing Matrices

4
Implementing Quaternions

5
Implementing Transforms

8
Creating Curves, Frames, and Tracks

9
Implementing Animation Clips

10
Mesh Skinning

11
Optimizing the Animation Pipeline

12
Blending between Animations

13
Implementing Inverse Kinematics

14

Using Dual Quaternions for Skinning

15

Rendering Instanced Crowds

Other Books You May Enjoy

Preface

Modern game animation is a bit of a black art. There are not many resources available that detail how to build a track-driven animation system, or advanced topics such as dual quaternion skinning. That is the void this book aims to fill. The goal of this book is to shed some light on the black art of animation programming and make the topic approachable for everyone.

This book takes a "theory to implementation" approach, where you will learn the theory of each topic discussed first. Once you understand the theory, you will implement it to get hands-on experience.

This book makes it a point to focus on the concepts and implementation details of animation programming, not the language or graphics API being used. By focusing on these fundamental concepts, you will be able to implement an animation system regardless of language or graphics API.

Who this book is for

This book is for programmers who want to learn how to build a modern animation system. The only requirement for following along with this book is some familiarity with C++. Other than that, everything is covered, from how to open a new window, to creating an OpenGL context, rendering an animated model, and advanced animation techniques.

What this book covers

Chapter 1, Creating a Game Window, explains how to create a new visual studio project, create a Win32 window, set up an OpenGL 3.3 render context, and enable vsynch. The code samples for this book are compiled against OpenGL 3.3. All the OpenGL code is compatible with the latest version of OpenGL and OpenGL 4.6.

Chapter 2, Implementing Vectors, covers vector math for game animation programming.

Chapter 3, Implementing Matrices, discusses matrix math for game animation programming.

Chapter 4, Implementing Quaternions, explains how to use quaternion math for game animation programming.

Chapter 5, Implementing Transforms, explains how to combine position, rotation, and scale into a transform object. These transform objects can be arranged in a hierarchy.

Chapter 6, Building an Abstract Renderer, shows you how to create an abstraction layer on top of OpenGL 3.3. The rest of this book will use this abstraction for rendering. By using an abstraction, we can focus on the core concepts of animation programming instead of the API being used to implement it. The abstraction layer targets OpenGL 3.3, but the code is valid with OpenGL 4.6 as well.

Chapter 7, Understanding the glTF File Format, introduces the glTF file format. glTF is a standard open file format that is supported by most 3D content creation tools. Being able to load a common format will let you load animation authored in almost any creation tool.

Chapter 8 Creating Curves, Frames, and Tracks, covers how to interpolate curves and how cruces can be used to animate transforms stored in a hierarchy.

Chapter 9, Implementing Animation Clips, explains how to implement animation clips. Animation clips modify a transform hierarchy over time.

Chapter 10, Mesh Skinning, covers how to deform a mesh so that it matches the pose generated by sampling an animation clip.

Chapter 11, Optimizing the Animation Pipeline, shows you how to optimize parts of the animation pipeline to make it faster and more production-ready.

Chapter 12, Blending between Animations, explains how to blend two animated poses together. This technique can be used to switch between two animations smoothly, without any visual popping.

Chapter 13, Implementing Inverse Kinematics, covers how to use inverse kinematics to make animations interact with the environment. For example, you'll learn how to make an animated character's foot not penetrate the ground on uneven terrain.

Chapter 14, Using Dual Quaternions for Skinning, covers dual quaternion math for game animation. Dual quaternions can be used to avoid pinching at animated joints.

Chapter 15, Rendering Instanced Crowds, shows how to encode animation data to a texture and move pose generation into a vertex shader. You will use this technique to render a large crowd using instancing.

To get the most out of this book

To get the most out of this book, some experience with C++ is expected. You don't have to be a hardened C++ master, but you should be able to debug simple C++ problems. Having some experience with OpenGL is a plus, but not required. No advanced C++ features are used. The provided code compiles against C++ 11 or the most recent version.

The code in this book is written against OpenGL 3.3 Core. The OpenGL code presented in this book is forward compatible; the highest compatible version of OpenGL at the time of publishing is 4.6. In Chapter 6, Building an Abstract Renderer, you will implement a thin abstraction layer on top of OpenGL. Throughout the rest of the book, you will be coding against this abstraction layer, rather than OpenGL directly.

The code presented should compile and run on just about any laptop running Windows 10 or a more recent version. The only hardware requirement to follow along with this book is access to a computer that can run Visual Studio 2019 or a more recent version.

The minimum hardware requirements for Visual Studio 2019 are:

- Windows 10, version 1703 or higher

- 1.8 Ghz or a faster processor

- 2GB of RAM

These requirements can be found online at: `https://docs.microsoft.com/en-us/visualstudio/releases/2019/system-requirements`

Download the example code files

You can download the example code files for this book from your account at `http://www.packt.com`. If you purchased this book elsewhere, you can visit `http://www.packt.com/support` and register to have the files emailed directly to you.

You can download the code files by following these steps:

1. Log in or register at `http://www.packt.com`.

2. Select the SUPPORT tab.

3. Click on Code Downloads & Errata.

4. Enter the name of the book in the Search box and follow the on-screen instructions.

Once the file is downloaded, please make sure that you unzip or extract the folder using the latest version of:

- WinRAR/7-Zip for Windows
- Zipeg/iZip / UnRarX for Mac
- 7-Zip/PeaZip for Linux

The code bundle for the book is also hosted on GitHub at https://github.com/PacktPublishing/Game-Animation-Programming. In case there's an update to the code, it will be updated on the existing GitHub repository.

We also have other code bundles from our rich catalog of books and videos available at https://github.com/PacktPublishing/. Check them out!

Conventions used

There are a number of text conventions used throughout this book.

CodeInText: Indicates code words in text, database table names, folder names, filenames, file extensions, pathnames, dummy URLs, user input, and Twitter handles. For example; "Mount the downloaded WebStorm-10*.dmg disk image file as another disk in your system."

A block of code is set as follows:

```
public:
    Pose();
    Pose(const Pose& p);
    Pose& operator=(const Pose& p);
    Pose(unsigned int numJoints);
```

Any command-line input or output is written as follows:

```
# cp /usr/src/asterisk-addons/configs/cdr_mysql.conf.sample
    /etc/asterisk/cdr_mysql.conf
```

Bold: Indicates a new term, an important word, or words that you see on the screen, for example, in menus or dialog boxes, also appear in the text like this. For example: "Select **System info** from the Administration panel."

> **Note**
>
> Warnings or important notes appear like this.
>
> Tips and tricks appear like this.

Get in touch

Feedback from our readers is always welcome.

General feedback: If you have questions about any aspect of this book, mention the book title in the subject of your message and email us at customercare@packtpub.com.

Get in touch with the author: The best way to get in touch with Gabor, the book's author, is on Twitter: @gszauer.

Errata: Although we have taken every care to ensure the accuracy of our content, mistakes do happen. If you have found a mistake in this book, we would be grateful if you would report this to us. Please visit, http://www.packt.com/submit-errata, selecting your book, clicking on the Errata Submission Form link, and entering the details.

Piracy: If you come across any illegal copies of our works in any form on the Internet, we would be grateful if you would provide us with the location address or website name. Please contact us at copyright@packt.com with a link to the material.

If you are interested in becoming an author: If there is a topic that you have expertise in and you are interested in either writing or contributing to a book, please visit http://authors.packtpub.com.

Reviews

Please leave a review. Once you have read and used this book, why not leave a review on the site that you purchased it from? Potential readers can then see and use your unbiased opinion to make purchase decisions, we at Packt can understand what you think about our products, and our authors can see your feedback on their book. Thank you!

For more information about Packt, please visit packt.com.

1
Creating a Game Window

In this chapter, you will set up a simple Win32 window and bind an OpenGL context to it. You will be using OpenGL 3.3 Core throughout this book. The actual OpenGL code is going to be very minimal.

Most OpenGL-specific code will be abstracted into helper objects and functions, which will allow you to focus on animation rather than any specific graphics APIs. You will write the abstraction layer in *Chapter 6, Building an Abstract Renderer*, but for now, it's important to create a window ready to be drawn to.

By the end of this chapter, you should be able to do the following:

- Open a Win32 window
- Create and bind an OpenGL 3.3 Core context
- Use glad to load OpenGL 3.3 Core functions
- Enable vsynch for the created window
- Understand the downloadable samples for this book

Technical requirements

To follow along with the code in this book, you will need a computer running Windows 10 with a recent version of Visual Studio installed. All of the downloadable code samples are built using Visual Studio 2019. You can download Visual Studio from `https://visualstudio.microsoft.com/`.

You can find all of the sample code for the book on GitHub at `https://github.com/PacktPublishing/Game-Animation-Programming`.

Creating an empty project

Throughout this book, you will be creating code from scratch as much as possible. Because of this, there will be very few external dependencies. To get started, follow these steps to create a new blank C++ project in Visual Studio:

1. Open Visual Studio and create a new project by going to **File|New|Project**:

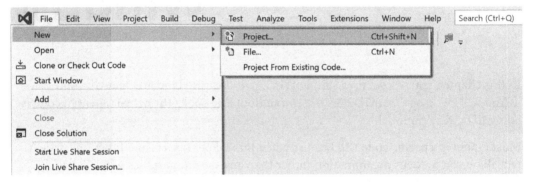

Figure 1.1: Creating a new Visual Studio project

2. You will see your project templates on the left-hand side of the window that pops up. Navigate to **Installed|Visual C++|Other**. Then, select **Empty Project**:

Figure 1.2: Creating an empty C++ project

3. Enter a project name and select a project location. Finally, click **Create**.

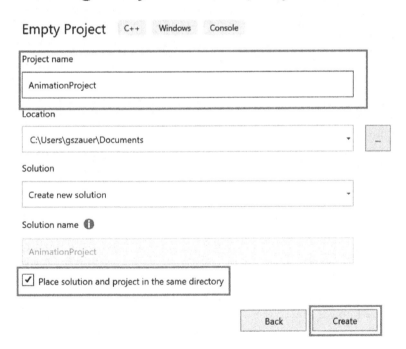

Figure 1.3: Specifying a new project name

If you have followed the preceding steps, you should have a new blank project. Throughout the rest of this chapter, you will add an application framework and an OpenGL-enabled window.

Creating the application class

It would be difficult to maintain a cluttered window entry function. Instead, you need to create an abstract Application class. This class will contain some basic functions, such as Initialize, Update, Render, and Shutdown. All of the code samples provided for this book will be built on top of the Application base class.

Create a new file, Application.h. The declaration of the Application class is provided in the following code sample. Add this declaration to the newly created Application.h file:

```
#ifndef _H_APPLICATION_
#define _H_APPLICATION_

class Application {
private:
    Application(const Application&);
    Application& operator=(const Application&);
public:
    inline Application() { }
    inline virtual ~Application() { }
    inline virtual void Initialize() { }
    inline virtual void Update(float inDeltaTime) { }
    inline virtual void Render(float inAspectRatio) { }
    inline virtual void Shutdown() { }
};

#endif
```

The Initialize, Update, Render, and Shutdown functions are the life cycle of an application. All these functions will be called directly from the Win32 window code. Update and Render take arguments. To update a frame, the delta time between the current and last frame needs to be known. To render a frame, the aspect ratio of the window must be known.

The life cycle functions are virtual. Each chapter in the downloadable materials for this book has an example that is a subclass of the `Application` class that demonstrates a concept from that chapter.

Next, you will be adding an OpenGL loader to the project.

Adding an OpenGL loader

There is some external code that this chapter depends on, called `glad`. When you create a new OpenGL context on Windows, it's created with a legacy OpenGL context. The extension mechanism of OpenGL will let you use this legacy context to create a new modern context.

Once the modern context is created, you will need to get function pointers to all OpenGL functions. The functions need to be loaded with `wglGetProcAdress`, which returns a function pointer.

Loading every OpenGL function in this fashion would be very time-consuming. This is where having an OpenGL loader comes in; `glad` will do all this work for you. An OpenGL loader is a library or some code that calls `wglGetProcAdress` on the functions that the OpenGL API defines.

There are several OpenGL loaders available on Windows.; this book will use `glad`. `glad` is a small library that consists of only a few files. It has a simple API; you call one function and get access to all the OpenGL functions. `glad` has a web-based interface; you can find it at `https://glad.dav1d.de/`.

Important note

When using an X Windows system, such as many popular Linux distributions, the function to load OpenGL functions is `glXGetProcAddress`. As with Windows, there are OpenGL loaders available for Linux as well. Not all OSes need an OpenGL loader; for example, macOS, iOS, and Android don't need a loader. Both iOS and Android run on OpenGL ES.

Getting glad

You can get `glad` from `https://glad.dav1d.de/`, a web-based generator:

1. Go to the site, select **Version 3.3** from the **gl** dropdown, and select **Core** from the **Profile** dropdown:

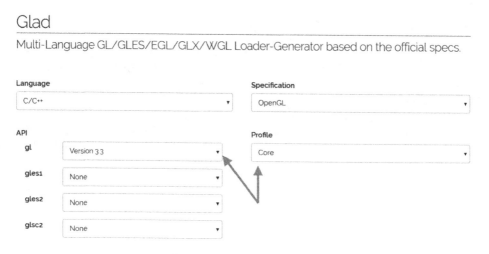

Figure 1.4: Configuring glad

2. Scroll to the bottom and hit the **Generate** button. This should start downloading a ZIP file that contains all of the required code.

The code presented in this book is forward compatible with OpenGL version 3.3 or a more recent version. If you want to use a newer OpenGL version, such as 4.6, change the gl dropdown under API to the desired version. You will be adding the contents of this ZIP file to your main project in the next section.

Adding glad to the project

Once `glad.zip` is downloaded, extract its contents. Add the following files from the ZIP file to your project. The directory structure does not need to be maintained; all of these files can be placed next to each other:

- `src/glad.c`
- `include/glad/glad.h`
- `include/KHR/khrplatform.h`

These files will be included as normal project files—you don't have to set up `include` paths—but that does mean that the contents of the files need to be edited:

1. Open `glad.c` and find the following #include:

   ```
   #include <glad/glad.h>
   ```

2. Replace the `include` path with the relative path of `glad.h`:

   ```
   #include "glad.h"
   ```

3. Similarly, open `glad.h` and find the following #include:

   ```
   #include <KHR/khrplatform.h>
   ```

4. Replace the `include` path with the relative path of `khrplatform.h`:

   ```
   #include "khrplatform.h"
   ```

`glad` should now be added to the project and there should be no compilation errors. In the next section, you will start implementing the Win32 window.

Creating a window

In this section, you will create a window. This means you will be using Win32 API calls directly to open a window and control its life cycle from code. You will also set up a debug console that can run alongside the window, which is useful for viewing logs.

> **Important note**
>
> An in-depth discussion of the Win32 API is beyond the scope of this book. For additional information on any of the Win32 APIs, refer to the Microsoft Developers Network (MSDN) at `https://docs.microsoft.com/en-us/windows/win32/api/`.

To make logging a bit easier, two windows will be open at the same time in debug mode. One will be the standard Win32 window, and the other will be a console window for viewing logs. This can be achieved by setting the linker conditionally. In debug mode, the application should link to the console subsystem. In release mode, it should link to the window subsystem.

Setting the linker subsystem can be done through the project's properties or in code using a #pragma comment. Once the subsystem is set to the console, the `WinMain` function can be called from `main`, which will launch a window that is attached to the console.

Additional linker actions, such as linking to external libraries, can be done from code, too. You will be using a #pragma command to link with OpenGL.

Start the window implementation by creating a new file, WinMain.cpp. This file will contain all of the window logic. Then, do the following:

1. Add the following code to the beginning of the file. It creates #define constants that reduce the amount of code that is brought in by including <windows.h>:

    ```
    #define _CRT_SECURE_NO_WARNINGS
    #define WIN32_LEAN_AND_MEAN
    #define WIN32_EXTRA_LEAN

    #include "glad.h"
    #include <windows.h>
    #include <iostream>
    #include "Application.h"
    ```

2. The window entry function and the window event processing function both need to be forward declared. These are the two Win32 functions that we will need to open a new window:

    ```
    int WINAPI WinMain(HINSTANCE, HINSTANCE, PSTR, int);
    LRESULT CALLBACK WndProc(HWND, UINT, WPARAM, LPARAM);
    ```

3. Use a #pragma comment to link to OpenGL32.lib in code, rather than going through the project's properties window. Add the following code to WinMain.cpp:

    ```
    #if _DEBUG
        #pragma comment( linker, "/subsystem:console" )
        int main(int argc, const char** argv) {
            return WinMain(GetModuleHandle(NULL), NULL,
                    GetCommandLineA(), SW_SHOWDEFAULT);
        }
    #else
        #pragma comment( linker, "/subsystem:windows" )
    #endif
    #pragma comment(lib, "opengl32.lib")
    ```

Now, a few OpenGL functions need to be declared. Creating a modern OpenGL context is done through wglCreateContextAttribsARB, but there is no reference to this function. This is one of the functions that needs to be loaded through wglGetProcAddress, as it's an extension function.

The function signature of `wglCreateContextAttribsARB` can be found in `wglext.h`. The `wglext.h` header is hosted by Khronos and can be found online in the OpenGL registry at `https://www.khronos.org/registry/OpenGL/index_gl.php`.

There is no need to include the entire `wglext.h` header file; you will only need the function relevant to creating a modern context. The following code is directly copied from the file. It contains the declarations for the relevant `#define` constants and the function pointer types:

```
#define WGL_CONTEXT_MAJOR_VERSION_ARB        0x2091
#define WGL_CONTEXT_MINOR_VERSION_ARB        0x2092
#define WGL_CONTEXT_FLAGS_ARB                0x2094
#define WGL_CONTEXT_CORE_PROFILE_BIT_ARB     0x00000001
#define WGL_CONTEXT_PROFILE_MASK_ARB         0x9126
typedef HGLRC(WINAPI* PFNWGLCREATECONTEXTATTRIBSARBPROC)
             (HDC, HGLRC, const int*);
```

The previous code defines a function pointer type for `wglCreatecontextAttribsARB`. In addition to this, there are `#define` constants that are needed to make an OpenGL 3.3 Core context. The samples for this book will have `vsynch` enabled, which can be done through `wglSwapIntervalEXT`.

As you will guess, this function needs to be loaded using OpenGL's extension mechanism, too. It also needs two additional support functions: `wglGetExtensionStringEXT` and `wglGetSwapIntervalEXT`. All three of these functions are found in `wgl.h`, which is hosted by Khronos in the OpenGL registry linked previously.

Instead of including `wgl.h`, add the following code to `WinMain.cpp`. The code defines function pointer signatures for `wglGetExtensionStringEXT`, `wglSwapIntervalEXT`, and `wglGetSwapIntervalEXT`, copied out of `wgl.h`:

```
typedef const char*
        (WINAPI* PFNWGLGETEXTENSIONSSTRINGEXTPROC) (void);
typedef BOOL(WINAPI* PFNWGLSWAPINTERVALEXTPROC) (int);
typedef int (WINAPI* PFNWGLGETSWAPINTERVALEXTPROC) (void);
```

The preceding code is required to work with OpenGL. It's common to copy the code instead of including these headers directly. In the next section, you will begin working on the actual window.

Global variables

Two global variables are required for easy window cleanup: a pointer to the currently running application and a handle to the global OpenGL **Vertex Array Object (VAO)**. Instead of each draw call having its own VAO, one will be bound for the entire duration of the sample.

To do this, create the following global variables:

```
Application* gApplication = 0;
GLuint gVertexArrayObject = 0;
```

Throughout the rest of this book, there will be no other global variables. Global variables can make the program state harder to track. The reason these two exist is to easily reference them when the application is shutting down later. Next, you will start implementing the WinMain function to open a new window.

Opening a window

Next, you need to implement the window entry function, WinMain. This function will be responsible for creating a window class, registering the window class, and opening a new window:

1. Start the definition of WinMain by creating a new instance of the Application class and storing it in the global pointer:

   ```
   int WINAPI WinMain(HINSTANCE hInstance, HINSTANCE
                      hPrevInstance, PSTR szCmdLine,
                      int iCmdShow) {
   gApplication = new Application();
   ```

2. Next, an instance of WNDCLASSEX needs to be filled out. There isn't anything special that goes into this; it's just a standard window definition. The only thing to look out for is whether the WndProc function is set correctly:

   ```
   WNDCLASSEX wndclass;
   wndclass.cbSize = sizeof(WNDCLASSEX);
   wndclass.style = CS_HREDRAW | CS_VREDRAW;
   wndclass.lpfnWndProc = WndProc;
   wndclass.cbClsExtra = 0;
   wndclass.cbWndExtra = 0;
   wndclass.hInstance = hInstance;
   wndclass.hIcon = LoadIcon(NULL, IDI_APPLICATION);
   wndclass.hIconSm = LoadIcon(NULL, IDI_APPLICATION);
   wndclass.hCursor = LoadCursor(NULL, IDC_ARROW);
   ```

```
wndclass.hbrBackground = (HBRUSH)(COLOR_BTNFACE + 1);
wndclass.lpszMenuName = 0;
wndclass.lpszClassName = "Win32 Game Window";
RegisterClassEx(&wndclass);
```

3. A new application window should launch in the center of the monitor. To do this, find the width and height of the screen using `GetSystemMetrics`. Then, adjust `windowRect` to the desired size around the center of the screen:

```
int screenWidth = GetSystemMetrics(SM_CXSCREEN);
int screenHeight = GetSystemMetrics(SM_CYSCREEN);
int clientWidth = 800;
int clientHeight = 600;
RECT windowRect;
SetRect(&windowRect,
        (screenWidth / 2) - (clientWidth / 2),
        (screenHeight / 2) - (clientHeight / 2),
        (screenWidth / 2) + (clientWidth / 2),
        (screenHeight / 2) + (clientHeight / 2));
```

4. To figure out the size of the window, not just the client area, the style of the window needs to be known. The following code sample creates a window that can be minimized or maximized but not resized. To resize the window, use a bitwise OR (`|`) operator with the `WS_THICKFRAME` defined:

```
DWORD style = (WS_OVERLAPPED | WS_CAPTION |
    WS_SYSMENU | WS_MINIMIZEBOX | WS_MAXIMIZEBOX);
// | WS_THICKFRAME to resize
```

5. Once the desired window style is defined, call the `AdjustWindowRectEx` function to adjust the size of the client rectangle to include all the window dressing in its size as well. When the final size is known, `CreateWindowEx` can be used to create the actual window. Once the window is created, store a reference to its device context:

```
AdjustWindowRectEx(&windowRect, style, FALSE, 0);
HWND hwnd = CreateWindowEx(0, wndclass.lpszClassName,
            "Game Window", style, windowRect.left,
            windowRect.top, windowRect.right -
            windowRect.left, windowRect.bottom -
            windowRect.top, NULL, NULL,
            hInstance, szCmdLine);
HDC hdc = GetDC(hwnd);
```

6. Now that the window is created, you will next create an OpenGL context. To do this, you first need to find the correct pixel format, and then apply it to the device context of the window. The following code shows you how to do this:

```
PIXELFORMATDESCRIPTOR pfd;
memset(&pfd, 0, sizeof(PIXELFORMATDESCRIPTOR));
pfd.nSize = sizeof(PIXELFORMATDESCRIPTOR);
pfd.nVersion = 1;
pfd.dwFlags = PFD_SUPPORT_OPENGL | PFD_DRAW_TO_WINDOW
              | PFD_DOUBLEBUFFER;
pfd.iPixelType = PFD_TYPE_RGBA;
pfd.cColorBits = 24;
pfd.cDepthBits = 32;
pfd.cStencilBits = 8;
pfd.iLayerType = PFD_MAIN_PLANE;
int pixelFormat = ChoosePixelFormat(hdc, &pfd);
SetPixelFormat(hdc, pixelFormat, &pfd);
```

7. With the pixel format set, create a temporary OpenGL context using `wglCreateContext`. This temporary context is only needed to get a pointer to `wglCreateContextAttribsARB`, which will be used to create a modern context:

```
HGLRC tempRC = wglCreateContext(hdc);
wglMakeCurrent(hdc, tempRC);
PFNWGLCREATECONTEXTATTRIBSARBPROC
   wglCreateContextAttribsARB = NULL;
wglCreateContextAttribsARB =
   (PFNWGLCREATECONTEXTATTRIBSARBPROC)
   wglGetProcAddress("wglCreateContextAttribsARB");
```

8. A temporary OpenGL context exists and is bound, so call the `wglCreateContextAttribsARB` function next. This function will return an OpenGL 3.3 Core context profile, bind it, and delete the legacy context:

```
const int attribList[] = {
    WGL_CONTEXT_MAJOR_VERSION_ARB, 3,
    WGL_CONTEXT_MINOR_VERSION_ARB, 3,
    WGL_CONTEXT_FLAGS_ARB, 0,
    WGL_CONTEXT_PROFILE_MASK_ARB,
    WGL_CONTEXT_CORE_PROFILE_BIT_ARB,
    0, };
HGLRC hglrc = wglCreateContextAttribsARB(
                hdc, 0, attribList);
```

```
wglMakeCurrent(NULL, NULL);
wglDeleteContext(tempRC);
wglMakeCurrent(hdc, hglrc);
```

9. With an OpenGL 3.3 Core context active, `glad` can be used to load all the OpenGL 3.3 Core functions. Call `gladLoadGL` to do this:

```
if (!gladLoadGL()) {
    std::cout << "Could not initialize GLAD\n";
}
else {
    std::cout << "OpenGL Version " <<
    GLVersion.major << "." << GLVersion.minor <<
      "\n";
}
```

10. An OpenGL 3.3 Core context should now be initialized, with all of the core OpenGL functions loaded. Next, you will enable `vsynch` on the window. `vsynch` is not a built-in function; it's an extension and, as such, support for it needs to be queried with `wglGetExtensionStringEXT`. The extension string for `vsynch` is `WGL_EXT_swap_control`. Check whether this is in the list of extension strings:

```
PFNWGLGETEXTENSIONSSTRINGEXTPROC
  _wglGetExtensionsStringEXT =
  (PFNWGLGETEXTENSIONSSTRINGEXTPROC)
  wglGetProcAddress("wglGetExtensionsStringEXT");
bool swapControlSupported = strstr(
  _wglGetExtensionsStringEXT(),
  "WGL_EXT_swap_control") != 0;
```

11. If the `WGL_EXT_swap_control` extension is available, it needs to be loaded. The actual function is `wglSwapIntervalEXT`, which can be found in `wgl.h`. Passing an argument to `wglSwapIntervalEXT` turns on `vsynch`:

```
int vsynch = 0;
if (swapControlSupported) {
    PFNWGLSWAPINTERVALEXTPROC wglSwapIntervalEXT =
        (PFNWGLSWAPINTERVALEXTPROC)
        wglGetProcAddress("wglSwapIntervalEXT");
    PFNWGLGETSWAPINTERVALEXTPROC
        wglGetSwapIntervalEXT =
        (PFNWGLGETSWAPINTERVALEXTPROC)
        wglGetProcAddress("wglGetSwapIntervalEXT");
    if (wglSwapIntervalEXT(1)) {
```

```
        std::cout << "Enabled vsynch\n";
        vsynch = wglGetSwapIntervalEXT();
    }
    else {
        std::cout << "Could not enable vsynch\n";
    }
}
else { // !swapControlSupported
    cout << "WGL_EXT_swap_control not supported\n";
}
```

12. There is just a little bit more housekeeping to do to finish setting up an OpenGL-enabled window. OpenGL 3.3 Core requires a VAO to be bound for all draw calls. Instead of creating a VAO for each draw call, you will create one global VAO that is bound in WinMain and never unbound until the window is destroyed. The following code creates this VAO and binds it:

```
glGenVertexArrays(1, &gVertexArrayObject);
glBindVertexArray(gVertexArrayObject);
```

13. Call the ShowWindow and UpdateWindow functions to display the current window; this is also a good place to initialize the global application. Depending on the amount of work that the application's Initialize function ends up doing, the window may appear frozen for a little bit:

```
ShowWindow(hwnd, SW_SHOW);
UpdateWindow(hwnd);
gApplication->Initialize();
```

14. You're now ready to implement the actual game loop. You will need to keep track of the last frame time to calculate the delta time between frames. In addition to game logic, the loop needs to handle window events by peeking at the current message stack and dispatching messages accordingly:

```
DWORD lastTick = GetTickCount();
MSG msg;
while (true) {
    if (PeekMessage(&msg, NULL, 0, 0, PM_REMOVE)) {
        if (msg.message == WM_QUIT) {
            break;
        }
        TranslateMessage(&msg);
        DispatchMessage(&msg);
    }
```

15. After the window events are processed, the `Application` instance needs to update and render. First, find the delta time between the last frame and this one, converting it into seconds. For example, a game that's running at 60 FPS should have a delta time of 16.6 milliseconds, or 0.0166 seconds:

```
DWORD thisTick = GetTickCount();
float dt = float(thisTick - lastTick) * 0.001f;
lastTick = thisTick;
if (gApplication != 0) {
    gApplication->Update(dt);
}
```

16. Rendering the currently running application needs just a little bit more housekeeping. Set the OpenGL viewport with `glViewport` every frame and clear the color, depth, and stencil buffer. In addition to this, make sure all OpenGL states are correct before rendering. This means that the correct VAO is bound, depth test and face culling are enabled, and the appropriate point size is set:

```
if (gApplication != 0) {
    RECT clientRect;
    GetClientRect(hwnd, &clientRect);
    clientWidth = clientRect.right -
                  clientRect.left;
    clientHeight = clientRect.bottom -
                   clientRect.top;

    glViewport(0, 0, clientWidth, clientHeight);
    glEnable(GL_DEPTH_TEST);
    glEnable(GL_CULL_FACE);
    glPointSize(5.0f);
    glBindVertexArray(gVertexArrayObject);

    glClearColor(0.5f, 0.6f, 0.7f, 1.0f);
    glClear(GL_COLOR_BUFFER_BIT |
    GL_DEPTH_BUFFER_BIT | GL_STENCIL_BUFFER_BIT);

    float aspect = (float)clientWidth /
                   (float)clientHeight;
    gApplication->Render(aspect);
}
```

17. After the current `Application` instance has updated and rendered, the back buffer needs to be presented. This is done by calling `SwapBuffers`. If `vsynch` is enabled, `glFinish` needs to be called right after `SwapBuffers`:

```
if (gApplication != 0) {
    SwapBuffers(hdc);
    if (vsynch != 0) {
        glFinish();
    }
}
```

18. That's it for the window loop. After the window loop exits, it's safe to return from the `WinMain` function:

```
} // End of game loop

if (gApplication != 0) {
    std::cout << "Expected application to
                    be null on exit\n";
    delete gApplication;
}

return (int)msg.wParam;
}
```

If you want to use a version of OpenGL other than 3.3, adjust the major and minor values in the `attribList` variable presented in Step 8. Even though the `WinMain` function is written, you still can't compile this file; it would fail because `WndProc` was never defined. The `WndProc` function handles events such as mouse motion or resizing for a window. In the next section, you will implement the `WndProc` function.

Creating the event handler

In order to have a properly functioning window, or to even compile the application, at this point, the event processing function, `WndProc`, must be defined. The implementation here will be very simple, mostly focusing on how to destroy the window:

1. Start implementing the `WndProc` function in `WinMain.cpp`:

```
LRESULT CALLBACK WndProc(HWND hwnd, UINT iMsg,
                    WPARAM wParam, LPARAM lParam) {
    switch (iMsg) {
```

2. When the `WM_CLOSE` message is received, you need to shut down the `Application` class and emit a destroy window message. Once the application is shut down, don't forget to delete it:

```
case WM_CLOSE:
    if (gApplication != 0) {
        gApplication->Shutdown();
        delete gApplication;
        gApplication = 0;
        DestroyWindow(hwnd);
    }
    else {
        std::cout << "Already shut down!\n";
    }
    break;
```

3. When the destroy message is received, the window's OpenGL resources need to be released. This means deleting the global vertex array object, and then deleting the OpenGL context:

```
case WM_DESTROY:
    if (gVertexArrayObject != 0) {
        HDC hdc = GetDC(hwnd);
        HGLRC hglrc = wglGetCurrentContext();

        glBindVertexArray(0);
        glDeleteVertexArrays(1, &gVertexArrayObject);
        gVertexArrayObject = 0;

        wglMakeCurrent(NULL, NULL);
        wglDeleteContext(hglrc);
        ReleaseDC(hwnd, hdc);

        PostQuitMessage(0);
    }
    else {
        std::cout << "Multiple destroy messages\n";
    }
    break;
```

4. The paint and erase background messages are safe to ignore since OpenGL is managing rendering to the window. If the message received isn't one of the messages already handled, forward it to the default window message function:

```
case WM_PAINT:
case WM_ERASEBKGND:
    return 0;
}

return DefWindowProc(hwnd, iMsg, wParam, lParam);
}
```

Now that you have written the windows event loop, you should be able to compile and run a blank window. In the following section, you'll explore the downloadable samples for this book.

Exploring the samples

All of the code presented in this book is available in the downloadable content for the book. There is one large sample, called AllChapters, which includes every sample in a single application. There is a Bin ZIP file that contains a pre-compiled executable of the AllChapters sample.

There are also individual folders for each chapter that contain multiple sub-folders. Every chapter contains Sample00, which is the code as it was written in the book with no additional content. The subsequently numbered samples add content.

The AllChapters sample looks a bit different from the samples in the individual chapter folders. This application uses Nuklear (https://github.com/vurtun/nuklear) to display its UI. The part of the UI that is displayed is a stats counter in the upper-right corner of the screen. It looks like this:

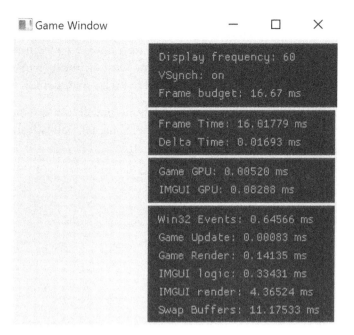

Figure 1.5: Stats counter for the AllChapters sample

The top box contains some general information about the display that the application opened on. This information contains the display frequency, whether `vsynch` is enabled, and what the frame budget is in milliseconds.

The second box down contains high-level frame timings. The time displayed will turn red if there was a stale frame in the last 60 frames. Some stale frames are unavoidable; if the frame rate drops to 59.9, the text will show red for a second. Seeing red here occasionally is OK; it's only a concern if the numbers are solid red.

The third box down contains two GPU timers; these measure how fast the sample is running on the GPU. This is useful for debugging any heavy draw calls. The final box contains CPU timers, which are helpful for figuring out which phase of the problem has a bottleneck.

> **Important note**
>
> Throughout this book, you will use C++ `stl` containers. The Standard Library is a bit slow in debug mode, mostly due to error checking. It's a good idea to profile any samples in release mode only.

These examples should do a fair job of demonstrating what you will learn in each of the upcoming chapters. They also provide an example for you to compare your code against.

Summary

In this chapter, you explored the process of setting up a new Win32 window. An OpenGL 3.3 Core context was set up to render to the window, with vsynch enabled. You learned about OpenGL loaders and how glad can load all the relevant OpenGL functions.

This window will serve as a foundation for you to build on; all future samples are built on the framework you created in this chapter. In the next chapter, you will start to explore some of the math required for rendering and animation.

2
Implementing Vectors

In this chapter, you will learn the basics of vector math. Much of what you will code throughout the rest of this book relies on having a strong understanding of vectors. Vectors will be used to represent displacement and direction.

By the end of this chapter, you will have implemented a robust vector library and will be able to perform a variety of vector operations, including component-wise and non-component-wise operations.

We will cover the following topics in this chapter:

- Introducing vectors
- Creating a vector
- Understanding component-wise operations
- Understanding non-component-wise operations
- Interpolating vectors
- Comparing vectors
- Exploring more vectors

> **Important information:**
>
> In this chapter, you will learn how to implement vectors in an intuitive,
> visual way that relies on code more than math formulas. If you are interested
> in math formulas or want some interactive examples to try out, go to
> `https://gabormakesgames.com/vectors.html`.

Introducing vectors

What is a vector? A vector is an n-tuple of numbers. It represents a displacement
measured as a magnitude and a direction. Each element of a vector is usually expressed
as a subscript, such as $(V_0, V_1, V_2, ... V_N)$. In the context of games, vectors usually have
two, three, or four components.

For example, a three-dimensional vector measures displacement on three unique
axes: x, y, and z. Elements of vectors are often subscripted with the axis they represent,
rather than an index. (V_X, V_Y, V_Z) and (V_0, V_1, V_2) are used interchangeably.

When visualizing vectors, they are often drawn as arrows. The position of the base of an
arrow does not matter because vectors measure displacement, not a position. The end of
the arrow follows the displacement of the arrow on each axis.

For example, all of the arrows in the following figure represent the same vector:

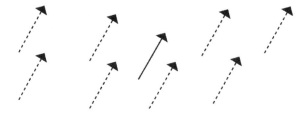

Figure 2.1: Vector (2, 5) drawn in multiple locations

Each arrow has the same length and points in the same direction, regardless of where it is
positioned. In the next section, you will start to implement the vector structure that will
be used throughout the rest of this book.

Creating a vector

Vectors will be implemented as structures, not classes. The vector struct will contain an
anonymous union that allows the vector's components to be accessed as an array or as
individual elements.

To declare the vec3 structure and the function headers, create a new file, vec3.h. Declare the new vec3 structure in this file. The vec3 struct needs three constructors—a default constructor, one that takes each component as an element, and one that takes a pointer to a float array:

```
#ifndef _H_VEC3_
#define _H_VEC3_

struct vec3 {
    union {
        struct  {
            float x;
            float y;
            float z;
        };
        float v[3];
    };
    inline vec3() : x(0.0f), y(0.0f), z(0.0f) { }
    inline vec3(float _x, float _y, float _z) :
        x(_x), y(_y), z(_z) { }
    inline vec3(float *fv) :
        x(fv[0]), y(fv[1]), z(fv[2]) { }
};

#endif
```

The anonymous union in the vec3 struct allows data to be accessed using .x, .y, and .z notation, or as a contiguous array using .v. Before moving on to implementing functions that work on the vec3 struct, you need to consider comparing floating point numbers and whether or not to use an epsilon value.

Epsilon

Comparing floating point numbers is difficult. Instead of comparing two floating point numbers directly, you need to compare them using an epsilon. An epsilon is an arbitrarily small positive number that is the minimum difference two numbers need to have to be considered different numbers. Declare an epsilon constant in vec3.h:

```
#define VEC3_EPSILON 0.000001f
```

> **Important note:**
> You can learn more about floating point comparison at
> `https://bitbashing.io/comparing-floats.html`

With the `vec3` structure created and the `vec3` epsilon defined, you are ready to start implementing some common vector operations. In the next section, you're going to start by learning and implementing several component-wise operations.

Understanding component-wise operations

Several vector operations are just component-wise operations. A component-wise operation is one that you perform on each component of a vector or on like components of two vectors. Like components are components that have the same subscript. The component-wise operations that you will implement are as follows:

- Vector addition
- Vector subtraction
- Vector scaling
- Multiplying vectors
- Dot product

Let's look at each of these in more detail.

Vector addition

Adding two vectors together yields a third vector, which has the combined displacement of both input vectors. Vector addition is a component-wise operation; to perform it, you need to add like components.

To visualize the addition of two vectors, draw the base of the second vector at the tip of the first vector. Next, draw an arrow from the base of the first vector to the tip of the second vector. This arrow represents the vector that is the result of the addition:

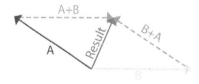

Figure 2.2: Vector addition

To implement vector addition in code, add like components of the input vectors. Create a new file, `vec3.cpp`. This is where you will define functions related to the `vec3` struct. Don't forget to include `vec3.h`. Overload the `+ operator` to perform vector addition. Don't forget to add the function signature to `vec3.h`:

```cpp
vec3 operator+(const vec3 &l, const vec3 &r) {
    return vec3(l.x + r.x, l.y + r.y, l.z + r.z);
}
```

When thinking about vector addition, remember that a vector represents a displacement. When adding two vectors, the result is the combined displacement of both input vectors.

Vector subtraction

As with adding vectors, subtracting vectors is also a component-wise operation. You can think of subtracting vectors as adding the negative of the second vector to the first vector. When visualized as an arrow, subtraction points from the tip of the second vector to the tip of the first one.

To visually subtract vectors, place both vectors so they share the same origin. Draw a vector from the tip of the second arrow to the tip of the first one. The resulting arrow is the subtraction result vector:

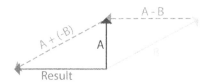

Figure 2.3: Vector subtraction

To implement vector subtraction, subtract like components. Implement the subtraction function by overloading the `- operator` in `vec3.cpp`. Don't forget to add the function declaration to `vec3.h`:

```cpp
vec3 operator-(const vec3 &l, const vec3 &r) {
    return vec3(l.x - r.x, l.y - r.y, l.z - r.z);
}
```

The steps and logic are very similar to vector addition. It might help to think of vector subtraction as adding a negative vector.

Scaling vectors

When a vector is scaled, it only changes in magnitude, not direction. As with addition and subtraction, scaling is a component-wise operation. Unlike addition and subtraction, a vector is scaled by a scalar, not another vector.

Visually, a scaled vector points in the same direction as the original vector, but it has a different length. The following figure shows two vectors: *(2, 1)* and *(2, 4)*. Both vectors share the same direction, but the magnitude of the second vector is longer:

Figure 2.4: Vector scaling

To implement vector scaling, multiply every component of the vector by the given scalar value.

Implement the scale function by overloading the * operator in vec3.cpp. Don't forget to add the function declaration to vec3.h:

```
vec3 operator*(const vec3 &v, float f) {
    return vec3(v.x * f, v.y * f, v.z * f);
}
```

Negating a vector can be done by scaling the vector by *-1*. When negating a vector, the vector maintains its magnitude but changes its direction.

Multiplying vectors

Vector multiplication can be considered a non-uniform scale. Instead of scaling every component of a vector by a scalar, to multiply two vectors, you scale every component of a vector by the like component of another vector.

You can implement vector multiplication by overloading the * operator in vec3.cpp. Don't forget to add the function declaration to vec3.h:

```
vec3 operator*(const vec3 &l, const vec3 &r) {
    return vec3(l.x * r.x, l.y * r.y, l.z * r.z);
}
```

The result generated by multiplying two vectors will have a different direction and magnitude.

Dot product

The dot product is used to measure how similar two vectors are. Given two vectors, the dot product returns a scalar value. The result of the dot product has the following properties:

- It is positive if the vectors point in the same direction.

- It is negative if the vectors point in opposite directions.

- It is 0 if the vectors are perpendicular.

If both input vectors have a unit length (you will learn about unit length vectors in the *Normal vectors* section of this chapter), the dot product will have a range of -1 to 1.

The dot product between two vectors, A and B, is equal to the length of A multiplied by the length of B multiplied by the cosine of the angle between the two vectors:

$$A \cdot B = |A||B| \cos \theta$$

The easiest way to calculate the dot product is to sum the products of like components in the input vectors:

$$A \cdot B = \sum_{i=0}^{n} A_i B_i$$

Implement the dot function in vec3.cpp. Don't forget to add the function definition to vec3.h:

```
float dot(const vec3 &l, const vec3 &r) {
    return l.x * r.x + l.y * r.y + l.z * r.z;
}
```

The dot product is one of the most used operations for video games. It's often used to check angles and in lighting calculations.

With the dot product, you have implemented the common component-wise operations of vectors. Next, you will learn about some of the non-component-wise operations that can be performed on vectors.

Understanding non-component-wise operations

Not all vector operations are component-wise; some operations require more math. In this section, you are going to learn how to implement common vector operations that are not component-based. These operations are as follows:

- How to find the length of a vector
- What a normal vector is
- How to normalize a vector
- How to find the angle between two vectors
- How to project vectors and what rejection is
- How to reflect vectors
- What the cross product is and how to implement it

Let's take a look at each one in more detail.

Vector length

Vectors represent a direction and a magnitude; the magnitude of a vector is its length. The formula for finding the length of a vector comes from trigonometry. In the following figure, a two-dimensional vector is broken down into parallel and perpendicular components. Notice how this forms a right triangle, with the vector being the hypotenuse:

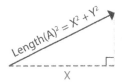

Figure 2.5: A vector broken down into parallel and perpendicular components

The length of the hypotenuse of a right triangle can be found with the Pythagorean theorem, $A^2 + B^2 = C^2$. This function extends to three dimensions by simply adding a Z component—$X^2 + Y^2 + Z^2 = length^2$.

You may have noticed a pattern here; the squared length of a vector equals the sum of its components. This could be expressed as a dot product—$Length^2(A) = dot(A, A)$:

> **Important note:**
> Finding the length of a vector involves a square root operation, which should be avoided when possible. When checking the length of a vector, the check can be done in squared space to avoid the square root. For example, if you wanted to check if the length of vector A is less than 5, that could be expressed as $(dot(A, A) < 5 * 5)$.

1. To implement the square length function, sum the result of squaring each component of the vector. Implement the `lenSq` function in `vec3.cpp`. Don't forget to add the function declaration to `vec3.h`:

```
float lenSq(const vec3& v) {
    return v.x * v.x + v.y * v.y + v.z * v.z;
}
```

2. To implement the length function, take the square root of the result of the square length function. Take care not to call `sqrtf` with 0. Implement the `lenSq` function in `vec3.cpp`. Don't forget to add the function declaration to `vec3.h`:

```
float len(const vec3 &v) {
    float lenSq = v.x * v.x + v.y * v.y + v.z * v.z;
    if (lenSq < VEC3_EPSILON) {
        return 0.0f;
    }
    return sqrtf(lenSq);
}
```

> **Important note:**
> You can find the distance between two vectors by taking the length of the difference between them. For example, *float distance = len(vec1 - vec2)*.

Normalizing vectors

A vector with a length of *1* is called a normal vector (or unit vector). Generally, unit vectors are used to represent a direction without a magnitude. The dot product of two unit vectors will always fall in the *-1* to *1* range.

Aside from the *0* vector, any vector can be normalized by scaling the vector by the inverse of its length:

1. Implement the `normalize` function in `vec3.cpp`. Don't forget to add the function declaration to `vec3.h`:

```
void normalize(vec3 &v) {
    float lenSq = v.x * v.x + v.y * v.y + v.z * v.z;
    if (lenSq < VEC3_EPSILON) { return; }
    float invLen = 1.0f / sqrtf(lenSq);
    v.x *= invLen;
    v.y *= invLen;
    v.z *= invLen;
}
```

2. Implement the `normalized` function in `vec3.cpp`. Don't forget to add the function declaration to `vec3.h`:

```
vec3 normalized(const vec3 &v) {
    float lenSq = v.x * v.x + v.y * v.y + v.z * v.z;
    if (lenSq < VEC3_EPSILON) { return v; }
    float invLen = 1.0f / sqrtf(lenSq);
    return vec3(
        v.x * invLen,
        v.y * invLen,
        v.z * invLen
    );
}
```

The `normalize` function takes a reference to a vector and normalizes it in place. The `normalized` function, on the other hand, takes a constant reference and does not modify the input vector. Instead, it returns a new vector.

The angle between vectors

If two vectors are of unit length, the angle between them is the cosine of their dot product:

$$\cos \theta = \widehat{A} \cdot \widehat{B}$$

If the two vectors are not normalized, the dot product needs to be divided by the product of the length of both vectors:

$$\cos \theta = \frac{A \cdot B}{|A||B|}$$

To find the actual angle, not just the cosine of it, we need to take the inverse of the cosine on both sides, which is the arccosine function:

$$\theta = \cos^{-1} \frac{A \cdot B}{|A||B|}$$

Implement the `angle` function in `vec3.cpp`. Don't forget to add the function declaration to `vec3.h`:

```
float angle(const vec3 &l, const vec3 &r) {
    float sqMagL = l.x * l.x + l.y * l.y + l.z * l.z;
    float sqMagR = r.x * r.x + r.y * r.y + r.z * r.z;

    if (sqMagL<VEC3_EPSILON || sqMagR<VEC3_EPSILON) {
        return 0.0f;
    }

    float dot = l.x * r.x + l.y * r.y + l.z * r.z;
    float len = sqrtf(sqMagL) * sqrtf(sqMagR);
    return acosf(dot / len);
}
```

> **Important note:**
>
> The `acosf` function returns angles in radians. To convert radians to degrees, multiply by `57.2958f`. To convert degrees to radians, multiply by `0.0174533f`.

Vector projection and rejection

Projecting vector *A* onto vector *B* yields a new vector that has the length of *A* in the direction of *B*. A good way to visualize vector projection is to imagine that vector *A* is casting a shadow onto vector *B*, as shown:

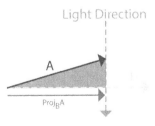

Figure 2.6: Vector A casting a shadow onto vector B

To calculate the projection of *A* onto *B* ($proj_B A$), vector *A* must be broken down into parallel and perpendicular components with respect to vector *B*. The parallel component is the length of *A* in the direction of *B*—this is the projection. The perpendicular component is the parallel component subtracted from *A*—this is the rejection:

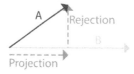

Figure 2.7: Vector projection and rejection showing parallel and perpendicular vectors

If the vector that is being projected onto (in this example, vector *B*) is a normal vector, then finding the length of *A* in the direction of *B* is a simple dot product between *A* and *B*. However, if neither input vector is normalized, the dot product needs to be divided by the length of vector *B* (the vector being projected onto).

Now that the parallel component of *A* with respect to *B* is known, vector *B* can be scaled by this component. Again, if *B* wasn't of unit length, the result will need to be divided by the length of vector *B*.

Rejection is the opposite of projection. To find the rejection of *A* onto *B*, subtract the projection of *A* onto *B* from vector *A*:

1. Implement the `project` function in `vec3.cpp`. Don't forget to add the function declaration to `vec3.h`:

```
vec3 project(const vec3 &a, const vec3 &b) {
    float magBSq = len(b);
    if (magBSq < VEC3_EPSILON) {
        return vec3();
    }
    float scale = dot(a, b) / magBSq;
    return b * scale;
}
```

2. Implement the `reject` function in `vec3.cpp`. Don't forget to declare this function in `vec3.h`:

```
vec3 reject(const vec3 &a, const vec3 &b) {
    vec3 projection = project(a, b);
    return a - projection;
}
```

Vector projection and rejection are generally used for gameplay programming. It is important that they are implemented in a robust vector library.

Vector reflection

Vector reflection can mean one of two things: a mirror-like reflection or a bounce-like reflection. The following figure shows the different types of reflections:

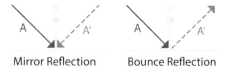

Mirror Reflection   Bounce Reflection

Figure 2.8: A comparison of the mirror and bounce reflections

The bounce reflection is more useful and intuitive than the mirror reflection. To make a bounce projection work, project vector *A* onto vector *B*. This will yield a vector that points in the opposite direction to the reflection. Negate this projection and subtract it twice from vector A. The following figure demonstrates this:

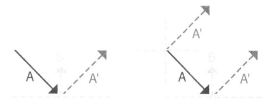

Figure 2.9: Visualizing a bounce reflection

Implement the `reflect` function in `vec3.cpp`. Don't forget to add the function declaration to `vec3.h`:

```
vec3 reflect(const vec3 &a, const vec3 &b) {
    float magBSq = len(b);
    if (magBSq < VEC3_EPSILON) {
        return vec3();
    }
    float scale = dot(a, b) / magBSq;
    vec3 proj2 = b * (scale * 2);
    return a - proj2;
}
```

Vector reflection is useful for physics and AI. We won't need to use reflection for animation, but it's good to have the function implemented in case it is needed.

Cross product

When given two input vectors, the cross product returns a third vector that is perpendicular to both input vectors. The length of the cross product equals the area of the parallelogram formed by the two vectors.

The following figure demonstrates what the cross product looks like visually. The input vectors don't have to be 90 degrees apart, but it's easier to visualize them this way:

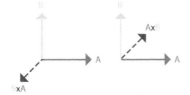

Figure 2.10: Visualizing the cross product

Finding the cross product involves some matrix math, which will be covered in more depth in the next chapter. For now, you need to create a 3x3 matrix, with the top row being the result vector. The second and third rows should be filled in with the input vectors. The value of each component of the result vector is the minor of that element in the matrix.

What exactly is the minor of an element in a 3x3 matrix? It's the determinant of a smaller, 2x2 sub-matrix. Assuming you want to find the value of the first component, ignore the first row and column, which yields a smaller 2x2 sub-matrix. The following figure shows the smaller sub-matrix for each component:

```
|R.x R.y R.z|  |R.x  *   * |  | *  R.y  * |  | *   *  R.z|
|A.x A.y A.z|  | *  A.y A.z|  |A.x  *  A.z|  |A.x A.y  * |
|B.x B.y B.z|  | *  B.y B.z|  |B.x  *  B.z|  |B.x B.y  * |
    Matrix       Submatrix X    Submatrix Y    Submatrix Z
```

Figure 2.11: The submatrix for each component

To find the determinant of a 2x2 matrix, you need to cross multiply. Multiply the top-left and bottom-right elements, then subtract the product of the top-right and bottom-left elements. The following figure shows this for each element of the resulting vector:

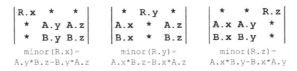

Figure 2.12: The determinant of each component in the result vector

Implement the `cross` product in `vec3.cpp`. Don't forget to add the function declaration to `vec3.h`:

```cpp
vec3 cross(const vec3 &l, const vec3 &r) {
    return vec3(
        l.y * r.z - l.z * r.y,
        l.z * r.x - l.x * r.z,
        l.x * r.y - l.y * r.x
    );
}
```

The dot product has a relationship to the cosine of the angle between two vectors and the cross product has a relationship to the sine of the angle between the two vectors. The length of the cross product between the two vectors is the product of both vectors, lengths, scaled by the sine of the angle between them:

$$||A \times B| = |A||B| \sin \theta$$

In the next section, you will learn how to interpolate between vectors using three different techniques.

Interpolating vectors

Two vectors can be interpolated linearly by scaling the difference between the two vectors and adding the result back to the original vector. This linear interpolation is often abbreviated to `lerp`. The amount to `lerp` by is a normalized value between *0* and *1*; this normalized value is often represented by the letter *t*. The following figure shows `lerp` between two vectors with several values for *t*:

t: 0.00   t: 0.25   t: 0.50   t: 0.75   t: 1.00

Figure 2.13: Linear interpolation

When *t = 0*, the interpolated vector is the same as the starting vector. When *t = 1*, the interpolated vector is the same as the end vector.

Implement the `lerp` function in `vec3.cpp`. Don't forget to add the function declaration to `vec3.h`:

```cpp
vec3 lerp(const vec3 &s, const vec3 &e, float t) {
    return vec3(
        s.x + (e.x - s.x) * t,
        s.y + (e.y - s.y) * t,
```

```
         s.z + (e.z - s.z) * t
    );
}
```

Linearly interpolating between two vectors will always take the shortest path from one vector to another. Sometimes, the shortest path isn't the best path; you may need to interpolate between two vectors along the shortest arc, instead. Interpolating on the shortest arc is called a spherical linear interpolation (slerp). The following figure shows the difference between the slerp and lerp processes for several values of *t*:

t: 0.00   t: 0.25   t: 0.50   t: 0.75   t: 1.00

Figure 2.14: Comparing slerp and lerp

To implement slerp, find the angle between the two input vectors. Assuming the angle is known, the formula for slerp is as follows

$$slerp(\hat{A}, \hat{B}, t) = \frac{sin\,(1-t)\theta}{sin\,\theta}\,\hat{A} + \frac{sin\,(t\theta)}{sin\theta}\,\hat{B}$$

Implement the slerp function in vec3.cpp. Don't forget to add the function declaration to vec3.h. Take care of when the value of *t* is close to *0*, as slerp will yield unexpected results. When the value of *t* is close to *0*, fall back on lerp or normalized lerp (nlerp) (which will be covered next):

```cpp
vec3 slerp(const vec3 &s, const vec3 &e, float t) {
    if (t < 0.01f) {
        return lerp(s, e, t);
    }

    vec3 from = normalized(s);
    vec3 to = normalized(e);

    float theta = angle(from, to);
    float sin_theta = sinf(theta);

    float a = sinf((1.0f - t) * theta) / sin_theta;
    float b = sinf(t * theta) / sin_theta;

    return from * a + to * b;
}
```

The last interpolation method to cover is `nlerp`. `nlerp` approximates `slerp`. Unlike `slerp`, `nlerp` is not constant in velocity. `nlerp` is much faster than `slerp` and easier to implement; just normalize the result of `lerp`. The following figure compares `lerp`, `slerp`, and `nlerp`, where *t = 0.25*:

Figure 2.15: Comparing lerp, slerp, and nlerp

Implement the `nlerp` function in `vec3.cpp`. Don't forget to add the function declaration to `vec3.h`:

```cpp
vec3 nlerp(const vec3 &s, const vec3 &e, float t) {
    vec3 linear(
        s.x + (e.x - s.x) * t,
        s.y + (e.y - s.y) * t,
        s.z + (e.z - s.z) * t
    );
    return normalized(linear);
}
```

Generally, `nlerp` is a better choice than `slerp`. It's a very close approximation and much cheaper to calculate. The only time it makes sense to use `slerp` instead is if constant interpolation velocity is required. Throughout this book, you will be using `lerp` and `nlerp` to interpolate between vectors.

In the next section, you will learn how to use an epsilon value to compare vectors for equality and inequality.

Comparing vectors

The last operation that needs to be implemented is vector comparison. Comparison is a component-wise operation; each element must be compared using an epsilon. Another way to measure whether two vectors are the same is to subtract them. If they were equal, subtracting them would yield a vector with no length.

Overload the == and != operators in vec3.cpp. Don't forget to add the function declarations to vec3.h:

```
bool operator==(const vec3 &l, const vec3 &r) {
    vec3 diff(l - r);
    return lenSq(diff) < VEC3_EPSILON;
}

bool operator!=(const vec3 &l, const vec3 &r) {
    return !(l == r);
}
```

> **Important note:**
> Finding the right epsilon value to use for comparison operations is difficult. In this chapter, you declared 0.000001f as the epsilon. This value is the result of some trial and error. To learn more about comparing floating point values, check out https://bitbashing.io/comparing-floats.html.

In the next section, you will implement vectors with two and four components. These vectors will only be used as a convenient way to store data; they won't actually need any math operations implemented on them.

Exploring more vectors

At some point later on in this book, you will need to utilize two- and four-component vectors as well. The two- and four-component vectors don't need any mathematical functions defined as they will be used exclusively as containers used to pass data to the GPU.

Unlike the three-component vector you have implemented, the two- and four-component vectors need to exist as both integer and floating point vectors. To avoid duplicating code, both structures will be implemented using a template:

1. Create a new file, vec2.h, and add the definition of the vec2 struct. All the vec2 constructors are inline; there is no need for a cpp file. The TVec2 struct is templated and typedef is used to declare vec2 and ivec2:

```
template<typename T>
struct TVec2 {
    union {
        struct {
            T x;
```

```
              T y;
          };
          T v[2];
      };
      inline TVec2() : x(T(0)), y(T(0)) { }
      inline TVec2(T _x, T _y) :
          x(_x), y(_y) { }
      inline TVec2(T* fv) :
          x(fv[0]), y(fv[1]) { }
  };

  typedef TVec2<float> vec2;
  typedef TVec2<int> ivec2;
```

2. Similarly, create a vec4.h file, which will hold the vec4 structure:

```
  template<typename T>
  struct TVec4 {
      union {
          struct {
              T x;
              T y;
              T z;
              T w;
          };
          T v[4];
      };
      inline TVec4<T>(): x((T)0),y((T)0),z((T)0),w((T)0){}
      inline TVec4<T>(T _x, T _y, T _z, T _w) :
          x(_x), y(_y), z(_z), w(_w) { }
      inline TVec4<T>(T* fv) :
          x(fv[0]), y(fv[ ]), z(fv[2]), w(fv[3]) { }
  };

  typedef TVec4<float> vec4;
  typedef TVec4<int> ivec4;
  typedef TVec4<unsigned int> uivec4;
```

The declaration of the vec2, ivec2, vec4, and ivec4 structs are all very similar to the declaration of the vec3 struct. All these structures can be accessed using component subscripts or as a pointer to a linear array of memory. They all have similar constructors, as well.

Summary

In this chapter, you have learned the vector math required to create a robust animation system. Animation is a math-heavy topic; the skills you have learned in this chapter are required to complete the rest of this book. You implemented all the common vector operations for three-component vectors. The vec2 and vec4 structures don't have a full implementation like vec3, but they are only used to send data to the GPU.

In the next chapter, you will continue to learn more about game-related math by learning about matrices.

3
Implementing Matrices

In the context of game animation, a matrix represents an affine transformation. It linearly maps points from one space to another. A mesh is represented by vertices, which are just points in space. These vertices are moved by multiplying them by a matrix.

In this chapter, you will learn matrix math and how to implement matrices in code. By the end of this chapter, you will have built a robust matrix library that can be used in any project. Matrices are important; they play a big role in the graphics pipeline. It's hard to render anything without using matrices.

You will only need to implement a square, 4 x 4 matrix. By the end of this chapter, you should be able to do the following:

- Understand what a matrix is
- Understand column-major matrix storage
- Multiply matrices together
- Invert a matrix
- Transform points and vectors by using a matrix
- Understand how to create matrices to view a three-dimensional world

> **Important information**
>
> In this chapter, you will implement a 4 x 4 matrix. The matrix implementation
> will rely on code to demonstrate concepts, rather than through the format of
> math definitions. If you're interested in the formal math behind matrices, check
> out `https://gabormakesgames.com/matrices.html`.

Technical requirements

There are two samples provided in the downloadable materials for the book for this
chapter. `Sample00` shows the matrix code as it is written throughout the chapter.
`Sample01` shows an alternative implementation that uses explicit lower-order matrices to
implement the matrix inverse function.

What is a matrix?

A matrix is a two-dimensional array of numbers. A square matrix is one whose width and
height are the same. In this chapter, you will implement a 4 x 4 matrix; that is, a matrix
with four rows and four columns. The elements of this matrix will be stored as a linear
array.

A 4 x 4 matrix can be thought of as four vectors that have four components each,
or an array of `vec4`s. If the vectors represent the columns of the matrix, the matrix
is column-major. If the vectors represent the rows of the matrix, it is row-major.

Assuming a 4 x 4 matrix contains the letters *A, B, C, D … P* of the alphabet, it can be
constructed as either a row- or column-major matrix. This is demonstrated in the
following *Figure 3.1*:

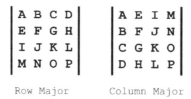

Figure 3.1: Comparing row- and column-major matrices

Most math books and OpenGL use column-major matrices. In this chapter, you will be implementing column-major matrices as well. Understanding what is in a matrix is important. The diagonal of the matrix contains scaling information, and the final column contains translation:

Figure 3.2: What is stored in a matrix?

The upper 3 x 3 submatrix contains three vectors; each of these is a basis vector for the matrix's rotation. The basis vectors are the up, right, and forward directions stored in the matrix. You might have noticed that the rotation and scale components occupy the same space in the matrix.

Matrix storage

Now that you know that the matrix layout is going to be column matrices, the next question is how to store the actual matrix. Matrix storage is a confusing topic.

Since a matrix is stored in memory as a linear array, let's figure out what elements should be placed where. A row-major matrix is stored in memory one row at a time. A column-major matrix is stored one column at a time.

Since both row- and column-major matrices contain the same vectors, the final linear mapping ends up being the same, regardless of the major of the matrix. The following *Figure 3.3* demonstrates this:

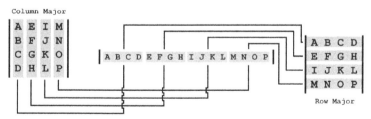

Figure 3.3: Matrix storage mapping to a linear array

The matrix class you will be building is a column-major matrix with column storage; this means there will be a discrepancy between the physical memory layout of the matrix and the logical placement of its elements. It's easy to treat a matrix with a linear memory layout as a row matrix but remember that each of those rows is actually a column.

> **Important note**
>
> The typical mapping of a two-dimensional grid to linear storage is `"row * numberOfColumns + column"`. This mapping won't work for storing a column-major matrix. When looking at a matrix, the element in column 2, row 3 should have a linear index of 7, but the previous mapping yields 14. Instead, to account for the column-major storage, the mapping formula is `"column * numberOfRows + row"`.

Understanding how a matrix is stored in memory is important, it's going to affect how data is stored and how APIs can access that data. In the next section, you will start to implement a matrix structure.

Creating a matrix

In this section, you will create a new 4 x 4 matrix. This matrix will be stored as a 16-element array of floats. A union will be used to allow access to the data in the matrix in an easier-to-use fashion:

> **Important note**
>
> The identity matrix is a special matrix that multiplies anything by the identity matrix results in the original matrix. The identity matrix does no mapping. An identity matrix contains 0 in all elements except the main diagonal, which is made up entirely of 1.

1. Create a new file, mat4.h. This file is needed to declare the mat4 struct.

2. Add the following structure declaration to mat4.h, which starts a union by declaring a flat array of 16 elements as the first member of the union:

```
struct mat4 {
    union {
        float v[16];
```

3. The next member of the union is a structure of `vec4` variables. Each of the `vec4` variables represents one column of the matrix; they are named after the basis vector stored in those columns:

```
struct {
    vec4 right;
    vec4 up;
    vec4 forward;
    vec4 position;
};
```

4. It might be useful to access members by element based on the basis vector. The following struct contains named pairs; the first letter represents the basis vector and the second letter represents the component of that vector:

```
struct {
//          row 1      row 2      row 3      row 4
/*col 1*/float xx;float xy;float xz;float xw;
/*col 2*/float yx;float yy;float yz;float yw;
/*col 3*/float zx;float zy;float zz;float zw;
/*col 4*/float tx;float ty;float tz;float tw;
};
```

5. The next struct will allow you to access the matrix using column-row notation:

```
struct {
    float c0r0;float c0r1;float c0r2;float c0r3;
    float c1r0;float c1r1;float c1r2;float c1r3;
    float c2r0;float c2r1;float c2r2;float c2r3;
    float c3r0;float c3r1;float c3r2;float c3r3;
};
```

6. The final struct will allow you to access the matrix using row-column notation:

```
struct {
    float r0c0;float r1c0;float r2c0;float r3c0;
    float r0c1;float r1c1;float r2c1;float r3c1;
    float r0c2;float r1c2;float r2c2;float r3c2;
    float r0c3;float r1c3;float r2c3;float r3c3;
};
}; // End union
```

7. Add an `inline` constructor that will create the identity matrix:

```
inline mat4() :
    xx(1), xy(0), xz(0), xw(0),
    yx(0), yy(1), yz(0), yw(0),
    zx(0), zy(0), zz(1), zw(0),
    tx(0), ty(0), tz(0), tw(1) {}
```

8. Add an `inline` constructor that will create a matrix from a float array:

```
inline mat4(float *fv) :
    xx( fv[0]), xy( fv[1]), xz( fv[2]), xw( fv[3]),
    yx( fv[4]), yy( fv[5]), yz( fv[6]), yw( fv[7]),
    zx( fv[8]), zy( fv[9]), zz(fv[10]), zw(fv[11]),
    tx(fv[12]), ty(fv[13]), tz(fv[14]), tw(fv[15]) { }
```

9. Add an `inline` constructor that will let you create a matrix by specifying each element inside the matrix:

```
inline mat4(
    float _00, float _01, float _02, float _03,
    float _10, float _11, float _12, float _13,
    float _20, float _21, float _22, float _23,
    float _30, float _31, float _32, float _33) :
    xx(_00), xy(_01), xz(_02), xw(_03),
    yx(_10), yy(_11), yz(_12), yw(_13),
    zx(_20), zy(_21), zz(_22), zw(_23),
    tx(_30), ty(_31), tz(_32), tw(_33) { }
}; // end mat4 struct
```

The matrix struct you just declared is the final `mat4` struct; the anonymous union provides five different ways of accessing matrix data. Matrix data can be accessed as a flat array, as four columns each stored as `vec4`, or as one of three mnemonics. The three mnemonics name elements using their basis vectors, their row and then column, or their column and then row.

Next, you will start working on functions that operate on the `mat4` structure. You will implement common matrix operations, such as adding, scaling, and multiplying matrices, and see how to use matrices to transform vectors and points.

Common matrix operations

In this section, you will learn how to implement some common matrix operations. These operations will be used in later chapters of this book to display animated models. Specifically, this section will cover how to compare, add, scale, and multiply matrices as well as how to transform vectors and points using matrices.

Comparing matrices

Comparing matrices is a component-wise operation. Two matrices are the same only if all their components are the same. To compare two matrices, loop through and compare all of their components. Since you are comparing floating point numbers, an epsilon should be used.

Create a new file, mat4.cpp. Implement the matrix equality and inequality operators in this file. The equality operator should check whether two matrices are the same; the inequality operator returns the opposite of the equality operator. Don't forget to add the function declarations to mat4.h:

```cpp
bool operator==(const mat4& a, const mat4& b) {
    for (int i = 0; i < 16; ++i) {
        if (fabsf(a.v[i] - b.v[i]) > MAT4_EPSILON) {
            return false;
        }
    }
    return true;
}

bool operator!=(const mat4& a, const mat4& b) {
    return !(a == b);
}
```

> **Important note**
> The MAT4_EPSILON constant should be defined in mat4.h. 0.000001f is a good default value to use.

When comparing matrices by component, you are checking for literal equality. There are other ways to define matrix equality; for example, regardless of shape, the volume of two matrices can be compared using their determinants. Matrix determinants will be covered later in this chapter.

In the next section, you will learn how to add matrices together.

Adding matrices

Two matrices can be added together by component. To add two matrices together, sum their respective components and store the result in a new matrix. Matrix addition can be used with scalar multiplication to interpolate or blend between multiple matrices. Later, you will learn how to use this property to implement animation skinning.

Implement the matrix addition function in mat4.cpp. Don't forget to add the function declaration to mat4.h:

```cpp
mat4 operator+(const mat4& a, const mat4& b) {
    return mat4(
        a.xx+b.xx, a.xy+b.xy, a.xz+b.xz, a.xw+b.xw,
        a.yx+b.yx, a.yy+b.yy, a.yz+b.yz, a.yw+b.yw,
        a.zx+b.zx, a.zy+b.zy, a.zz+b.zz, a.zw+b.zw,
        a.tx+b.tx, a.ty+b.ty, a.tz+b.tz, a.tw+b.tw
    );
}
```

Matrix addition is simple but it will play a big role in displaying an animated mesh. In the next section, you will learn how to scale a matrix by a scalar value.

Scaling a matrix

Matrices can be scaled by floating point numbers; this kind of scaling is a component-wise operation. To scale a matrix, multiply every element by the provided floating point number.

Implement matrix scaling in mat4.cpp. Don't forget to add the function declaration to mat4.h:

```cpp
mat4 operator*(const mat4& m, float f) {
    return mat4(
        m.xx * f, m.xy * f, m.xz * f, m.xw * f,
        m.yx * f, m.yy * f, m.yz * f, m.yw * f,
        m.zx * f, m.zy * f, m.zz * f, m.zw * f,
        m.tx * f, m.ty * f, m.tz * f, m.tw * f
    );
}
```

Scaling matrices and then adding them allows you to "lerp" or "mix" between two matrices, so long as both matrices represent a linear transform. In the next section, you will learn how to multiply matrices together.

Matrix multiplication

Matrix multiplication combines the transformation of two matrices into one matrix. Two matrices can only be multiplied together if their inner dimensions are the same. The following are some examples:

- A 4 x **4** and a **4** x 4 matrix could be multiplied together, since both inner dimensions are 4.

- A 4 x **4** and a **4** x 1 matrix could be multiplied together, since both inner dimensions are 4.

- A 4 x **4** and a **1** x 4 matrix could not be multiplied together, since the inner dimensions, 4 and 1, don't match.

The resulting matrix from a matrix multiplication will have the outer dimensions of the matrices being multiplied together. The following is an example:

- A **4** x 4 and a 4 x **4** matrix would yield a 4 x 4 matrix.

- A **4** x 4 and a 4 x **1** matrix would yield a 4 x 1 matrix.

- A **1** x 4 and a 4 x **2** matrix would yield a 1 x 2 matrix.

Assume there are two matrices, A and B. Matrix A translates 10 units on the X axis. Matrix B rotates by 30 degrees around the Y axis. If the matrices where to be multiplied as $A * B$, the resulting matrix would rotate by 30 degrees around the Y axis then translate 10 units on the X axis.

Matrix multiplication is not cumulative. Consider the last example but multiply $B * A$, instead. When multiplying $B * A$, the resulting matrix will translate 10 units on the X axis and then rotate 30 degrees around the Y axis. Multiplication order matters; $A * B$ is not the same as $B * A$.

This brings up a new question—what order should matrices be multiplied together in? If $M = A * B * C$, in what order do those matrices concatenate? A, B, and then C or C, B, and then A? If it's A, B, and then C, the matrix multiplication is defined as left to right. But if it's C, B, and then A, the matrix multiplication is right to left.

To maintain consistency with OpenGL, in this chapter you will be implementing right-to-left multiplication. But how are two matrices multiplied together? Each element of a matrix has a row and a column. The resulting value for any element is the dot product of that row from the left matrix and that column forms the right matrix.

For example, suppose you want to find the value of the element in row 2 column 3 when multiplying two matrices. This means taking the dot product of row 2 from the left-hand side matrix and column 3 from the right-hand side matrix. *Figure 3.4* demonstrates this:

$$
\begin{array}{ccc}
\text{Result} & \text{Matrix A} & \text{Matrix B} \\
\begin{vmatrix} R_{00} & R_{01} & R_{02} & R_{03} \\ R_{10} & R_{11} & R_{12} & R_{13} \\ R_{20} & R_{21} & R_{22} & R_{23} \\ R_{30} & R_{31} & R_{32} & R_{33} \end{vmatrix}
=
\begin{vmatrix} A_{00} & A_{01} & A_{02} & A_{03} \\ A_{10} & A_{11} & A_{12} & A_{13} \\ A_{20} & A_{21} & A_{22} & A_{23} \\ A_{30} & A_{31} & A_{32} & A_{33} \end{vmatrix}
*
\begin{vmatrix} B_{00} & B_{01} & B_{02} & B_{03} \\ B_{10} & B_{11} & B_{12} & B_{13} \\ B_{20} & B_{21} & B_{22} & B_{23} \\ B_{30} & B_{31} & B_{32} & B_{33} \end{vmatrix}
\end{array}
$$

$$
R_{23} = \text{Dot}([A_{20}, A_{21}, A_{22}, A_{23}], [B_{03}, B_{13}, B_{23}, B_{33}])
$$

Figure 3.4: Multiplying matrices

You might have noticed, in the previous figure, that even though the matrices are column-major, the subscript of the elements appears as row first, then column. The subscript references the physical topology of the matrix; it has nothing to do with what is stored in the matrix or how the matrix is laid out. Subscript indices remain the same, no matter what major the matrix is. Perform the following steps to implement matrix multiplication:

1. To keep the code for multiplying matrices short, you will need to create a helper macro. This macro will assume that there are two matrices, a and b. The macro will take two numbers, the row of a and the column of b, to dot together and the result will bet the dot product of the two. Define the M4D macro in mat4.cpp:

```
#define M4D(aRow, bCol) \
    a.v[0 * 4 + aRow] * b.v[bCol * 4 + 0] + \
    a.v[1 * 4 + aRow] * b.v[bCol * 4 + 1] + \
    a.v[2 * 4 + aRow] * b.v[bCol * 4 + 2] + \
    a.v[3 * 4 + aRow] * b.v[bCol * 4 + 3]
```

2. With the M4D macro in place, implement the matrix multiplication function in mat4.cpp. Don't forget to add the function declaration to mat4.h. Remember that the (2, 1) element, for example, should take the dot product of row 2 from matrix a and column 1 of matrix b:

```
mat4 operator*(const mat4 &a, const mat4 &b) {
    return mat4(
        M4D(0,0), M4D(1,0), M4D(2,0), M4D(3,0),//Col 0
        M4D(0,1), M4D(1,1), M4D(2,1), M4D(3,1),//Col 1
        M4D(0,2), M4D(1,2), M4D(2,2), M4D(3,2),//Col 2
        M4D(0,3), M4D(1,3), M4D(2,3), M4D(3,3) //Col 3
    );
}
```

The most important property of matrix multiplication is that it combines the transformation encoded in both matrices into a single matrix. This is useful because you can pre-multiply certain matrices to perform fewer multiplications per frame. Next, you will learn about how matrices can apply their transformation data to vectors and points.

Transforming vectors and points

Transforming points and vectors is done in the same way as multiplying matrices. In fact, the vector being transformed can be thought of as a matrix with 4 columns and 1 row. This means transforming vectors is a matter of multiplying a 4 x 4 and a 4 x 1 matrix together.

When a matrix transforms a vector, it affects both the orientation and scale of the vector. When a matrix transforms a point, it just translates the point in space. So, what's the difference between vectors and points? The w component of a vector is 0 and the W component of a point is 1. The following steps will guide you through implementing matrix-vector multiplication:

1. To make the matrix-vector multiplication a little easier to read, you will need to once again create a macro. This macro will take the row of a matrix and perform a dot product of that row against the provided column vector. Implement the M4VD macro in mat4.cpp:

```
#define M4V4D(mRow, x, y, z, w) \
    x * m.v[0 * 4 + mRow] + \
    y * m.v[1 * 4 + mRow] + \
    z * m.v[2 * 4 + mRow] + \
    w * m.v[3 * 4 + mRow]
```

2. With the M4V4D macro in place, implement the matrix-vector multiplication function in mat4.cpp. Don't forget to add the function definition to mat4.h:

```
vec4 operator*(const mat4& m, const vec4& v) {
    return vec4(
        M4V4D(0, v.x, v.y, v.z, v.w),
        M4V4D(1, v.x, v.y, v.z, v.w),
        M4V4D(2, v.x, v.y, v.z, v.w),
        M4V4D(3, v.x, v.y, v.z, v.w)
    );
}
```

3.   Most of the data in this book will be stored as three-component vectors, not four. There is no need to create a new four-component vector every time one needs to be transformed by a matrix; instead, you will create a specialized function for just this occasion.

4.   Define a new function in mat4.cpp: transformVector. Don't forget to add the function declaration to mat4.h. This function will take vec3 and transform it using the provided matrix, assuming the vector represents the direction and magnitude:

```
vec3 transformVector(const mat4& m, const vec3& v) {
    return vec3(
        M4V4D(0, v.x, v.y, v.z, 0.0f),
        M4V4D(1, v.x, v.y, v.z, 0.0f),
        M4V4D(2, v.x, v.y, v.z, 0.0f)
    );
}
```

5.   Next, define the transformPoint function in mat4.cpp. It should multiply the vector and the matrix, assuming that the W component of the vector is 1:

```
vec3 transformPoint(const mat4& m, const vec3& v) {
    return vec3(
        M4V4D(0, v.x, v.y, v.z, 1.0f),
        M4V4D(1, v.x, v.y, v.z, 1.0f),
        M4V4D(2, v.x, v.y, v.z, 1.0f)
    );
}
```

6.   Define an overload for transformPoint that takes an additional W component. The W component is a reference—it is a read-write. After the function is executed, the w component holds the value for W, if the input vector had been vec4:

```
vec3 transformPoint(const mat4& m, const vec3& v, float& w) {
    float _w = w;
    w = M4V4D(3, v.x, v.y, v.z, _w);
    return vec3(
        M4V4D(0, v.x, v.y, v.z, _w),
        M4V4D(1, v.x, v.y, v.z, _w),
        M4V4D(2, v.x, v.y, v.z, _w)
    );
}
```

Throughout the rest of this book, most data is stored in `vec3` structures. This means `transformVector` and `transformPoint` will be used, rather than the overloaded multiplication operator. This should help reduce ambiguity as to what the data being transformed is. Next, you will learn how to invert a matrix.

Inverting a matrix

Multiplying a matrix by its inverse will always result in the identity matrix. An inverted matrix has the opposite mapping of the non-inverted matrix. Not all matrices have an inverse. Only matrices with a non-zero determinant can be inverted.

Inverting matrices is an important operation; the view matrix that is used to transform three-dimensional objects to be displayed on-screen is the inverse of the camera's position and rotation. Another place where inverted matrices become important is skinning, which will be covered in *Chapter 10, Mesh Skinning*.

Finding the inverse of a matrix is rather complicated as it needs other support functions (such as transpose and adjugate). In this section, you will build these support functions first and then build the inverse function after they have all been built. So firstly, we need to transpose the matrix.

Transpose

To transpose a matrix, flip every element of the matrix across its main diagonal. For example, the *2, 1* element would become the *1, 2* element. Elements where both subscripts are the same, such as *1, 1*, will remain the same:

1. Implement the `transpose` function in `mat4.cpp`. Don't forget to add the function declaration to `mat4.h`:

```
#define M4SWAP(x, y) \
    {float t = x; x = y; y = t; }

void transpose(mat4 &m) {
    M4SWAP(m.yx, m.xy);
    M4SWAP(m.zx, m.xz);
    M4SWAP(m.tx, m.xw);
    M4SWAP(m.zy, m.yz);
    M4SWAP(m.ty, m.yw);
    M4SWAP(m.tz, m.zw);
}
```

2. Create a `transposed` function in `mat4.cpp`. The `transposed` function modifies a matrix that is passed into it. Don't forget to add the function declaration to `mat4.h`:

```cpp
mat4 transposed(const mat4 &m) {
    return mat4(
        m.xx, m.yx, m.zx, m.tx,
        m.xy, m.yy, m.zy, m.ty,
        m.xz, m.yz, m.zz, m.tz,
        m.xw, m.yw, m.zw, m.tw
    );
}
```

Transposing a matrix is useful if you need to convert a matrix from row-major to column-major or the other way around. In the next section, you will learn how to calculate the determinant of a square matrix.

Determinant and minors of lower-order matrices

To find the determinant of a 4 x 4 matrix, it's important to first understand what the determinant and minor of lower-order matrices are. The determinant function is recursive; to find the determinant of a 4 x 4 matrix, we need to find the determinants of several 3 x 3 and 2 x 2 matrices as well.

The determinant of a matrix is always a scalar value; only square matrices have a determinant. The determinant of a matrix remains the same if the matrix is transposed.

In the following sections, you will learn how to find the determinant of 2 x 2 matrices, the matrix of minors for any sized matrices, and the cofactor of any sized matrices. These methods are the building blocks of Laplace expansion, which you will use to find the determinant of any sized matrices.

A 2 x 2 determinant

To find the determinant of a 2 x 2 matrix, subtract the product of the diagonal elements. The following diagram demonstrates this:

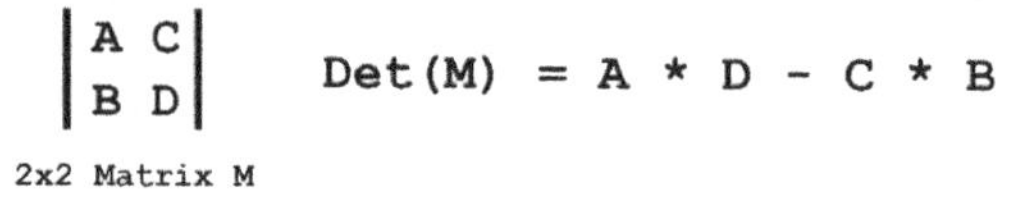

$$\begin{vmatrix} A & C \\ B & D \end{vmatrix} \qquad Det(M) = A * D - C * B$$

2x2 Matrix M

Figure 3.5: A 2 x 2 matrix and the formula for the determinant

Minor

Every element in a matrix has a minor. The minor of an element is the determinant of a smaller matrix that eliminates the row and column of the element. For example, consider a 3 x 3 matrix—what is the minor of element *2, 1*?

First, eliminate row 2 and column 1 from the matrix. This will result in a smaller 2 x 2 matrix. The determinant of this 2 x 2 matrix is the minor of element *2, 1*. The following diagram demonstrates this:

$$\begin{vmatrix} M_{00} & * & M_{02} \\ M_{10} & * & M_{12} \\ * & M_{21} & * \end{vmatrix} \quad \texttt{minor(M}_{21}\texttt{)} \ = \ \texttt{det(}\begin{vmatrix} M_{00} & M_{02} \\ M_{10} & M_{12} \end{vmatrix}\texttt{)}$$

Figure 3.6: The minor of element 2, 1 in a 3 x 3 matrix

This formula works for higher-dimension matrices as well. For example, the minor of an element in a 4 x 4 matrix is the determinant of some smaller, 3 x 3 matrix. A matrix of minors is a matrix where every element is the minor of the corresponding element from the input matrix.

Cofactor

To find the cofactor of a matrix, first, calculate the matrix of minors. After the matrix of minors is known, multiply every element, *(i, j)*, in the matrix by *-1* to the *i + j* power. The value of Add $-1^{(i+j)}$ power forms a convenient checkerboard pattern with + always being at the top left:

$$\begin{vmatrix} + & - & + & - \\ - & + & - & + \\ + & - & + & - \\ - & + & - & + \end{vmatrix} \quad \begin{vmatrix} + & - & + \\ - & + & - \\ + & - & + \end{vmatrix} \quad \begin{vmatrix} + & - \\ - & + \end{vmatrix}$$

Figure 3.7: A checkerboard pattern of -1 to the i + j power

The preceding diagram shows the checkerboard pattern that Add $-1^{(i+j)}$ creates. Notice how the pattern always starts with a positive element in the top left.

Laplace expansion

The determinant (if one exists) of any square matrix can be found through Laplace expansion. To perform this, first find the cofactor matrix. Next, multiply every element in the first row of the original matrix by the corresponding element in the first row of the cofactor matrix. The determinant is the sum of these multiplications:

$$|M| = \sum_{i=1}^{n} M_{1i} cofactor(M_{1i})$$

Adjugate

The final operation before you can invert a matrix is to find the adjugate of a matrix. The adjugate of a matrix is the transpose of the cofactor matrix. Implementing the adjugate is simple since you already know how to find the cofactor of a matrix and how to transpose a matrix.

Inverse

To find the inverse of a matrix, divide the adjugate of the matrix by its determinant. Since the scalar matrix division is not defined, you will need to multiply the adjugate by the reciprocal of the determinant.

> **Important note**
>
> In this chapter, you will build a matrix multiplication function that uses macros to avoid the need for lower-order matrices. The Chapter03/ Sample01 sample in the downloadable materials for this book provides an implementation that utilizes lower-order matrices and is easier to work through with a debugger.

To implement a matrix inverse function, you will first need to be able to find the determinant and adjugate of a 4 x 4 matrix. Both functions rely on being able to find the minor of an element in the matrix:

1. Create a new macro in mat4.cpp. This macro will find the minor of one element in the matrix, given an array of floats, and three rows and three columns to cut from the matrix:

```
#define M4_3X3MINOR(x, c0, c1, c2, r0, r1, r2) \
    (x[c0*4+r0] * (x[c1*4+r1]*x[c2*4+r2]-x[c1*4+r2]* \
    x[c2*4+r1])-x[c1*4+r0] * (x[c0*4+r1]*x[c2*4+r2]- \
```

```
        x[c0*4+r2]*x[c2*4+r1])+x[c2*4+r0]*(x[c0*4+r1]* \
        x[c1*4+r2]-x[c0*4+r2]*x[c1*4+r1]))
```

2. With the M4_3X3MINOR macro defined, implement the determinant function in mat4.cpp. Since the determinant will multiply each element by the cofactor, some of the values need to be negated. Don't forget to add the function declaration to mat4.h:

```
float determinant(const mat4& m) {
    return  m.v[0] *M4_3X3MINOR(m.v, 1, 2, 3, 1, 2, 3)
          - m.v[4] *M4_3X3MINOR(m.v, 0, 2, 3, 1, 2, 3)
          + m.v[8] *M4_3X3MINOR(m.v, 0, 1, 3, 1, 2, 3)
          - m.v[12]*M4_3X3MINOR(m.v, 0, 1, 2, 1, 2, 3);
}
```

3. Next, implement the adjugate function in mat4.cpp. Don't forget to add the function declaration to mat4.h. Use the M4_3X3MINOR macro to find the matrix of minors, then negate the appropriate elements to create the cofactor matrix. Finally, return the transpose of the cofactor matrix:

```
mat4 adjugate(const mat4& m) {
    //Cof (M[i, j]) = Minor(M[i, j]] * pow(-1, i + j)
    mat4 cofactor;
    cofactor.v[0] = M4_3X3MINOR(m.v, 1, 2, 3, 1, 2, 3);
    cofactor.v[1] =-M4_3X3MINOR(m.v, 1, 2, 3, 0, 2, 3);
    cofactor.v[2] = M4_3X3MINOR(m.v, 1, 2, 3, 0, 1, 3);
    cofactor.v[3] =-M4_3X3MINOR(m.v, 1, 2, 3, 0, 1, 2);
    cofactor.v[4] =-M4_3X3MINOR(m.v, 0, 2, 3, 1, 2, 3);
    cofactor.v[5] = M4_3X3MINOR(m.v, 0, 2, 3, 0, 2, 3);
    cofactor.v[6] =-M4_3X3MINOR(m.v, 0, 2, 3, 0, 1, 3);
    cofactor.v[7] = M4_3X3MINOR(m.v, 0, 2, 3, 0, 1, 2);
    cofactor.v[8] = M4_3X3MINOR(m.v, 0, 1, 3, 1, 2, 3);
    cofactor.v[9] =-M4_3X3MINOR(m.v, 0, 1, 3, 0, 2, 3);
    cofactor.v[10]= M4_3X3MINOR(m.v, 0, 1, 3, 0, 1, 3);
    cofactor.v[11]=-M4_3X3MINOR(m.v, 0, 1, 3, 0, 1, 2);
    cofactor.v[12]=-M4_3X3MINOR(m.v, 0, 1, 2, 1, 2, 3);
    cofactor.v[13]= M4_3X3MINOR(m.v, 0, 1, 2, 0, 2, 3);
    cofactor.v[14]=-M4_3X3MINOR(m.v, 0, 1, 2, 0, 1, 3);
    cofactor.v[15]= M4_3X3MINOR(m.v, 0, 1, 2, 0, 1, 2);
    return transposed(cofactor);
}
```

4. Now that the `determinant` and `adjugate` functions are finished, the
    implementation of the `inverse` function for a 4 x 4 matrix should be
    straightforward. Implement the `inverse` function in `mat4.cpp`.
    Don't forget to add the function declaration to `mat4.h`:

```cpp
mat4 inverse(const mat4& m) {
    float det = determinant(m);

    if (det == 0.0f) {
        cout << " Matrix determinant is 0\n";
        return mat4();
    }
    mat4 adj = adjugate(m);

    return adj * (1.0f / det);
}
```

5. The `inverse` function takes a constant matrix reference and returns a new matrix
    that is the inverse of the provided matrix. Implement an `invert` convenience
    function in `mat4.cpp`. This convenience function will invert the matrix inline,
    modifying the argument. Don't forget to add the function declaration to `mat4.h`:

```cpp
void invert(mat4& m) {
    float det = determinant(m);

    if (det == 0.0f) {
        std::cout << "Matrix determinant is 0\n";
        m = mat4();
        return;
    }

    m = adjugate(m) * (1.0f / det);
}
```

Inverting matrices is a relatively expensive function. Matrices that only encode the
position and rotation can be inverted faster because the inverse of a 3 x 3 rotation matrix
is the same as its transpose.

You will learn how to implement this fast inverse in the next section when implementing
the `lookAt` function.

Creating camera matrices

Matrices are also used for camera transformations, including perspective transforms. A perspective transform maps a frustum to NDC space. NDC space typically has a range of -1 to +1 on all axes. Unlike world/eye coordinates, NDC space is left-handed.

In this section, you will learn how to create camera transformation matrices. The first camera matrix is a frustum, which looks like a pyramid with the tip cut off. A frustum represents everything that is visible to the camera. You will also learn how to create different projections and how to implement a "look at" function that lets you easily create a view matrix.

Frustum

Visually, a frustum looks like a pyramid with the tip cut off. A frustum has six sides; it represents the space that a camera can see. Create the frustum function in mat4.cpp. This function takes left, right, bottom, top, near, and far values:

```
mat4 frustum(float l, float r, float b,
             float t, float n, float f) {
    if (l == r || t == b || n == f) {
        std::cout << "Invalid frustum\n";
        return mat4(); // Error
    }
    return mat4(
        (2.0f * n) / (r - l),0, 0, 0,
        0,    (2.0f * n) / (t - b), 0, 0,
        (r+l)/(r-l), (t+b)/(t-b), (-(f+n))/(f-n), -1,
        0, 0, (-2 * f * n) / (f - n), 0
    );
}
```

> **Important note**
>
> The details of deriving the frustum matrix are beyond the scope of this book. For more information on how to derive the function, check out http://www.songho.ca/opengl/gl_projectionmatrix.html.

The frustum function can be used to construct a view frustum, but the function parameters are not intuitive. In the next section, you will learn how to create a view frustum from more intuitive arguments.

Perspective

A perspective matrix is built from a field of view (typically in degrees), an aspect ratio, and near and far distances. It serves as an easy way to create a view frustum.

Implement the `perspective` function in `mat4.cpp`. Don't forget to add the function declaration to `mat4.h`:

```
mat4 perspective(float fov, float aspect, float n,float f){
    float ymax = n * tanf(fov * 3.14159265359f / 360.0f);
    float xmax = ymax * aspect;

    return frustum(-xmax, xmax, -ymax, ymax, n, f);
}
```

The `perspective` function will be used in almost all visual graphics demonstrations throughout the rest of this book. It's a really convenient way of creating a view frustum.

Orthographic

An orthographic projection has no perspective to it. An orthographic projection maps linearly to NDC space. Orthographic projections are often used for two-dimensional games. It's often used to achieve an isometric perspective.

Implement the `ortho` function in `mat4.cpp`. Don't forget to add the function declaration to `mat4.h`:

```
mat4 ortho(float l, float r, float b, float t,
           float n, float f) {
    if (l == r || t == b || n == f) {
        return mat4(); // Error
    }
    return mat4(
        2.0f / (r - 1), 0, 0, 0,
        0, 2.0f / (t - b), 0, 0,
        0, 0, -2.0f / (f - n), 0,
        -((r+l)/(r-1)),-((t+b)/(t-b)),-((f+n)/(f-n)), 1
    );
}
```

Orthographic view projections are generally useful for displaying UI or other two-dimensional elements.

Look at

The view matrix is the inverse of the camera's transformation (the position, rotation, and scale of the camera). Instead of having to create the camera's transform matrix and then invert it, you will be implementing a lookAt function that generates this matrix directly.

A lookAt function typically takes a position, the target point at which the camera is looking and a reference up direction. The rest of the work is finding the inverted basis vectors and figuring out where the position is.

Since the basis vectors are orthonormal, their inverse is the same as their transpose. The position can be calculated by negating the dot product of the position column vector with the inverted basis vectors.

Implement the lookAt function in mat4.cpp. Don't forget to add the function declaration to mat4.h. Remember, the view matrix maps the game world forward to the positive Z axis:

```
mat4 lookAt(const vec3& position, const vec3& target,
            const vec3& up) {
    vec3 f = normalized(target - position) * -1.0f;
    vec3 r = cross(up, f); // Right handed
    if (r == vec3(0, 0, 0)) {
        return mat4(); // Error
    }
    normalize(r);
    vec3 u = normalized(cross(f, r)); // Right handed

    vec3 t = vec3(
        -dot(r, position),
        -dot(u, position),
        -dot(f, position)
    );

    return mat4(
        // Transpose upper 3x3 matrix to invert it
        r.x, u.x, f.x, 0,
        r.y, u.y, f.y, 0,
        r.z, u.z, f.z, 0,
        t.x, t.y, t.z, 1
    );
}
```

The `lookAt` function is the most convenient way of constructing a view matrix. All of the code samples throughout the rest of this book will use the `lookAt` function to set up a view matrix.

Summary

In this chapter, you learned the math required to work with four-dimensional square matrices and implemented a reusable matrix library. Matrices are commonly used to encode transformation information; they are used at almost every step of the graphics pipeline to display models on screen.

In the next chapter, you will learn about encoding rotation data using quaternions.

4
Implementing Quaternions

In this chapter, you will learn about quaternions. Quaternions are used to encode rotations. A quaternion is a complex number in an $x_i + y_j + z_k + w$ form. Think of i, j, and k as placeholders that each represent a three-dimensional axis. w is a real number. While quaternions don't directly encode an angle axis pair, it's easy to think of them as just that—a rotation about an arbitrary axis.

By the end of this chapter, you should have a strong understanding of what quaternions are and how to use them and you will have implemented a robust quaternion class in code. This chapter will cover the following topics:

- Different methods for creating quaternions
- Retrieving the angle and axis of a quaternion
- Basic component-wise operations
- The length and dot product of two quaternions
- Inverting quaternions
- Combining quaternions

- Transforming vectors by quaternions
- Interpolating between quaternions
- Converting quaternions and matrices

Why are quaternions important? Most humanoid animations are created using only rotations—no translation or scale is needed. Think about an elbow joint, for example. The natural motion of an elbow only rotates. If you want to translate the elbow through space, you rotate the shoulder. Quaternions encode rotations and they interpolate well.

> **Important information:**
>
> In this chapter, you will implement quaternions with an intuitive, code-first approach. If you are interested in the more formal math behind quaternions, check out `https://gabormakesgames.com/quaternions.html`.

Creating quaternions

Quaternions are used to encode rotation data. In code, quaternions will have four components. They resemble `vec4` in that they have an `x`, `y`, `z`, and `w` component. As with `vec4`, the `w` component comes last.

The `quat` structure should have two constructors. The default constructor creates an identity quaternion, `(0, 0, 0, 1)`. The `(0, 0, 0, 1)` identity quaternion is like `1`. Any number multiplied by `1` remains the same. Similarly, any quaternion multiplied by the identity quaternion remains the same:

Create a new file, `quat.h`, to declare the quaternion structure. The `quat` structure is going to be used throughout the rest of this book to represent rotations:

```
#ifndef _H_QUAT_
#define _H_QUAT_
#include "vec3.h"
#include "mat4.h"

struct quat {
    union {
        struct {
            float x;
            float y;
            float z;
            float w;
```

```
    };
    struct {
        vec3 vector;
        float scalar;
    };
    float v[4];
};

inline quat() :
    x(0), y(0), z(0), w(1) { }
inline quat(float _x, float _y, float _z, float _w)
            : x(_x), y(_y), z(_z), w(_w) {}
};
#endif
```

The anonymous union inside the `quat` structure will allow you to access the data inside a quaternion through X, Y, Z, and W subscript notation, as a vector and scalar pair, or as an array of floating-point values.

Next, you're going to learn how to start creating quaternions.

Angle axis

Quaternions are often created using an axis of rotation and an angle. A rotation about an axis by θ can be represented on a sphere as any directed arc whose length is $\frac{1}{2}\theta$ on the plane perpendicular to the rotation axis. Positive angles yield a counterclockwise rotation around the axis.

Create a new file, `quat.cpp`. Implement the `angleAxis` function in `quat.cpp`. Don't forget to add the function declaration to `quat.h`:

```cpp
#include "quat.h"
#include <cmath>

quat angleAxis(float angle, const vec3& axis) {
    vec3 norm = normalized(axis);
    float s = sinf(angle * 0.5f);

    return quat(norm.x * s,
                norm.y * s,
                norm.z * s,
                cosf(angle * 0.5f)
    );
}
```

Why $\frac{1}{2}\theta$? A quaternion can track two full rotations, which is *720* degrees. This makes the period of a quaternion *720* degrees. The period of sin/cos is *360* degrees. Dividing θ by *2* maps the range of a quaternion to the range of sin/cos.

In this section, you learned how the angle and axis of a rotation are encoded in a quaternion. In the next section, you will learn how to build an angle and an axis for the rotation between two vectors and encode that into a quaternion.

Creating rotations from one vector to another

Any two-unit vectors can represent points on a sphere. The shortest arc between these points lies on a plane that contains both points and the center of the sphere. This plane is perpendicular to the axis of rotation between those two vectors.

To find the axis of rotation, normalize the input vectors. Find the cross product of the input vectors. This is the axis of rotation. Find the angle between the input vectors. From *Chapter 2, Implementing Vectors*, the formula for the angle between two vectors is $\theta = cos^{-1}\left(\frac{v0 \cdot v1}{|v0||v1|}\right)$. Since both input vectors are normalized, this simplifies to $\theta = cos^{-1}\left(\widehat{v1} \cdot \widehat{v2}\right)$, which means that the cosine of θ is the dot product of the input vectors:

$$\widehat{v1} \cdot \widehat{v2} = cos\ \theta$$

You will recall from *Chapter 2, Implementing Vectors*, that the dot product has a relationship to the cosine of the angle between two vectors, and that the cross product has a relationship to the sine of the angle between two vectors. When creating quaternions, the dot and cross product have the following properties:

$$\widehat{v1} \times \widehat{v2} = axis * sin\ \theta$$

$$\widehat{v1} \cdot \widehat{v2} = cos\ \theta$$

The cross product can be expanded into x, y, and z components and the previous equation starts to look like the code for creating a quaternion from an angle and an axis of rotation. Finding the angle between the two vectors would be expensive, but the half-angle can be counted without knowing what the angle is.

To find the half-angle, find the halfway vector between the *v1* and *v2* input vectors. Construct a quaternion using *v1* and this halfway vector. This will create a quaternion that results in the desired rotation.

There is one edge case—what happens when *v1* and *v2* are parallel? Or if *v1*== *-v2* ? The cross product that's used to find the axis of rotation would yield a *0* vector. If this edge case happens, find the most perpendicular vector between the two vectors to create a pure quaternion.

Perform the following steps to implement the `fromTo` function:

1. Begin to implement the `fromTo` function in `quat.cpp` and add the function declaration to `quat.h`. Start by normalizing the `from` and `to` vectors, making sure they are not the same vector:

```
quat fromTo(const vec3& from, const vec3& to) {
    vec3 f = normalized(from);
    vec3 t = normalized(to);
    if (f == t) {
        return quat();
    }
```

2. Next, check whether the two vectors are opposites of each other. If they are, the most orthogonal axis of the `from` vector can be used to create a pure quaternion:

```
    else if (f == t * -1.0f) {
        vec3 ortho = vec3(1, 0, 0);
        if (fabsf(f.y) <fabsf(f.x)) {
            ortho = vec3(0, 1, 0);
        }
        if (fabsf(f.z)<fabs(f.y) && fabs(f.z)<fabsf(f.x)){
            ortho = vec3(0, 0, 1);
        }
        vec3 axis = normalized(cross(f, ortho));
        return quat(axis.x, axis.y, axis.z, 0);
    }
```

3. Finally, create a half vector between the `from` and `to` vectors. Use the cross product of the half vector and the starting vector to calculate the axis of rotation and the dot product of the two to find the angle of rotation:

```
    vec3 half = normalized(f + t);
    vec3 axis = cross(f, half);
    return quat(axis.x, axis.y, axis.z, dot(f, half));
}
```

The `fromTo` function is one of the most intuitive ways of creating a quaternion. Next, you're going to learn how to retrieve the angle and the axis that define a quaternion.

Retrieving quaternion data

Since a quaternion can be created from an angle and an axis, it's reasonable to expect to be able to retrieve the same angle and axis from the quaternion. To retrieve the axis of rotation, normalize the vector part of the quaternion. The angle of rotation is double the inverse cosine of the real component.

Implement the getAngle and getAxis functions in quat.cpp and add function declarations for both in quat.h:

```cpp
vec3 getAxis(const quat& quat) {
    return normalized(vec3(quat.x, quat.y, quat.z));
}

float getAngle(const quat& quat) {
    return 2.0f * acosf(quat.w);
}
```

Being able to retrieve the angle and the axis that defines a quaternion will be needed later for some quaternion operations.

Next, you're going to learn about the component-wise operations that are commonly performed on quaternions.

Common quaternion operations

Like vectors, quaternions also have component-wise operations. Common component-wise operations are adding, subtracting, multiplying, or negating quaternions. Component-wise quaternion multiplication multiplies a quaternion by a single scalar value.

Since these functions are component-wise, they just perform the appropriate action on similar components of the input quaternions. Implement these functions in quat.cpp and add declarations for each function in quat.h:

```cpp
quat operator+(const quat& a, const quat& b) {
    return quat(a.x+b.x, a.y+b.y, a.z+b.z, a.w+b.w);
}

quat operator-(const quat& a, const quat& b) {
    return quat(a.x-b.x, a.y-b.y, a.z-b.z, a.w-b.w);
}

quat operator*(const quat& a, float b) {
```

```
        return quat(a.x * b, a.y * b, a.z * b, a.w * b);
}

quat operator-(const quat& q) {
    return quat(-q.x, -q.y, -q.z, -q.w);
}
```

These component-wise operations don't have much practical use by themselves. They are the building blocks for building the rest of the quaternion functionality on. Next, you're going to learn about the different ways to compare quaternions.

Comparison operations

Comparing two quaternions can be done component-wise. Two quaternions can represent the same rotation even if they are not identical on a component level. This happens because a quaternion and its inverse rotate to the same spot but they take different routes:

1. Overload the == and != operators in quat.cpp. Add the declaration for these functions to quat.h:

    ```
    bool operator==(const quat& left, const quat& right) {
        return (fabsf(left.x - right.x) <= QUAT_EPSILON &&
                fabsf(left.y - right.y) <= QUAT_EPSILON &&
                fabsf(left.z - right.z) <= QUAT_EPSILON &&
                fabsf(left.w - right.w) <= QUAT_EPSILON);
    }

    bool operator!=(const quat& a, const quat& b) {
        return !(a == b);
    }
    ```

2. To test whether two quaternions represent the same rotation, the absolute difference between the two needs to be tested. Implement the sameOrientation function in quat.cpp. Add the function declaration to quat.h:

    ```
    bool sameOrientation(const quat&l, const quat&r) {
        return (fabsf(l.x - r.x) <= QUAT_EPSILON  &&
                fabsf(l.y - r.y) <= QUAT_EPSILON  &&
                fabsf(l.z - r.z) <= QUAT_EPSILON  &&
                fabsf(l.w - r.w) <= QUAT_EPSILON) ||
               (fabsf(l.x + r.x) <= QUAT_EPSILON  &&
                fabsf(l.y + r.y) <= QUAT_EPSILON  &&
    ```

```
                    fabsf(l.z + r.z) <= QUAT_EPSILON  &&
                    fabsf(l.w + r.w) <= QUAT_EPSILON);
    }
```

Most of the time, you will want to use the equality operator to compare quaternions. The `sameOrientation` function is not as useful because the rotation that a quaternion takes can be changed if the quaternion is inverted.

In the next section, you will learn how to implement a quaternion dot product.

Dot product

Like with vectors, the dot product measures how similar two quaternions are. The implementation is the same as the vector implementation. Multiply like components and sum the result.

Implement the quaternion dot product function in `quat.cpp` and add its declaration to `quat.h`:

```
float dot(const quat& a, const quat& b) {
    return a.x * b.x + a.y * b.y + a.z * b.z + a.w * b.w;
}
```

Like vectors, the length of a quaternion is the dot product of the quaternion with itself. In the next section, you will learn how to find the squared length and length of a quaternion.

Length and squared length

Like vectors, the squared length of a quaternion is the same as the dot product of the quaternion with itself. The length of a quaternion is the square root of the square length:

1. Implement the `lenSq` function in `quat.cpp` and declare the function in `quat.h`:

```
float lenSq(const quat& q) {
    return q.x * q.x + q.y * q.y + q.z * q.z + q.w * q.w;
}
```

2. Implement the `len` function in `quat.cpp`. Don't forget to add the function declaration to `quat.h`:

```
float len(const quat& q) {
    float lenSq = q.x*q.x + q.y*q.y + q.z*q.z + q.w*q.w;
    if (lenSq< QUAT_EPSILON) {
        return 0.0f;
```

```
    }
    return sqrtf(lenSq);
}
```

Quaternions that represent a rotation should always have a length of *1*. In the next section, you will learn about unit quaternions, which always have a length of *1*.

Unit quaternions

Quaternions can be normalized just like vectors. Normalized quaternions represent only a rotation and non-normalized quaternions introduce a skew. In the context of game animation, quaternions should be normalized to avoid adding a skew to the transform.

To normalize a quaternion, divide each component of the quaternion by its length. The resulting quaternion's length will be *1*. This can be implemented as follows:

1. Implement the `normalize` function in `quat.cpp` and declare it in `quat.h`:

```cpp
void normalize(quat& q) {
    float lenSq = q.x*q.x + q.y*q.y + q.z*q.z + q.w*q.w;
    if (lenSq < QUAT_EPSILON) {
        return;
    }
    float i_len = 1.0f / sqrtf(lenSq);

    q.x *= i_len;
    q.y *= i_len;
    q.z *= i_len;
    q.w *= i_len;
}
```

2. Implement the `normalized` function in `quat.cpp`, and declare it in `quat.h`:

```cpp
quat normalized(const quat& q) {
    float lenSq = q.x*q.x + q.y*q.y + q.z*q.z + q.w*q.w;
    if (lenSq < QUAT_EPSILON) {
        return quat();
    }
    float il = 1.0f / sqrtf(lenSq); // il: inverse length

    return quat(q.x * il, q.y * il, q.z * il,q.w * il);
}
```

There is a fast way of inverting any unit quaternion. In the next section, you will learn how to find the conjugate and inverse of a quaternion and their relationship when it comes to unit quaternions.

Conjugate and inverse

Games mostly use normalized quaternions, which comes in handy when inverting quaternions. The inverse of a normalized quaternion is its conjugate. The conjugate of a quaternion flips its axis of rotation:

1. Implement the `conjugate` function in `quat.cpp` and remember to declare the function in `quat.h`:

```cpp
quat conjugate(const quat& q) {
    return quat(
        -q.x,
        -q.y,
        -q.z,
         q.w
    );
}
```

2. The proper inverse of a quaternion is the conjugate divided by the squared length of the quaternion. Implement the quaternion `inverse` function in `quat.cpp`. Add the function declaration to `quat.h`:

```cpp
quat inverse(const quat& q) {
    float lenSq = q.x*q.x + q.y*q.y + q.z*q.z + q.w*q.w;
    if (lenSq < QUAT_EPSILON) {
        return quat();
    }
    float recip = 1.0f / lenSq;
    return quat(-q.x * recip,
                -q.y * recip,
                -q.z * recip,
                 q.w * recip
    );
}
```

If you need to find out whether a quaternion is normalized or not, check the squared length. The squared length of a normalized quaternion is always *1*. If a quaternion is normalized, its conjugate and inverse are the same. This means you can use the faster `conjugate` function, instead of the `inverse` function. In the next section, you will learn how to multiply two quaternions together.

Multiplying quaternions

Two quaternions can be concatenated by multiplying them together. Like with matrices, the operation is carried out from right to left; the right quaternion's rotation is applied first and then the left quaternion's.

Assume you have two quaternions, q and p. They are subscripted with 0, 1, 2, and 3, which correspond to the X, Y, Z, and W components, respectively. These quaternions can be expressed in *ijk* notation, as shown:

$$q = q_0 i + q_1 j + q_2 k + q_3$$
$$p = p_0 i + p_1 j + p_2 k + p_3$$

To multiply these two quaternions together, distribute the components of p to the components of q. Distributing the real component is simple. Distributing p_3 to q would look like this:

$$p_3 q_0 i + p_3 q_1 j + p_3 q_2 k + p_3 q_3$$

Distributing the imaginary components looks very similar. The real and imaginary parts are combined separately; the order of imaginary components matters. For example, distributing $p_0 i$ to q would look like this:

$$p_0 q_0 i^2 + p_0 q_1 ij + p_0 q_2 ik + p_0 q_3 i$$

Fully distributing p to q looks like this:

$$p_0 q_0 i^2 + p_0 q_1 ij + p_0 q_2 ik + p_0 q_3 i$$
$$p_1 q_0 ji + p_1 q_1 j^2 + p_1 q_2 jk + p_1 q_3 j$$
$$p_2 q_0 ki + p_2 q_1 kj + p_2 q_2 k^2 + p_2 q_3 k$$
$$p_3 q_0 i + p_3 q_1 j + p_3 q_2 k + p_3 q_3$$

Start simplifying for the case when imaginary numbers are squared. The square root of an imaginary number is *-1*. If you raise *-1* to the power of *-1*, the result is also *-1*. This means that any instance of i^2, j^2, or k^2 can be replaced by *-1*, like so:

$$p_0q_0(-1) + p_0q_1ij + p_0q_2ik + p_0q_3i$$
$$p_1q_0ji + p_1q_1(-1) + p_1q_2jk + p_1q_3j$$
$$p_2q_0ki + p_2q_1kj + p_2q_2(-1) + p_2q_3k$$
$$p_3q_0i + p_3q_1j + p_3q_2k + p_3q_3$$

What about the rest of the imaginary numbers? When talking about quaternions, *ijk= -1*, the squared value of each of these components is also *-1*, which means that $i^2 = j^2 = k^2 = ijk$. This property of quaternions can be used to simplify the rest of the equation.

Take *jk*, for example. Start with *ijk= -1* and try to isolate *jk* to one side of the equation. To do this, multiply both sides by *i*, leaving you with *i(ijk)= -i*. Distribute *i*, which will leave you with i^2 *jk= -i*. You already know that the value of i^2 is *-1*. Substitute it to get *-jk= -i*. Multiply both sides by *-1* and you have found the value of *jk— jk=i*.

The values for *ki* and *ij* can be found in a similar way; they are *ki=j* and *k=ij*. You can now substitute any instances of *ki* with *j*, *ij* with *k*, and *jk* with *i*. Substituting these values leaves you with the following:

$$p_0q_0(-1) + p_0q_1k + p_0q_2ik + p_0q_3i$$
$$p_1q_0ji + p_1q_1(-1) + p_1q_2i + p_1q_3j$$
$$p_2q_0j + p_2q_1kj + p_2q_2(-1) + p_2q_3k$$
$$p_3q_0i + p_3q_1j + p_3q_2k + p_3q_3$$

The remaining imaginary numbers are *ik*, *ji*, and *kj*. Like the cross product, the order matters: *ik= -ki*. From this, you can assume that *ik= -j*, *ji= -k*, and *kj= -1*. Substituting these values leaves you with the following:

$$p_0q_0(-1) + p_0q_1k + p_0q_2(-j) + p_0q_3i$$
$$p_1q_0(-k) + p_1q_1(-1) + p_1q_2i + p_1q_3j$$
$$p_2q_0j + p_2q_1(-i) + p_2q_2(-1) + p_2q_3k$$
$$p_3q_0i + p_3q_1j + p_3q_2k + p_3q_3$$

Numbers with different imaginary components cannot be added together. Re-arrange the preceding formula so that like imaginary components are next to each other. This results in the final equation for quaternion multiplication:

$$+p_0q_3i + p_1q_2i - p_2q_1i + p_3q_0i$$
$$-p_0q_2j + p_1q_3j + p_2q_0j + p_3q_1j$$
$$+p_0q_1k - p_1q_0k + p_2q_3k + p_3q_2k$$
$$-p_0q_0 - p_1q_1 - p_2q_2 + p_3q_3$$

To implement this formula in code, change from this subscripted *ijk* notation back to vector notation with X, Y, Z, and W subscripts. Implement the quaternion multiplication function in quat.cpp and don't forget to add the function declaration to quat.h:

```cpp
quat operator*(const quat& Q1, const quat& Q2) {
    return quat(
        Q2.x*Q1.w + Q2.y*Q1.z - Q2.z*Q1.y + Q2.w*Q1.x,
        -Q2.x*Q1.z + Q2.y*Q1.w + Q2.z*Q1.x + Q2.w*Q1.y,
        Q2.x*Q1.y - Q2.y*Q1.x + Q2.z*Q1.w + Q2.w*Q1.z,
        -Q2.x*Q1.x - Q2.y*Q1.y - Q2.z*Q1.z + Q2.w*Q1.w
    );
}
```

When looking at the preceding code, notice that the real part of the quaternion has one positive component, but the vector part has one negative component. Re-arrange the quaternion so that the negative numbers are always last. Write it down using vector notation:

$$qp_x = p_x\,q_w + p_w\,q_x + p_y\,q_z - p_z\,q_y$$

$$qp_y = p_y\,q_w + p_w\,q_y + p_z\,q_x - p_x\,q_z$$

$$qp_z = p_z\,q_w + p_w\,q_z + p_x\,q_y - p_y\,q_x$$

$$qp_w = p_w\,q_w - p_x\,q_x - p_y\,q_y - p_z\,q_z$$

There are two interesting parts in the preceding equation. If you look closely at the last two columns of the first three rows, the columns with the subtraction are the cross product. The first two columns are just scaling the vector parts of each quaternion by the scalar parts of the others.

If you look at the last row, the dot product is in there with the negative of the dot product. The last row is basically multiplying the real parts of both quaternions, then subtracting the dot product of their vector parts. This means that an alternate multiplication implementation could look like this:

```
quat operator*(const quat& Q1, const quat& Q2) {
   quat result;
   result.scalar = Q2.scalar * Q1.scalar -
   dot(Q2.vector, Q1.vector);
   result.vector = (Q1.vector * Q2.scalar) +
   (Q2.vector * Q1.scalar)+cross(Q2.vector, Q1.vector);
   return result;
}
```

The original implementation is a bit more performant since it doesn't need to invoke other functions. The sample code for this book will use the first implementation.

Next, you will learn how to transform vectors by quaternions.

Transforming vectors

To multiply a vector and a quaternion, you first have to turn the vector into a pure quaternion. What is a pure quaternion? It's a quaternion whose W component is 0 and the vector part is normalized. Assume you have a quaternion, q, and a vector, v. First, turn v into a pure quaternion, represented as v':

$$v = (x, y, z)$$

$$v' = (\hat{v}_x, \hat{v}_y, \hat{v}_z, 0)$$

Next, multiply q by v' then multiply the result by the inverse of q. The result of this multiplication is a pure quaternion whose vector part contains the rotated vector. The quaternion becomes the following:

$$r = (q * v' * q^{-1}).xyz$$

Why is v' multiplied by q and then q^{-1}? Multiplying by q will rotate the vector twice as much as the rotation of q. Multiplying by q^{-1} brings the vector back into the expected range. This formula can be simplified further.

Deriving this formula is outside the scope of this book. Given a quaternion, q, and a vector, v, the simplified vector quaternion multiplication formula is listed as follows. q_v refers to the vector part of the quaternion and q_s refers to the real (or scalar) part:

$$2(q_v \cdot v)q_v + (q_s^2 - q_v \cdot q_v)v + 2q_s(q_v \times v)$$

Implement the preceding formula for quaternion vector multiplication in quat.cpp. Don't forget to add the function declaration to quat.h:

```
vec3 operator*(const quat& q, const vec3& v) {
    return q.vector * 2.0f * dot(q.vector, v) +
        v * (q.scalar * q.scalar - dot(q.vector, q.vector)) +
        cross(q.vector, v) * 2.0f * q.scalar;
}
```

Multiplying a vector by a quaternion will always yield a vector that is rotated by the quaternion. In the next section, you're going to learn about interpolating between quaternions.

Interpolating quaternions

Quaternions can be interpolated in a similar fashion to vectors. Quaternion interpolation is used to animate rotation between two keyframes. Since most skeletal animation is achieved by rotating joints over time, interpolating between quaternions is going to be a very common operation.

Neighborhood

A quaternion represents a rotation, not an orientation. Rotating from one part of a sphere to another can be achieved by one of two rotations. The rotation can take the shortest or the longest arc. Generally, having quaternions travel along the shortest arc is desirable. When interpolating between two quaternions, which path will be taken—the shortest arc or the longest?

This problem is called neighborhooding. To solve it, check the dot product of the quaternions being interpolated. If the dot product is positive, the shorter arc will be taken. If the dot product is negative, the longer arc will be taken.

If the dot product is negative, how can you correct the interpolation to take the shortest arc? The answer is to negate one of the quaternions. An example of quaternion neighborhooding is provided in the following code sample:

```
quat SampleFunction(const quat& a, const quat& b) {
    if (dot(a, b) < 0.0f) {
        b = -b;
    }
    return slerp(a, b, 0.5f);
}
```

You only need to neighborhood quaternions when interpolating between them. Next, you will learn how to mix linear interpolation (`lerp`), normalized linear interpolation (`nlerp`), and spherical linear interpolation (`slerp`) quaternions. Remember that these functions expect the quaternion to already be in its desired neighborhood.

Understanding the mix function

When mixing two or more quaternions together, each quaternion is scaled by some weight value, then the resulting scaled quaternions are added together. All the weights of all input quaternions must add up to *1*.

If all input quaternions are of unit length, the resulting quaternion will be of unit length as well. This function achieves the same result as `lerp` does, but it's not really a `lerp` function as the quaternion still travels on an arc. To avoid any confusion, this function will be called `mix`, not `lerp`.

The `mix` function assumes that the input quaternions are in the desired neighborhood. Implement the `mix` function in `quat.cpp` and don't forget to add the function declaration to `quat.h`:

```
quat mix(const quat& from, const quat& to, float t) {
    return from * (1.0f - t) + to * t;
}
```

Understanding the nlerp function

`nlerp` between quaternions is a fast and good approximation for spherical interpolation. Its implementation is almost the same as the `nlerp` implementation of the `vec3` class.

Like `mix`, `nlerp` also assumes the input vectors are in the desired neighborhood. Implement the `nlerp` function in `quat.cpp` and don't forget to add the function declaration to `quat.h`:

```
quat nlerp(const quat& from, const quat& to, float t) {
    return normalized(from + (to - from) * t);
}
```

Introduction to slerp

`slerp` should only be used if consistent velocity is required. In most cases, `nlerp` will be a better interpolation method. Depending on the interpolation step size, `slerp` may end up falling back to `nlerp` anyway.

In order to spherically interpolate between two quaternions, create a delta quaternion between the two. Adjust the angle of the delta quaternion, then concatenate it with the starting quaternion using quaternion multiplication.

How can the angle of a quaternion be adjusted? To adjust the angle of a quaternion, raise it to the desired power. For example, to adjust the quaternion to only rotate halfway, you would raise it to the power of *0.5*.

Power

To raise a quaternion to some power, it needs to be decomposed into an angle and an axis. Then, the angle can be adjusted by the power and a new quaternion can be built from the adjusted angle and axis. If a quaternion rotates around the *v* axis by an θ angle, raising it to some power, *t*, would be done as follows:

$$\left(v \sin\left(\frac{t\theta}{2}\right), \cos\left(\frac{t\theta}{2}\right) \right)$$

Implement the `power operator` in `quat.cpp`. Don't forget to add the function declaration to `quat.h`:

```
quat operator^(const quat& q, float f) {
    float angle = 2.0f * acosf(q.scalar);
    vec3 axis = normalized(q.vector);

    float halfCos = cosf(f * angle * 0.5f);
    float halfSin = sinf(f * angle * 0.5f);

    return quat(axis.x * halfSin,
                axis.y * halfSin,
                axis.z * halfSin,
```

```
                    halfCos
        );
}
```

Implementing slerp

Now that you know how to raise a quaternion to a power, implementing `slerp` becomes straightforward. If the start and end quaternions are very close together, `slerp` tends to produce unexpected results. If the start and end quaternions are close together, fall back on `nlerp`.

To interpolate between two quaternions, find the delta quaternion from the start rotation to the end rotation. This delta quaternion is the interpolation path. Raise the angle to the power of how much the two quaternions are being interpolated between (usually represented as *t*) and multiply the start quaternion back.

Implement the `slerp` function in `quat.cpp`. Don't forget to add the function declaration to `quat.h`. Like the other interpolation functions, `slerp` assumes that the quaternions being interpolated are in the desired neighborhoods:

```
quat slerp(const quat& start, const quat& end, float t) {
    if (fabsf(dot(start, end)) > 1.0f - QUAT_EPSILON) {
        return nlerp(start, end, t);
    }

    quat delta = inverse(start) * end;
    return normalized((delta ^ t) * start);
}
```

The input vectors to `slerp` should be normalized, which means you could use `conjugate` instead of `inverse` in the `slerp` function. Most of the time, `nlerp` will be used over `slerp`. In the next section, you will learn how to create a quaternion that points in a specific direction.

Look rotation

Given a direction and a reference for which way is up, it's possible to create a quaternion that looks in that direction with the correct orientation. This function will be called `lookRotation`—not `lookAt`, to avoid any confusion with the matrix `lookAt` function.

To implement the `lookRotation` function, find a quaternion that rotates to the desired direction. To do this, create a quaternion between the world `forward` vector *(0, 0, 1)* and the `desired direction`. This quaternion will rotate to the `right` target, but with no regard for what direction up might be.

To correct the up direction of this quaternion, you first have to find a vector that is perpendicular to the current forward direction and the desired up direction. This can be done by taking the cross product of the two vectors.

The result of this cross product will be used to construct three orthogonal vectors—the forward vector, this new vector, and a vector that points up. The one you just found would point to the right.

Next, you need to find a vector that is perpendicular to both the `forward` and `right` directions; this will be the orthonormal up vector. To find this vector, take the cross product of the direction and this `right` vector and the result is the object space up vector.

Find a quaternion that rotates from the desired up vector to the object up vector. Multiply the quaternion that rotates to the target direction and the quaternion that rotates from `desired up` to `object up`.

Implement the `lookRotation` function in `quat.cpp`. Don't forget to add the function declaration to `quat.h`:

```cpp
quat lookRotation(const vec3& direction, const vec3& up) {
    // Find orthonormal basis vectors
    vec3 f = normalized(direction); // Object Forward
    vec3 u = normalized(up); // Desired Up
    vec3 r = cross(u, f); // Object Right
    u = cross(f, r); // Object Up

    // From world forward to object forward
    quat worldToObject = fromTo(vec3(0, 0, 1), f);

    // what direction is the new object up?
    vec3 objectUp = worldToObject * vec3(0, 1, 0);
    // From object up to desired up
    quat u2u = fromTo(objectUp, u);

    // Rotate to forward direction first
    // then twist to correct up
    quat result = worldToObject * u2u;
```

```
    // Don't forget to normalize the result
    return normalized(result);
}
```

The matrix `lookAt` function creates a view matrix, which is the inverse of the camera transform. This means the rotation of `lookAt` and the result of `lookRotation` are going to be the inverse of each other. In the next section, you will learn how to convert matrices to quaternions and quaternions to matrices.

Converting between quaternions and matrices

Since both matrices and quaternions can be used to encode rotation data, it will be useful to be able to convert between them. To make converting between the two easier, you have to start thinking about rotation in terms of basis vectors, which are the vectors that represent the *x*, *y*, and *z* axes.

The upper 3 x 3 sub-matrix of a 4 x 4 matrix contains three basis vectors. The first column is the `right` vector, the second is the `up` vector, and the third is the `forward` vector. Using only the `forward` and `up` vectors, the `lookRotation` function can be used to convert a matrix into a quaternion.

To convert a quaternion into a matrix, simply multiply the world basis vectors, which are the *x*, *y*, and *z* axes of the world, by the quaternion. Store the resulting vectors in the appropriate components of the matrix:

1. Implement the `quatToMat4` function in `quat.cpp`. Don't forget to add the function declaration to `quat.h`:

```
mat4 quatToMat4(const quat& q) {
    vec3 r = q * vec3(1, 0, 0);
    vec3 u = q * vec3(0, 1, 0);
    vec3 f = q * vec3(0, 0, 1);

    return mat4(r.x, r.y, r.z, 0,
                u.x, u.y, u.z, 0,
                f.x, f.y, f.z, 0,
                0  , 0  , 0  , 1
    );
}
```

2. A matrix stores both rotation and scale data using some of the same components. To address this, the basis vectors need to be normalized and the cross product needs to be used to make sure that the resulting vectors are orthogonal. Implement the `mat4ToQuat` function in `quat.cpp` and don't forget to add the function declaration to `quat.h`:

```
quat mat4ToQuat(const mat4& m) {
    vec3 up = normalized(vec3(m.up.x, m.up.y, m.up.z));
    vec3 forward = normalized(
        vec3(m.forward.x, m.forward.y, m.forward.z));
    vec3 right = cross(up, forward);
    up = cross(forward, right);

    return lookRotation(forward, up);
}
```

Being able to convert quaternions to matrices will be useful later when you need to pass rotation data to a shader. Shaders don't know what a quaternion is, but they have built-in functionality to deal with matrices. Converting matrices to quaternions is going to be useful for debugging and in the case where an external data source only provides rotations as matrices.

Summary

In this chapter, you implemented a robust quaternion library. Quaternions are important to the rest of this book as all animated rotation data is recorded as quaternions. You learned how to create quaternions and common quaternion operations, combine quaternions with multiplication, transform vectors by quaternions, interpolate quaternions and utility functions to create quaternions given a forward and up direction, and convert between matrices and quaternions.

In the next chapter, you will use your combined knowledge of vectors, matrices, and quaternions to define a transformation object.

5
Implementing Transforms

In this chapter, you will implement a structure that holds position, rotation, and scale data. This structure is a transform. A transform maps from one space to another space. Position, rotation, and scale could also be stored in a 4x4 matrix, so why would you want to use an explicit transform struct instead of a matrix? The answer is interpolation. Matrices don't interpolate well, but transform structures do.

Interpolating between two matrices is difficult because rotation and scale are stored in the same components of the matrix. Because of this, interpolating between two matrices doesn't yield the result you would expect. Transforms solve this problem by storing the position, rotation, and scale components separately.

In this chapter, you will implement a transform structure and the common operations that you need to be able to perform in transforms. By the end of this chapter, you should be able to do the following:

- Understand what a transform is
- Understand how to combine transforms
- Convert between transforms and matrices
- Understand how to apply transforms to points and vectors

> **Important information**
>
> In this chapter, you will implement a transform structure that represents position, rotation, and scale. To find out more about transforms, how they relate to matrices, and how they fit into game hierarchies, check out `http://gabormakesgames.com/transforms.html`.

Creating the transform

Transforms are simple structures. A transform contains a position, rotation, and scale. Position and scale are vectors and rotation is a quaternion. Transforms can be combined hierarchically, but this parent-child relationship should not be a part of the actual transform structure. The following steps will guide you through creating a transform structure:

1. Create a new file, `Transform.h`. This file is required to declare the transform structure.

2. Begin declaring the `Transform` structure in this new file. Start with the properties of the transform—`position`, `rotation`, and `scale`:

    ```
    struct Transform {
        vec3 position;
        quat rotation;
        vec3 scale;
    ```

3. Create a constructor that takes a position, rotation, and scale. This constructor should assign these values to the appropriate members of the Transform struct:

    ```
    Transform(const vec3& p, const quat& r, const vec3& s) :
        position(p), rotation(r), scale(s) {}
    ```

4. A blank transform should have no position or rotation and a scale of one. By default, the `scale` component will be created as `(0, 0, 0)`. To solve this, the default constructor of the `Transform` struct needs to initialize the `scale` to the correct value:

    ```
    Transform() :
        position(vec3(0, 0, 0)),
        rotation(quat(0, 0, 0, 1)),
        scale(vec3(1, 1, 1))
    {}
    }; // End of transform struct
    ```

The `Transform` structure is fairly straightforward; all of its members are public. A transform has a position, rotation, and scale. The default constructor sets the position vector to *0*, the rotation quaternion to identity, and the scale vector to *1*. The transformation created by the default constructor has no effect.

In the next section, you will learn how to combine transforms in a similar way to matrices or quaternions.

Combining transforms

Consider a skeleton, as an example. At each joint, you could place a transform to describe the motion of the joint. When you rotate your shoulder, the elbow attached to that shoulder also moves. To apply the shoulder transformation to all connected joints, the transform on each joint must be combined with its parent joint's transform.

Transforms can be combined in the same way as matrices and quaternions and the effects of two transforms can be combined into one transform. To keep things consistent, combining transforms should maintain a right-to-left combination order. Unlike matrices and quaternions, this `combine` function will not be implemented as a multiplication function.

Combining the scale and rotation of two transforms is simple—multiply them together. Combining the position is a bit harder. The combined position needs to be affected by the `rotation` and `scale` components as well. When finding the combined position, remember the order of transformations: scale first, rotate second, and translate last.

Create a new file, `Transform.cpp`. Implement the `combine` function and don't forget to add the function declaration to `Transform.h`:

```
Transform combine(const Transform& a, const Transform& b) {
    Transform out;

    out.scale = a.scale * b.scale;
    out.rotation = b.rotation * a.rotation;

    out.position = a.rotation * (a.scale * b.position);
    out.position = a.position + out.position;

    return out;
}
```

In later chapters, the `combine` function will be used to organize transforms into a hierarchy. In the next section, you will learn how to invert transforms, which is again similar to inverting matrices and quaternions.

Inverting transforms

You already know that a transform maps from one space into another space. It's possible to reverse that mapping and map the transform back into the original space. As with matrices and quaternions, transforms can also be inverted.

When inverting scale, keep in mind that 0 can't be inverted. The case where scale is 0 will need to be treated specially

Implement the `inverse` transform method in `Transform.cpp`. Don't forget to declare the method in `Transform.h`:

```
Transform inverse(const Transform& t) {
    Transform inv;

    inv.rotation = inverse(t.rotation);

    inv.scale.x = fabs(t.scale.x) < VEC3_EPSILON ?
                  0.0f : 1.0f / t.scale.x;
    inv.scale.y = fabs(t.scale.y) < VEC3_EPSILON ?
                  0.0f : 1.0f / t.scale.y;
    inv.scale.z = fabs(t.scale.z) < VEC3_EPSILON ?
                  0.0f : 1.0f / t.scale.z;

    vec3 invTrans = t.position * -1.0f;
    inv.position = inv.rotation * (inv.scale * invTrans);

    return inv;
}
```

Inverting a transform can be done to remove the effects of one transform from another transform. Consider a character moving through a level. Once the level is over, you might want to move the character back to the origin before starting the next level. You could multiply the transform of the character by its inverse.

In the next section, you will learn how to mix two or more transforms together.

Mixing transforms

You have transforms that represent joints at two specific points in time. To make the model appear animated, you need to interpolate or mix between the transformation of these frames.

It's possible to interpolate between vectors and quaternions, the building blocks of a transform. So it's possible to interpolate between transforms as well. Instead of interpolation, this operation is typically called blend or mix. When mixing two transforms together, linearly interpolate the position, rotation, and scale of the input transforms.

Implement the `mix` function in `Transform.cpp`. Don't forget to declare the function in `Transform.h`:

```cpp
Transform mix(const Transform& a,const Transform& b,float t){
    quat bRot = b.rotation;
    if (dot(a.rotation, bRot) < 0.0f) {
        bRot = -bRot;
    }

    return Transform(
        lerp(a.position, b.position, t),
        nlerp(a.rotation, bRot, t),
        lerp(a.scale, b.scale, t));
}
```

Being able to mix transformations together is important for creating smooth transitions between animations. Here, you implemented a linear blend between transforms. In the next section, you will learn how to convert a `transform` into a `mat4`.

Converting transforms to matrices

Shader programs work well with matrices. They don't have a native representation of a transform structure. You could port the transform code into GLSL, but that's not the best solution. Instead, you could convert a transform into a matrix right before submitting it as a shader uniform.

Since transforms encode data that could be stored in matrices, it's possible to convert a transform into a matrix. To convert a transform into a matrix, the matrix needs to be thought of in terms of vectors.

First, find the basis vectors by multiplying the orientation of the global basis vectors by the transform's rotation. Next, scale the basis vectors by the scale of the transform. This yields the final basis vectors to fill the upper 3x3 sub-matrix. The position goes directly into the last column of the matrix.

Implement the from `Transform` method in `Transform.cpp`. Don't forget to add the function declaration to `Transform.h`:

```
mat4 transformToMat4(const Transform& t) {
    // First, extract the rotation basis of the transform
    vec3 x = t.rotation * vec3(1, 0, 0);
    vec3 y = t.rotation * vec3(0, 1, 0);
    vec3 z = t.rotation * vec3(0, 0, 1);

    // Next, scale the basis vectors
    x = x * t.scale.x;
    y = y * t.scale.y;
    z = z * t.scale.z;

    // Extract the position of the transform
    vec3 p = t.position;

    // Create matrix
    return mat4(
        x.x, x.y, x.z, 0, // X basis (& Scale)
        y.x, y.y, y.z, 0, // Y basis (& scale)
        z.x, z.y, z.z, 0, // Z basis (& scale)
        p.x, p.y, p.z, 1  // Position
    );
}
```

Graphics APIs work with matrices not transforms. In later chapters, transforms will be converted into matrices before being sent to a shader. In the next section, you will learn how to do the opposite, which is converting matrices into transforms.

Converting matrices into transforms

External file formats might store transformation data as matrices. glTF, for example, can store the transform of a node as the position, rotation, and scale, or as a single 4x4 matrix. To make the transform code robust, you need to be able to convert matrices to transforms.

Converting a matrix to a transform is more difficult than converting a transform to a matrix. Extracting the rotation of the matrix is simple; you have already implemented a function to turn a 4x4 matrix into a quaternion. Extracting the position is also simple; copy the last column of the matrix into a vector. Extracting the scale is more difficult.

Recall that the order of operations for a transform is to scale, rotate, and then translate. This means that if you had three matrices—*S*, *R*, and *T*—that represent scale, rotation, and translation, respectively, they would combine into a transform matrix, *M*, as follows:

$$M = SRT$$

To find the scale, first, ignore the translation part of the matrix, *M* (zero out the translation vector). This leaves you with *M = SR*. To remove the rotation component of the matrix, multiply *M* by the inverse of *R*. That should leave only the scale component. Well, not exactly. The result would leave a matrix that contains a scale and some skew information.

The way we will extract the scale from this scale-skew matrix is to simply take the main diagonal as the scale-skew matrix. While this will work most of the time, it's not perfect. The scale that is acquired should be considered a lossy scale, as the value can contain skew data as well, which makes the scale inaccurate.

> **Important note**
>
> It is possible to decompose a matrix into translation, rotation, scale, skew, and the sign of the determinant. However, this decomposition is expensive and not well suited to real-time applications. To learn more, check out *Matrix Animation and Polar Decomposition* by Ken Shoemake and Tom Duff at https://research.cs.wisc.edu/graphics/Courses/838-s2002/Papers/polar-decomp.pdf.

Implement the toTransform function in Transform.cpp. Don't forget to add the function declaration to Transform.h:

```
Transform mat4ToTransform(const mat4& m) {
    Transform out;

    out.position = vec3(m.v[12], m.v[13], m.v[14]);
    out.rotation = mat4ToQuat(m);

    mat4 rotScaleMat(
        m.v[0], m.v[1], m.v[2], 0,
        m.v[4], m.v[5], m.v[6], 0,
        m.v[8], m.v[9], m.v[10], 0,
        0, 0, 0, 1
    );
    mat4 invRotMat = quatToMat4(inverse(out.rotation));
    mat4 scaleSkewMat = rotScaleMat * invRotMat;

    out.scale = vec3(
```

```
        scaleSkewMat.v[0],
        scaleSkewMat.v[5],
        scaleSkewMat.v[10]
    );

    return out;
}
```

It's important that you're able to convert matrices to transforms because you don't always control what format the data you are dealing with comes in. For example, a model format might store matrices instead of transforms.

By now, you have probably noticed that transforms and matrices can generally do the same things. In the next section, you will learn how to transform points and vectors using transforms, in a similar way to how it's done with matrices.

Transforming points and vectors

The Transform structure can be used to move points and vectors in space. Imagine a ball bouncing up and down. The bounce of the ball is derived from the Transform structure, but how do you know where to move each vertex of the ball? You need to transform all the vertices using the Transform structure (or a matrix) to properly display the ball.

Using a transform to modify points and vectors is like combining two transforms. To transform a point, first, apply the scale, then rotation, and finally, the translation of the transform. To transform a vector, follow the same steps, but don't add the position:

1. Implement the transformPoint function in Transform.cpp. Don't forget to add the function declaration to Transform.h:

```
vec3 transformPoint(const Transform& a, const vec3& b) {
    vec3 out;

    out = a.rotation * (a.scale * b);
    out = a.position + out;

    return out;
}
```

2. Implement the `transformVector` function in `Transform.cpp`. Don't forget to add the function declaration to `Transform.h`:

```
vec3 transformVector(const Transform& a, const vec3& b) {
    vec3 out;

    out = a.rotation * (a.scale * b);

    return out;
}
```

The `transformPoint` function does the same thing that multiplying a matrix and a point does, just one step at a time. `scale` is applied first, then `rotation`, and `translation`, last. When you're dealing with a vector instead of a point, the same order applies, except the translation is ignored.

Summary

In this chapter, you learned how to implement a transformation as a discreet structure that contains a position, rotation, and scale. In many ways, the `Transform` class holds the same data that you would normally store in a matrix.

You learned how to combine, invert, and mix between transforms, as well as how to use transforms to move points and rotate vectors. Transforms are going to be essential moving forward, as they are used to animate the armature or skeleton of game models.

The reason you need an explicit `Transform` struct is that matrices don't interpolate well. Interpolating transforms is very important for animation. It's how you create in-between poses to display two given keyframes.

In the next chapter, you will learn how to write a light abstraction layer on top of OpenGL to make rendering in future chapters easier.

6
Building an Abstract Renderer

This book focuses on animation, not rendering. However, rendering an animated model is important. In order to avoid getting caught up in any specific graphics APIs, in this chapter, you will build an abstraction layer on top of OpenGL. This will be a thin abstraction layer, but it will let you work on your animation in later chapters without having to do anything OpenGL-specific.

The abstract renderer you will implement in this chapter is very lightweight. It doesn't have a lot of features, only the ones you need to display animated models. This should make porting the renderer to other APIs straightforward.

By the end of this chapter, you should be able to render some debug geometry to the window using the abstract rendering code you will create. On a higher level, you will learn the following:

- How to create shaders
- How to store mesh data in buffers
- How to bind those buffers as shader attributes
- How to send uniform data to a shader

- How to render with index buffers

- How to load textures

- Basic OpenGL concepts

- Creating and working with simple shaders

Technical requirements

Some familiarity with OpenGL will make this chapter much easier to follow. OpenGL, lighting models, and shader tricks are out of the scope of this book. For more information on these topics, check out `https://learnopengl.com/`.

Working with shaders

The most important part of the abstraction layer is the `Shader` class. To draw something, you must bind a shader and attach some attributes and uniforms to it. The shader describes how the thing being drawn should be transformed and shaded, while attributes define what is being drawn.

In this section, you will implement a `Shader` class that can compile vertex and fragment shaders. The `Shader` class will also return uniform and attribute indices.

The Shader class declaration

When implementing the `Shader` class, you will need to declare several protected helper functions. These functions will keep the public API of the class clean; they are used for things such as reading a file into a string or calling an OpenGL code to compile the shader:

1. Create a new file to declare the `Shader` class in; call it `Shader.h`. The `Shader` class should have a handle to the OpenGL shader object and maps for attribute and uniform indices. These dictionaries have a string for a key (the name of the attribute or uniform) and `unsigned int` for a value (the index of the uniform or attribute):

```
class Shader {
private:
    unsigned int mHandle;

    std::map<std::string, unsigned int> mAttributes;
    std::map<std::string, unsigned int> mUniforms;
```

2. The copy constructor and assignment operator of the Shader class should be disabled. The Shader class is not intended to be copied by value since it holds a handle to a GPU resource:

```
private:
    Shader(const Shader&);
    Shader& operator=(const Shader&);
```

3. Next, you need to declare the helper function in the Shader class. The ReadFile function will read the contents of a file into std::string. The CompileVertexShader and CompileFragmentShader functions compile shader source code and return an OpenGL handle. The LinkShader function will link two shaders into a shader program. The PopulateAttribute and PopulateUniform functions will fill out the attribute and uniform dictionaries:

```
private:
    std::string ReadFile(const std::string& path);
    unsigned int CompileVertexShader(
                    const std::string& vertex);
    unsigned int CompileFragmentShader(
                    const std::string& fragment);
    bool LinkShaders(unsigned int vertex,
                    unsigned int fragment);

    void PopulateAttributes();
    void PopulateUniforms();
```

4. The default constructor of the class will create an empty Shader object. The overload constructor will call the Load method, which loads shaders from files and compiles them. The destructor will release the OpenGL shader handle that the Shader class is holding on to:

```
public:
    Shader();
    Shader(const std::string& vertex,
           const std::string& fragment);
    ~Shader();

    void Load(const std::string& vertex,
              const std::string& fragment);
```

5. Before a shader is used, it will need to be bound with the Bind function. Similarly, after it is no longer in use, it can be unbound with the UnBind function. The GetAttribute and GetUniform functions perform lookups in the appropriate dictionaries. The GetHandle function returns the shader's OpenGL handle:

```
    void Bind();
    void UnBind();

    unsigned int GetAttribute(const std::string& name);
    unsigned int GetUniform(const std::string& name);
    unsigned int GetHandle();
};
```

Now that the Shader class declaration is done, you will implement it in the next section.

Implementing the Shader class

Create a new file, Shader.cpp, to implement the Shader class in. The Shader class implementation hides almost all of the actual OpenGL code from the caller. Because most OpenGL calls are abstracted this way, in later chapters, you only have to call the abstraction layer, not the OpenGL functions, directly.

Uniform arrays are used throughout this book. When a uniform array is encountered in a shader (for example, modelMatrices[120]) the uniform name returned by glGetActiveUniform is the first element of the array. In this example, that would be modelMatrices[0]. When you encounter a uniform array, you want to loop through all the array indices and get the explicit uniform indices for each element, but you also want to store the uniform name without any subscripts:

1. Both Shader constructors must create a new shader program handle by calling glCreateProgram. The constructor variant that takes two strings calls the Load function with the strings. Since mHandle is always a program handle, the destructor needs to delete the handle:

```
Shader::Shader() {
    mHandle = glCreateProgram();
}

Shader::Shader(const std::string& vertex,
               const std::string& fragment) {
    mHandle = glCreateProgram();
    Load(vertex, fragment);
}
```

```
Shader::~Shader() {
    glDeleteProgram(mHandle);
}
```

2. The `ReadFile` helper function converts a file into a string using `std::ifstream` to read the contents of the file into `std::stringstream`. The string stream can be used to return the contents of the file as a string:

```
std::string Shader::ReadFile(const std::string& path) {
    std::ifstream file;
    file.open(path);
    std::stringstream contents;
    contents << file.rdbuf();
    file.close();
    return contents.str();
}
```

3. The `CompileVertexShader` function is boilerplate code for compiling an OpenGL vertex shader. First, create the shader object with `glCreateShader`, then set the source for the shader with `glShaderSource`. Finally, compile the shader with `glCompileShader`. Check for errors with `glGetShaderiv`:

```
unsigned int Shader::CompileVertexShader(
                            const string& vertex) {
    unsigned int v = glCreateShader(GL_VERTEX_SHADER);
    const char* v_source = vertex.c_str();
    glShaderSource(v, 1, &v_source, NULL);
    glCompileShader(v);
    int success = 0;
    glGetShaderiv(v, GL_COMPILE_STATUS, &success);
    if (!success) {
        char infoLog[512];
        glGetShaderInfoLog(v, 512, NULL, infoLog);
        std::cout << "Vertex compilation failed.\n";
        std::cout << "\t" << infoLog << "\n";
        glDeleteShader(v);
        return 0;
    };
    return v;
}
```

4. The `CompileFragmentShader` function is almost identical to the `CompileVertexShader` function. The only real difference is the argument to `glCreateShader`, indicating that you are creating a fragment shader, not a vertex shader:

```cpp
unsigned int Shader::CompileFragmentShader(
                            const std::string& fragment) {
    unsigned int f = glCreateShader(GL_FRAGMENT_SHADER);
    const char* f_source = fragment.c_str();
    glShaderSource(f, 1, &f_source, NULL);
    glCompileShader(f);
    int success = 0;
    glGetShaderiv(f, GL_COMPILE_STATUS, &success);
    if (!success) {
        char infoLog[512];
        glGetShaderInfoLog(f, 512, NULL, infoLog);
        std::cout << "Fragment compilation failed.\n";
        std::cout << "\t" << infoLog << "\n";
        glDeleteShader(f);
        return 0;
    };
    return f;
}
```

5. The `LinkShaders` helper function is also boilerplate. Attach the shaders to the shader program handle that the constructor created. Link the shaders by calling `glLinkProgram` and check for errors with `glGetProgramiv`. Once the shaders are linked, you only need the program; the individual shader objects can be deleted with `glDeleteShader`:

```cpp
bool Shader::LinkShaders(unsigned int vertex,
                         unsigned int fragment) {
    glAttachShader(mHandle, vertex);
    glAttachShader(mHandle, fragment);
    glLinkProgram(mHandle);
    int success = 0;
    glGetProgramiv(mHandle, GL_LINK_STATUS, &success);
    if (!success) {
        char infoLog[512];
        glGetProgramInfoLog(mHandle, 512, NULL, infoLog);
        std::cout << "ERROR: Shader linking failed.\n";
        std::cout << "\t" << infoLog << "\n";
        glDeleteShader(vertex);
        glDeleteShader(fragment);
```

```
            return false;
        }

        glDeleteShader(vertex);
        glDeleteShader(fragment);

        return true;
    }
```

6. The `PopulateAttributes` function enumerates all the attributes stored inside the shader program, then stores them as a key-value pair, where the key is the name of the attribute and the value is its location. You can count the number of active attributes in a shader program with the `glGetProgramiv` function, passing `GL_ACTIVE_ATTRIBUTES` as the parameter name. Then, loop through all the attributes by index and use `glGetActiveAttrib` to get the name of each attribute. Finally, call `glGetAttribLocation` to get the location of each attribute:

```
void Shader::PopulateAttributes() {
    int count = -1;
    int length;
    char name[128];
    int size;
    GLenum type;

    glUseProgram(mHandle);
    glGetProgramiv(mHandle, GL_ACTIVE_ATTRIBUTES,
                   &count);

    for (int i = 0; i < count; ++i) {
        memset(name, 0, sizeof(char) * 128);
        glGetActiveAttrib(mHandle, (GLuint)i, 128,
                          &length, &size, &type, name);
        int attrib = glGetAttribLocation(mHandle, name);
        if (attrib >= 0) {
            mAttributes[name] = attrib;
        }
    }

    glUseProgram(0);
}
```

7. The `PopulateUniforms` helper function is very similar to the
    `PopulateAttributes` helper function. `glGetProgramiv` needs to
    take `GL_ACTIVE_UNIFORMS` as the parameter name and you need to call
    `glGetActiveUniform` and `glGetUniformLocation`:

```
void Shader::PopulateUniforms() {
    int count = -1;
    int length;
    char name[128];
    int size;
    GLenum type;
    char testName[256];

    glUseProgram(mHandle);
    glGetProgramiv(mHandle, GL_ACTIVE_UNIFORMS, &count);

    for (int i = 0; i < count; ++i) {
        memset(name, 0, sizeof(char) * 128);
        glGetActiveUniform(mHandle, (GLuint)i, 128,
                           &length, &size, &type, name);

        int uniform=glGetUniformLocation(mHandle, name);
        if (uniform >= 0) { // Is uniform valid?
```

8. When a valid uniform is encountered, you need to determine whether the uniform
    is an array or not. To do this, search for the array bracket ([) in the uniform name.
    If the bracket is found, the uniform is an array:

```
std::string uniformName = name;
// if name contains [, uniform is array
std::size_t found = uniformName.find('[');
if (found != std::string::npos) {
```

9. If you encounter a uniform array, erase everything out of the string, starting with [.
    This will leave you with only the uniform name. Then, enter a loop where you try to
    retrieve every index from the array by appending [+ index +] to the uniform
    name. Once the first invalid index is found, break the loop:

```
uniformName.erase(uniformName.begin() +
    found, uniformName.end());
    unsigned int uniformIndex = 0;
    while (true) {
        memset(testName,0,sizeof(char)*256);
            sprintf(testName, "%s[%d]",
```

```
                          uniformName.c_str(),
                          uniformIndex++);
                int uniformLocation =
                          glGetUniformLocation(
                          mHandle, testName);
                if (uniformLocation < 0) {
                    break;
                }
                mUniforms[testName]=uniformLocation;
            }
        }
```

10. At this point, uniformName contains the name of the uniform. If that uniform was an array, the [0] part of the name has been removed. Store the uniform index by name in mUniforms:

```
            mUniforms[uniformName] = uniform;
        }
    }

    glUseProgram(0);
}
```

11. The final helper function is the Load function, which is responsible for loading the actual shaders. This function takes two strings, which are either filenames or inline shader definitions. Once the shaders are read, call the Compile, Link, and Populate helper functions to load the shader:

```
void Shader::Load(const std::string& vertex,
                  const std::string& fragment) {
    std::ifstream f(vertex.c_str());
    bool vertFile = f.good();
    f.close();

    f = std::ifstream(vertex.c_str());
    bool fragFile = f.good();
    f.close();

    std::string v_source = vertex;
    if (vertFile) {
        v_source = ReadFile(vertex);
    }

    std::string f_source = fragment;
```

```
    if (fragFile) {
        f_source = ReadFile(fragment);
    }

    unsigned int vert = CompileVertexShader(v_source);
    unsigned int f = CompileFragmentShader(f_source);
    if (LinkShaders(vert, frag)) {
        PopulateAttributes();
        PopulateUniforms();
    }
}
```

12. The `Bind` function needs to set the current shader program to active, while `UnBind` should make sure no `Shader` objects are active. The `GetHandle` helper function returns the OpenGL handle to the `Shader` object:

```
void Shader::Bind() {
    glUseProgram(mHandle);
}

void Shader::UnBind() {
    glUseProgram(0);
}

unsigned int Shader::GetHandle() {
    return mHandle;
}
```

13. Finally, you need a way of retrieving the bind slots for attributes and uniforms. The `GetAttribute` function will check whether a given attribute name is present in the attribute map. If it is, the integer representing it is returned. If it is not, 0 is returned. 0 is a valid attribute index, so in case of an error, an error message is logged as well:

```
unsigned int Shader::GetAttribute(
                      const std::string& name) {
    std::map<std::string, unsigned int>::iterator it =
                               mAttributes.find(name);
    if (it == mAttributes.end()) {
        cout << "Bad attrib index: " << name << "\n";
        return 0;
    }
    return it->second;
}
```

14. The GetUniform function is implemented almost identically to the
    GetAttribute function, except instead of the attribute map, it works on the
    uniform map:

```cpp
unsigned int Shader::GetUniform(const std::string& name){
    std::map<std::string, unsigned int>::iterator it =
                                    mUniforms.find(name);
    if (it == mUniforms.end()) {
        cout << "Bad uniform index: " << name << "\n";
        return 0;
    }
    return it->second;
}
```

The Shader class has methods to retrieve indices for uniforms and attributes. In the
next section, you will start implementing an Attribute class to hold vertex data that is
passed to shaders.

Working with buffers (attributes)

Attributes are per-vertex data in the graphics pipeline. A vertex is made up of attributes.
For example, a vertex has a position and a normal, which are both attributes. The most
common attributes are as follows:

- Position: Often in local space
- Normal: The direction the vertex points in
- UV or texture coordinate: The normalized (x,y) coordinate on a texture
- Color: A vector3 representing the color of a vertex

Attributes can have different data types. Throughout this book, you will implement
support for integers, floats, and vector attributes. For vector attributes, two-, three-, and
four-dimensional vectors will be supported.

The Attribute class declaration

Create a new file, `Attribute.h`. The `Attribute` class will be declared in this new file. The `Attribute` class will be templated. This will ensure that if an attribute is meant to be `vec3`, you cannot accidentally load `vec2` into it:

1. The attribute class will contain two member variables, one for the OpenGL attribute handle one to count how much data the `Attribute` class contains. Since the attribute data lives on the GPU and you don't want to have multiple handles to the same data, the copy constructor and `assignment operator` should be disabled:

    ```
    template<typename T>
    class Attribute {
    protected:
        unsigned int mHandle;
        unsigned int mCount;
    private:
        Attribute(const Attribute& other);
        Attribute& operator=(const Attribute& other);
    ```

2. The `SetAttribPointer` function is special, as it will need to be implemented once for each type of attribute that will be supported. This will be done explicitly in the `.cpp` file, later:

    ```
    void SetAttribPointer(unsigned int slot);
    ```

3. Declare the constructor and destructor of the Attribute class as public functions:

    ```
    public:
        Attribute();
        ~Attribute();
    ```

4. The `Attribute` class needs a `Set` function, which will upload an array of data to the GPU. Each element in the array represents the attribute for one vertex. We need a way of binding and unbinding attributes from bind slots defined by the shader, as well as accessors for the count and handle of the attribute:

    ```
    void Set(T* inputArray, unsigned int arrayLength);
    void Set(std::vector<T>& input);

    void BindTo(unsigned int slot);
    void UnBindFrom(unsigned int slot);

    unsigned int Count();
    ```

```
        unsigned int GetHandle();
};
```

Now that you have declared the `Attribute` class, you will be implementing it in the next section.

Implementing the Attribute class

Create a new file, `Attribtue.cpp`. You will be implementing the `Attribute` class in this file as follows:

1. The `Attribute` class is templated, but none of its functions are marked as inline. The template specializations for each attribute type will live in the `Attribute. cpp` file. Add specializations for the integer, floating point, `vec2`, `vec3`, `vec4`, and `ivec4` types:

    ```
    template Attribute<int>;
    template Attribute<float>;
    template Attribute<vec2>;
    template Attribute<vec3>;
    template Attribute<vec4>;
    template Attribute<ivec4>;
    ```

2. The constructor should generate an OpenGL buffer and store it in the handle of the `Attribute` class. The destructor is responsible for freeing the handle that the `Attribute` class is holding on to:

    ```
    template<typename T>
    Attribute<T>::Attribute() {
        glGenBuffers(1, &mHandle);
        mCount = 0;
    }

    template<typename T>
    Attribute<T>::~Attribute() {
        glDeleteBuffers(1, &mHandle);
    }
    ```

3. The `Attribute` class has two simple getters, one to retrieve the count and one to retrieve the OpenGL handle. The count represents how many total attributes there are:

```
template<typename T>
unsigned int Attribute<T>::Count() {
    return mCount;
}

template<typename T>
unsigned int Attribute<T>::GetHandle() {
    return mHandle;
}
```

4. The `Set` function takes an array and a length. It then binds the buffer that the `Attribute` class is holding on to and uses `glBufferData` to fill the buffer with data. There is a convenience function for `Set` that takes a vector reference instead of an array. It calls the actual `Set` function:

```
template<typename T>
void Attribute<T>::Set(T* inputArray,
                       unsigned int arrayLength) {
    mCount = arrayLength;
    unsigned int size = sizeof(T);

    glBindBuffer(GL_ARRAY_BUFFER, mHandle);
    glBufferData(GL_ARRAY_BUFFER, size * mCount,
                 inputArray, GL_STREAM_DRAW);
    glBindBuffer(GL_ARRAY_BUFFER, 0);
}

template<typename T>
void Attribute<T>::Set(std::vector<T>& input) {
    Set(&input[0], (unsigned int)input.size());
}
```

5. The `SetAttribPointer` function wraps `glVertesAttribPointer` or `glVertesAttribIPointer`. The arguments and which function to call are different based on what the type of the `Attribute` class is. To remove any ambiguity, provide explicit implementations for all supported template types. Start by implementing the `int`, `ivec4`, and `float` types:

```
template<>
void Attribute<int>::SetAttribPointer(unsigned int s) {
```

```
    glVertexAttribIPointer(s, 1, GL_INT, 0, (void*)0);
}
template<>
void Attribute<ivec4>::SetAttribPointer(unsigned int s){
    glVertexAttribIPointer(s, 4, GL_INT, 0, (void*)0);
}
template<>
void Attribute<float>::SetAttribPointer(unsigned int s){
    glVertexAttribPointer(s,1,GL_FLOAT,GL_FALSE,0,0);
}
```

6. Implement the `vec2`, `vec3`, and `vec4` types next. These are all very similar to the `float` type. The only difference is the second argument to `glVertexAttribPointer`:

```
template<>
void Attribute<vec2>::SetAttribPointer(unsigned int s) {
    glVertexAttribPointer(s,2,GL_FLOAT,GL_FALSE,0,0);
}
template<>
void Attribute<vec3>::SetAttribPointer(unsigned int s){
    glVertexAttribPointer(s,3,GL_FLOAT,GL_FALSE,0,0);
}
template<>
void Attribute<vec4>::SetAttribPointer(unsigned int s){
    glVertexAttribPointer(s,4,GL_FLOAT,GL_FALSE,0,0);
}
```

7. The last two functions of the `Attribute` class need to bind and unbind the attribute to a slot specified in the `Shader` class. Since the `glVertexAttribPointer` function is different based on the templated type of the `Attribute` class, `Bind` will call the `SetAttribPointer` helper function:

```
template<typename T>
void Attribute<T>::BindTo(unsigned int slot) {
    glBindBuffer(GL_ARRAY_BUFFER, mHandle);
    glEnableVertexAttribArray(slot);
    SetAttribPointer(slot);
    glBindBuffer(GL_ARRAY_BUFFER, 0);
}

template<typename T>
void Attribute<T>::UnBindFrom(unsigned int slot) {
    glBindBuffer(GL_ARRAY_BUFFER, mHandle);
```

```
        glDisableVertexAttribArray(slot);
        glBindBuffer(GL_ARRAY_BUFFER, 0);
    }
```

`Attribute` data changes per vertex. There is another type of data you will need to set: uniforms. Unlike attributes, uniforms remain the same throughout the execution of your shader program. You will implement uniforms in the next section.

Working with uniforms

Unlike attributes, uniforms are constant data; they are set once. The value of a uniform remains the same for all vertices processed. Uniforms can be created as arrays, a feature you will use in later chapters to implement mesh skinning.

Like the `Attribute` class, the `Uniform` class will also be templated. Unlike attributes, however, there will never be an instance of a `Uniform` class. It only needs public static functions. For each uniform type, there are three functions: one to set an individual uniform value, one to set an array of uniform values, and a convenience function that sets an array of values but uses a vector for input.

The Uniform class declaration

Create a new file, `Uniform.h`. You will be implementing the `Uniform` class in this new file. The `Uniform` class will never be instantiated since there won't be any instances of this class. Disable the constructor and copy the constructor, assignment operator, and destructor. What the class will have is three overloads of a static `Set` function. The `Set` function will need to be specified for each template type:

```
template <typename T>
class Uniform {
private:
    Uniform();
    Uniform(const Uniform&);
    Uniform& operator=(const Uniform&);
    ~Uniform();
public:
    static void Set(unsigned int slot, const T& value);
    static void Set(unsigned int slot,T* arr,unsigned int len);
    static void Set(unsigned int slot, std::vector<T>& arr);
};
```

You just finalized the declaration of the `Uniform` class. In the next section, you will start implementing the `Uniform` class.

Implementing the Uniform class

Create a new file, Uniform.cpp. You will be implementing the Uniform class in this new file. Like the Attribute class, the Uniform class is also templated.

In OpenGL, uniforms are set with the glUniform*** family of functions. There are different functions for integers, floating point numbers, vectors, matrices, and so on. You want to provide implementations for the Set method for each of these types but avoid writing nearly identical code.

To avoid having to write code that's almost identical, you will declare a #define macro. This macro will take three arguments—the OpenGL function to call, the template type of the Uniform class, and the data type of the OpenGL function:

1. Add the following code to define the template specifications for the supported uniform types:

```
template Uniform<int>;
template Uniform<ivec4>;
template Uniform<ivec2>;
template Uniform<float>;
template Uniform<vec2>;
template Uniform<vec3>;
template Uniform<vec4>;
template Uniform<quat>;
template Uniform<mat4>;
```

2. You only need to implement one of the Set methods for each type—the one that takes an array and a length. The other Set method overloads are for convenience. Implement the two convenience overloads—one of them is for setting a single uniform, the other is for setting a vector. Both overloads should just call the Set function:

```
template <typename T>
void Uniform<T>::Set(unsigned int slot,const T& value){
    Set(slot, (T*)&value, 1);
}

template <typename T>
void Uniform<T>::Set(unsigned int s,std::vector<T>& v){
    Set(s, &v[0], (unsigned int)v.size());
}
```

3. Create a UNIFORM_IMPL macro. The first argument will be which OpenGL
    function to call, the second is the type of structure that is being used, and the
    last argument is the data type of the same structure. The UNIFORM_IMPL macro
    assembles these pieces of information into a function declaration:

```
#define UNIFORM_IMPL(gl_func, tType, dType) \
template<> void Uniform<tType>::Set(unsigned int slot,\
                tType* data, unsigned int length) {\
    gl_func(slot, (GLsizei)length, (dType*)&data[0]); \
}
```

4. Call the UNIFORM_IMPL macro for each uniform data type to generate the
    appropriate Set functions. The only data type this method won't work for is mat4:

```
UNIFORM_IMPL(glUniform1iv, int, int)
UNIFORM_IMPL(glUniform4iv, ivec4, int)
UNIFORM_IMPL(glUniform2iv, ivec2, int)
UNIFORM_IMPL(glUniform1fv, float, float)
UNIFORM_IMPL(glUniform2fv, vec2, float)
UNIFORM_IMPL(glUniform3fv, vec3, float)
UNIFORM_IMPL(glUniform4fv, vec4, float)
UNIFORM_IMPL(glUniform4fv, quat, float)
```

5. The Set function for matrices needs to be specified manually; otherwise, the
    UNIFORM_IMPL macro won't work. This is because the glUniformMatrix4fv
    function takes an additional Boolean argument asking whether the matrix should
    be transposed or not. Set the transposed Boolean to false:

```
template<> void Uniform<mat4>::Set(unsigned int slot,
        mat4* inputArray, unsigned int arrayLength) {
    glUniformMatrix4fv(slot, (GLsizei)arrayLength,
                    false, (float*)&inputArray[0]);
}
```

In this section, you built an abstraction layer on top of the concept of uniforms. In the
next section, you will implement index buffers, which are like attributes.

Working with index buffers

Index buffers are a type of attribute. Unlike attributes, an index buffer is bound to GL_ELEMENT_ARRAY_BUFFER and can be used to draw primitives. Because of this, you will implement index buffers in their own class, rather than reuse the Attribute class.

The IndexBuffer class declaration

Create a new file, IndexBuffer.h. You will be adding the declaration of the IndexBuffer class to this new file. Like an Attribute object, IndexBuffer will contain an OpenGL handle and a count, with getter functions for both.

The copy constructor and assignment operator need to be disabled to avoid having multiple IndexBuffer objects referencing the same OpenGL buffer. The Set function takes an unsigned integer array and the length of the array, but there is a convenience overload that takes a vector as well:

```cpp
class IndexBuffer {
public:
    unsigned int mHandle;
    unsigned int mCount;
private:
    IndexBuffer(const IndexBuffer& other);
    IndexBuffer& operator=(const IndexBuffer& other);
public:
    IndexBuffer();
    ~IndexBuffer();

    void Set(unsigned int* rr, unsigned int len);
    void Set(std::vector<unsigned int>& input);

    unsigned int Count();
    unsigned int GetHandle();
};
```

In this section, you declared a new IndexBuffer class. In the next section, you will start to implement the actual index buffer.

Implementing the IndexBuffer class

An index buffer allows you to render a model using indexed geometry. Think of a human model; almost all triangles in the mesh will be connected. This means many triangles might share a single vertex. Instead of storing every single vertex, only unique vertices are stored. A buffer that indexes into the list of unique vertices, the index buffer, is used to create triangles out of the unique vertices, as follows:

1. Create a new file, `IndexBuffer.cpp`. You will be implementing the `IndexBuffer` class in this file. The constructor needs to generate a new OpenGL buffer and the destructor needs to delete that buffer:

```
IndexBuffer::IndexBuffer() {
    glGenBuffers(1, &mHandle);
    mCount = 0;
}

IndexBuffer::~IndexBuffer() {
    glDeleteBuffers(1, &mHandle);
}
```

2. The getter functions for count and the OpenGL handle inside of the `IndexBuffer` object are trivial:

```
unsigned int IndexBuffer::Count() {
    return mCount;
}

unsigned int IndexBuffer::GetHandle() {
    return mHandle;
}
```

3. The `Set` function of the `IndexBuffer` class needs to bind `GL_ELEMENT_ARRAY_BUFFER`. Other than that, the logic is the same as it was for attributes:

```
void IndexBuffer::Set(unsigned int* inputArray, unsigned
int arrayLengt) {
    mCount = arrayLengt;
    unsigned int size = sizeof(unsigned int);

    glBindBuffer(GL_ELEMENT_ARRAY_BUFFER, mHandle);
    glBufferData(GL_ELEMENT_ARRAY_BUFFER, size * mCount,
inputArray, GL_STATIC_DRAW);
    glBindBuffer(GL_ELEMENT_ARRAY_BUFFER, 0);
}
```

```
void IndexBuffer::Set(std::vector<unsigned int>& input) {
    Set(&input[0], (unsigned int)input.size());
}
```

In this section, you built an abstraction around index buffers. In the next section, you will learn how index buffers and attributes can be used to render geometry.

Rendering geometry

You have classes for dealing with vertex data, uniforms, and index buffers, but no code to draw any of it. Drawing will be handled by four global functions. You will have two Draw functions and two DrawInstanced functions. You will be able to draw geometry with or without an index buffer.

Create a new file, Draw.h. You will be implementing the Draw function in this file, as follows:

1. Declare an enum class that defines what primitive should be used for drawing. Most of the time, you will only need lines, points, or triangles, but some additional types may be useful:

```
enum class DrawMode {
    Points,
    LineStrip,
    LineLoop,
    Lines,
    Triangles,
    TriangleStrip,
    TriangleFan
};
```

2. Next, declare the Draw function. There are two overloads for the Draw function—one takes an index buffer and a draw mode and the other takes a vertex count and a draw mode:

```
void Draw(IndexBuffer& inIndexBuffer, DrawMode mode);
void Draw(unsigned int vertexCount, DrawMode mode);
```

3. Like `Draw`, declare two `DrawInstanced` functions. These functions have a similar signature but take an extra argument—`instanceCount`. This `instanceCount` variable controls how many instances of the geometry will be rendered:

```
void DrawInstanced(IndexBuffer& inIndexBuffer,
        DrawMode mode, unsigned int instanceCount);
void DrawInstanced(unsigned int vertexCount,
        DrawMode mode, unsigned int numInstances);
```

Create a new file, `Draw.cpp`. You will implement the drawing-related functionality in this file, as follows:

1. You need to be able to convert the `DrawMode` enum into `GLenum`. We will do this with a static helper function. The only thing this function needs to do is figure out what the input draw mode is and return the appropriate `GLenum` value:

```
static GLenum DrawModeToGLEnum(DrawMode input) {
    switch (input) {
        case DrawMode::Points: return  GL_POINTS;
        case DrawMode::LineStrip: return GL_LINE_STRIP;
        case DrawMode::LineLoop: return  GL_LINE_LOOP;
        case DrawMode::Lines: return  GL_LINES;
        case DrawMode::Triangles: return  GL_TRIANGLES;
        case DrawMode::TriangleStrip:
                    return  GL_TRIANGLE_STRIP;
        case DrawMode::TriangleFan:
                    return   GL_TRIANGLE_FAN;
    }
    cout << "DrawModeToGLEnum unreachable code hit\n";
    return 0;
}
```

2. The `Draw` and `DrawInstanced` functions that take a vertex count are simple to implement. `Draw` needs to call `glDrawArrays` and `DrawInstanced` needs to call `glDrawArraysInstanced`:

```
void Draw(unsigned int vertexCount, DrawMode mode) {
    glDrawArrays(DrawModeToGLEnum(mode), 0, vertexCount);
}

void DrawInstanced(unsigned int vertexCount,
    DrawMode mode, unsigned int numInstances) {
```

```
            glDrawArraysInstanced(DrawModeToGLEnum(mode),
                              0, vertexCount, numInstances);
}
```

3. The `Draw` and `DrawInstanced` functions that take an index buffer need to bind the index buffer to `GL_ELEMENT_ARRAY_BUFFER` and then call `glDrawElements` and `glDrawElementsInstanced`:

```
void Draw(IndexBuffer& inIndexBuffer, DrawMode mode) {
    unsigned int handle = inIndexBuffer.GetHandle();
    unsigned int numIndices = inIndexBuffer.Count();

    glBindBuffer(GL_ELEMENT_ARRAY_BUFFER, handle);
    glDrawElements(DrawModeToGLEnum(mode),
                   numIndices, GL_UNSIGNED_INT, 0);
    glBindBuffer(GL_ELEMENT_ARRAY_BUFFER, 0);
}

void DrawInstanced(IndexBuffer& inIndexBuffer,
        DrawMode mode, unsigned int instanceCount) {
    unsigned int handle = inIndexBuffer.GetHandle();
    unsigned int numIndices = inIndexBuffer.Count();

    glBindBuffer(GL_ELEMENT_ARRAY_BUFFER, handle);
    glDrawElementsInstanced(DrawModeToGLEnum(mode),
        numIndices, GL_UNSIGNED_INT, 0, instanceCount);
    glBindBuffer(GL_ELEMENT_ARRAY_BUFFER, 0);
}
```

So far, you have written code to load shaders, create and bind GPU buffers, and pass uniforms to shaders. Now that the drawing code is implemented as well, you can start displaying geometry.

In the next section, you will learn how to work with textures to make the rendered geometry look more interesting.

Working with textures

All the shaders you will write in this book assume that the diffused color of what is being rendered comes from a texture. Textures will be loaded from `.png` files. All image loading will be done through `stb_image`.

Stb is a collection of single-file public domain libraries. We're only going to use the image loader; you can find the entire stb collection on GitHub at https://github.com/nothings/stb.

Adding stb_image

You will be loading textures using stb_image. You can get a copy of the header file from https://github.com/nothings/stb/blob/master/stb_image.h. Add the stb_image.h header file to the project.

Create a new file, stb_image.cpp. This file just needs to declare the stb_image implementation macro and include the header file. It should look like this:

```
#define STB_IMAGE_IMPLEMENTATION
#include "stb_image.h"
```

The Texture class declaration

Create a new file, Texture.h. You will be declaring the Texture class in this file. The Texture class only needs a few important functions. It needs to be able to load a texture from a file, bind a texture index to a uniform index, and deactivate a texture index.

In addition to the core functions, the class should have a default constructor, a convenience constructor that takes a file path, a destructor, and a getter for the OpenGL handle contained inside of the Texture class. The copy constructor and assignment operator should be disabled to avoid having two Texture classes reference the same OpenGL texture handle:

```
class Texture {
protected:
    unsigned int mWidth;
    unsigned int mHeight;
    unsigned int mChannels;
    unsigned int mHandle;
private:
    Texture(const Texture& other);
    Texture& operator=(const Texture& other);
public:
    Texture();
    Texture(const char* path);
    ~Texture();

    void Load(const char* path);
```

```
    void Set(unsigned int uniform, unsigned int texIndex);
    void UnSet(unsigned int textureIndex);
    unsigned int GetHandle();
};
```

Implementing the Texture class

Create a new file, `Texture.cpp`. The definition of the `Texture` class will go in this file. The default constructor of the `Texture` class needs to set all member variables to `0`, then generate an OpenGL handle.

The `Load` function is probably the most important function in the `Texture` class; it's responsible for loading image files. The actual parsing of the image files will be handled by `stbi_load`:

1. The convenience constructor generates a new handle, then calls the `Load` function, which will initialize the rest of the class member variables, since every instance of the `Texture` class holds a valid texture handle:

    ```
    Texture::Texture() {
        mWidth = 0;
        mHeight = 0;
        mChannels = 0;
        glGenTextures(1, &mHandle);
    }

    Texture::Texture(const char* path) {
        glGenTextures(1, &mHandle);
        Load(path);
    }

    Texture::~Texture() {
        glDeleteTextures(1, &mHandle);
    }
    ```

2. `stbi_load` takes a path to the image file and references to the width, height, and number of channels in the image. The last argument specifies the number of components per pixel. By setting it to `4`, all textures are loaded with RGBA channels. Next, use `glTexImage2D` to upload the texture to the GPU and `glGenerateMipmap` to generate the appropriate mipmaps for the image. Set the wrap mode to repeat:

    ```
    void Texture::Load(const char* path) {
        glBindTexture(GL_TEXTURE_2D, mHandle);
    ```

```
    int width, height, channels;
    unsigned char* data = stbi_load(path, &width,
                                    &height,
                                    &channels, 4);
    glTexImage2D(GL_TEXTURE_2D, 0, GL_RGBA, width,
        height, 0, GL_RGBA, GL_UNSIGNED_BYTE, data);
    glGenerateMipmap(GL_TEXTURE_2D);
    stbi_image_free(data);

    glTexParameteri(GL_TEXTURE_2D, GL_TEXTURE_WRAP_S,
                    GL_REPEAT);
    glTexParameteri(GL_TEXTURE_2D, GL_TEXTURE_WRAP_T,
                    GL_REPEAT);

    glTexParameteri(GL_TEXTURE_2D,GL_TEXTURE_MIN_FILTER,
                    GL_NEAREST_MIPMAP_LINEAR);
    glTexParameteri(GL_TEXTURE_2D,GL_TEXTURE_MAG_FILTER,
                    GL_LINEAR);

    glBindTexture(GL_TEXTURE_2D, 0);

    mWidth = width;
    mHeight = height;
    mChannels = channels;
}
```

3. The Set function needs to activate a texture unit, bind the handle that the Texture class contains to that texture unit, then set the specified uniform index to contain the texture unit that is currently bound. The Unset function unbinds the current texture from the specified texture unit:

```
void Texture::Set(unsigned int uniformIndex,
                  unsigned int textureIndex) {
    glActiveTexture(GL_TEXTURE0 + textureIndex);
    glBindTexture(GL_TEXTURE_2D, mHandle);
    glUniform1i(uniformIndex, textureIndex);
}

void Texture::UnSet(unsigned int textureIndex) {
    glActiveTexture(GL_TEXTURE0 + textureIndex);
    glBindTexture(GL_TEXTURE_2D, 0);
    glActiveTexture(GL_TEXTURE0);
}
```

4.   The `GetHandle` getter function is simple:

```
unsigned int Texture::GetHandle() {
    return mHandle;
}
```

The `Texture` class will always load textures using the same mipmap level and wrapping parameters. For the samples in this book, that should be enough. You may want to try adding getters and setters for these properties.

In the next section, you will implement vertex and fragment shader programs, which is the last step needed to draw something.

Simple shaders

The rendering abstraction is done. Before drawing anything, you need to write shaders to direct how things are going to be drawn. In this section, you will write a vertex and a fragment shader. The fragment shader will be used throughout the rest of this book and the vertex shaders used in later sections of this book will be variations of the one presented here.

The vertex shader

The vertex shader is responsible for putting each vertex of a model through the model, view, and projection pipeline and for passing any required lighting data to the fragment shader. Create a new file, `static.vert`. You will be implementing the vertex shader in this file.

The vertex shader takes three uniforms—a model, a view, and a projection matrix. These uniforms are needed to transform a vertex. Each individual vertex is made up of three attributes—a position, a normal, and some texture coordinates.

The vertex shader outputs three variables to the fragment shader, the normal and fragment positions in the world space, and the texture coordinates:

```
#version 330 core

uniform mat4 model;
uniform mat4 view;
uniform mat4 projection;

in vec3 position;
in vec3 normal;
in vec2 texCoord;
```

```
out vec3 norm;
out vec3 fragPos;
out vec2 uv;

void main() {
    gl_Position = projection * view * model *
                    vec4(position, 1.0);

    fragPos = vec3(model * vec4(position, 1.0));
    norm = vec3(model * vec4(normal, 0.0f));
    uv = texCoord;
}
```

This is a minimal vertex shader; it only puts the vertex through a model view and projection pipeline. This shader can be used to display static geometry or CPU skinned meshes. In the next section, you will implement a fragment shader.

The fragment shader

Create a new file, lit.frag. The fragment shader in this file will be used throughout the rest of the book. Some chapters will introduce new vertex shaders, but the fragment shader is always going to remain as this one.

The fragment shader takes the object's diffused color from a texture, then applies a single-directional light. The lighting model is just *N* dot *L*. Because there is no ambient term to the light, some parts of the model can appear as all black:

```
#version 330 core

in vec3 norm;
in vec3 fragPos;
in vec2 uv;

uniform vec3 light;
uniform sampler2D tex0;

out vec4 FragColor;

void main() {
    vec4 diffuseColor = texture(tex0, uv);

    vec3 n = normalize(norm);
    vec3 l = normalize(light);
```

```
    float diffuseIntensity = clamp(dot(n, 1), 0, 1);

    FragColor = diffuseColor * diffuseIntensity;
}
```

> **Important information:**
> Want to learn more about lighting models in OpenGL? Go to
> `https://learnopengl.com/Lighting/Basic-Lighting`.

This is a simple fragment shader; the diffuse color is obtained by sampling a texture and the intensity is a simple directional light.

Summary

In this chapter, you learned how to write an abstraction layer on top of the OpenGL API. For the most part, you will be using these classes to draw things throughout the rest of the book, but a few stray OpenGL calls might find their way into our code here and there.

Abstracting OpenGL in this fashion will let future chapters focus on animation without having to worry about the underlying API. It should be straightforward to port this API to other backends as well.

There are two samples for this chapter—Chapter06/Sample00, which is the code used up to this point, and Chapter06/Sample01, which shows a simple textured and lit plane rotating in place. Sample01 is a good example of how to use the code you have written so far.

Sample01 also includes a utility class, DebugDraw, that won't be covered in this book. The class is found in DebugDraw.h and DebugDraw.cpp. The DebugDraw class can be used to draw debug lines quickly with a simple API. The DebugDraw class is not very efficient; it's only meant to be used for debugging.

In the next chapter, you will start to explore the glTF file format. glTF is a standard format that can store both mesh and animation data. It's the format that the rest of this book will be using.

7
Exploring the glTF File Format

In this chapter, we will explore glTF, a file format that contains everything you need to display animated models. It's a standard format that most three-dimensional content creation applications can export to and allows you to load any arbitrary model.

This chapter focuses on the file format itself. Later chapters will focus on implementing loading parts of glTF files as they become relevant. By the end of this chapter, you should have a solid understanding of the glTF file format.

This chapter will focus on building the following skills:

- Understanding what data is inside of a glTF file
- Implementing a glTF loading using cgltf
- Learning how to export glTF files from Blender

Technical requirements

This chapter will cover every concept of glTF files that you will need to load and display animated models. The chapter, however, is not a complete guide to the file format. Before reading this chapter, take a few minutes to familiarize yourself with the glTF format by reading the reference guide at `https://www.khronos.org/files/gltf20-reference-guide.pdf`.

You will be using cgltf (`https://github.com/jkuhlmann/cgltf`) to parse glTF files. If a glTF file isn't displaying properly, it might be a bad file. If you suspect a file might be bad, check it against the glTF reference viewer at `https://gltf-viewer.donmccurdy.com/`.

Exploring how glTF files are stored

glTF files are stored as either plain text JSON files or in a more compact binary representation. The plain text variant commonly has a `.gltf` extension, while the binary variant commonly has a `.glb` extension.

There might be multiple files. A glTF file can choose to embed large chunks of binary data—even textures—or it can choose to store them in external files. This is reflected in the following screenshot of Blender3D's glTF export options:

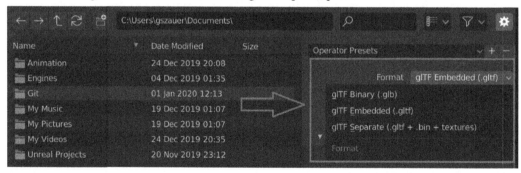

Figure 7.1: Blender3D's glTF export options

Sample files provided with the downloadable content for this book are stored as glTF embedded files (`.gltf`). This is the plain text variant of glTF that can be inspected with any text editor. More importantly, it's a single file to keep track of. Even though the files provided with this book are in the glTF embedded format, the final code will support loading the binary format and separate files (`.bin`) as well.

Now that you've explored the different ways a glTF file can be stored, let's get ready to learn what's stored inside glTF files. The glTF file was intended to store an entire scene, not just a single model. In the next section, you will explore the intended use of glTF files.

glTF files store a scene, not a model

It's important to know that glTF files are meant to represent an entire three-dimensional scene, not just a single animated model. As such, glTF has support for features you won't need to use for animation, such as cameras and PBR materials. For animation, we only care about using a small subset of the supported features. Let's outline what they are.

A glTF file can contain different types of meshes. It contains static meshes, such as props. These meshes are only moved by the animation of the node they are attached to; it can contain morph targets. Morph animation can be used for things such as facial expressions.

A glTF file can also contain skinned meshes. These are the meshes you will use to animate characters. Skinned meshes describe how the vertices of a model are affected by the transform hierarchy (or skeleton) of the model. With a skinned mesh, each vertex of a mesh can be bound to a joint in the hierarchy. As the hierarchy animates, the mesh is deformed.

The fact that glTF is intended to describe a scene, not a single model, is going to make some of the loading code a bit tricky. In the next section, you will start to explore what the actual content of a glTF file is from a high-level perspective.

Exploring the glTF format

The root of a glTF file is the scene. A glTF file can contain one or more scenes. A scene contains one or more nodes. A node can have a skin, a mesh, an animation, a camera, a light, or blend weights attached to it. Meshes, skins, and animations each store large chunks of information in buffers. To access a buffer, they contain an accessor that contains a buffer view, which in turn contains the buffer.

A description provided through text can be very hard to follow. The following diagram illustrates the file layout described. Since glTF is a scene description format, there are a decent number of data types that we don't have to care about. The next section explores these:

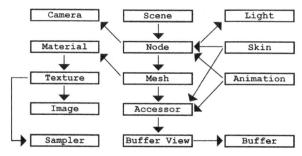

Figure 7.2: The contents of a glTF file

Now that you have an idea of what is stored in a glTF file, the following section will explore the parts of the file format needed for skinned animation.

The parts you need for animation

When using glTF files to load animated models, the required components of the file are the scene, nodes, meshes, and skins. This is a small subset to work with; these bits and their relationships are highlighted in the following diagram. The relationship between these data types can be depicted as follows:

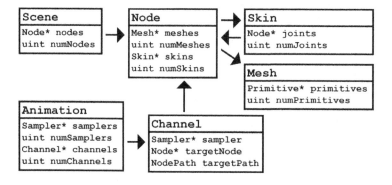

Figure 7.3: Parts of a glTF file used for skinned animation

The preceding diagram omits much of the data that is in each data structure, instead focusing only on what you will need to implement skinned animation. In the next section, we will explore what parts of a glTF file are not required for skinned animation.

The parts you don't need for animation

To implement skinned animations, you won't need lights, cameras, materials, textures, images, and samplers. In the following section, you will explore how to actually read data from glTF files.

Accessing data

Accessing data gets a little tricky, but it's not too difficult. Mesh, skin, and animation objects all contain a glTF accessor. This **accessor** references a **buffer view** and the buffer view references a **buffer**. The following diagram demonstrates this relationship:

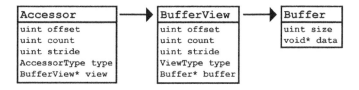

Figure 7.4: Accessing data in a glTF file

Given these three separate steps, how can you access the buffer data? In the next section, you will learn how data is interpreted from buffers using buffer views and finally, accessors.

Buffer

Think of a buffer as an OpenGL buffer. It's just a large, linear array of values. This is analogous to the `Attributes` class you built in *Chapter 6, Building An Abstract Renderer*. The `Set` function of the `Attributes` class calls `glBufferData`, which has the following signature:

```
void glBufferData(GLenum target, GLsizeiptr size,
                  void * data, GLenum usage);
```

A buffer in glTF contains all the information needed to call the `glBufferData` function. It contains a size, a void pointer, and optional offsets, which only modify the source pointer and the size. Think of a glTF buffer as everything needed to fill an OpenGL buffer with data.

In the next section, you will learn how buffer views are used in conjunction with buffers.

Buffer view

A buffer is just some large chunk of data. There is no context for what is stored inside the buffer. This is where the buffer view comes in. The buffer view describes what is in a buffer. If a buffer contains the information for `glBufferData`, then a buffer view contains some of the parameters to call `glVertexAttribPointer`. The `glVertexAttribPointer` function has the following signature:

```
void glVertexAttribPointer(GLuint index, GLint size,
                           GLenum type, GLboolean normalized,
                           GLsizei stride, void * pointer);
```

The buffer view contains `type`, which determines whether the view is a vertex buffer or an index buffer. This is important since a vertex buffer is bound to GL_ARRAY_BUFFER, but an index buffer is bound to GL_ELEMENT_ARRAY_BUFFER. In *Chapter 6*, *Building An Abstract Renderer*, we built two different classes for these different buffer types.

Like the buffer, the buffer view also contains some optional offsets that further modify the location of the source pointer and its size. In the following section, you will explore how to use accessors, which describe the contents of the buffer view.

Accessor

An accessor stores higher-level information. Most importantly, the accessor describes the type of data you are dealing with, such as `scalar`, `vec2`, `vec3`, or `vec4`. The `size` argument of `glVertexAttribPointer` is determined using this data.

The accessor answers questions such as whether the data is normalized and what the storage mode of the data is. The accessor also contains additional offset, size, and stride information on top of what the buffer and buffer view already contain.

The next section will demonstrate how data can be loaded into a linear scalar array from a glTF file.

Example

Even with the relationship of the accessor, buffer view, and buffer laid out, parsing data might still be a bit confusing. To try to clear it up a bit, let's explore how you could convert an accessor to a flat list of floating-point values. The following code is intended to be a sample; it will not be used in the rest of this book:

```
vector<float> GetPositions(const GLTFAccessor& accessor) {
    // Accessors and sanity checks
    assert(!accessor.isSparse);
    const GLTFBufferView& bufferView = accessor.bufferView;
```

```
        const GLTFBuffer& buffer = bufferView.buffer;

        // Resize result
        // GetNumComponents Would return 3 for a vec3, etc.
        uint numComponents = GetNumComponents(accessor);
        vector<float> result;
        result.resize(accessor.count * numComponents);

        // Loop trough every element in the accessor
        for (uint i = 0; i < accessor.count; ++i) {
            // Find where in the buffer the data actually starts
            uint offset = accessor.offset + bufferView.offset;
            uint8* data = buffer.data;
            data += offset + accessor.stride * i;

            // Loop trough every component of current element
            float* target = result[i] * componentCount;
            for (uint j = 0; j < numComponents; ++j) {
                // Omitting normalization
                // Omitting different storage types
                target[j] = data + componentCount * j;
            } // End loop of every component of current element
        } // End loop of every accessor element
        return result;
    }
```

The code for parsing glTF files can get verbose; in the previous code sample, the glTF file was already parsed. Most of the work in loading glTF files is actually in parsing the binary or JSON data. In the next section, we will explore how the cgltf library can be used to parse glTF files.

Exploring cgltf

In the last section, we explored what it would take to convert a glTF accessor into a linear array of floating-point numbers. The code omitted some of the more complicated tasks, such as normalizing the data or dealing with different storage types.

The sample code provided also assumed that the data would have already been parsed out of the JSON (or binary) format. Writing a JSON parser is out of the scope of this book but dealing with glTF files is not.

To help manage some of the complexity of loading glTF files, as well as to avoid having to write a JSON parser from scratch, the next section will teach you how to use cgltf to load JSON files. Cgltf is a single header glTF loading library; you can find it on GitHub at `https://github.com/jkuhlmann/cgltf`. In the next section, we will start to integrate cgltf into our project.

Integrating cgltf

To integrate cgltf into a project, download the header file from GitHub at `https://github.com/jkuhlmann/cgltf/blob/master/cgltf.h`. Then, add this header file to the project. Next, add a new `.c` file to the project and name it `cgltf.c`. This file should contain the following code:

```
#pragma warning(disable : 26451)
#define _CRT_SECURE_NO_WARNINGS
#define CGLTF_IMPLEMENTATION
#include "cgltf.h"
```

CGLTF is now integrated into the project. In this chapter, you will implement code that parses a glTF file. How to load the contents of the glTF file into runtime data will be covered in later chapters as the code for that runtime data is written. In the following section, we will learn how to implement the glTF parsing code.

Creating a glTF loader

In this section, we will explore how to load a glTF file using cgltf. The code to load the file into a runtime data structure, `cgltf_data`, is simple. In future chapters, you will learn how to parse the contents of this `cgltf_data` struct.

To load a file, you need to create an instance of `cgltf_options`. You won't need to set any option flags; just instantiate the `cgltf_options` struct with 0 for all member values. Next, declare a `cgltf_data` pointer. The address this pointer will be passed to is `cgltf_parse_file`. After `cgltf_parse_file` has filled in the `cgltf_data` structure, you are ready to parse the contents of the file. To free the `cgltf_data` structure later, call `cgltf_free`:

1. Create a new file, `GLTFLoader.h` that includes `cgltf.h`. Add function declarations for the `LoadGLTFFile` and `FreeGLTFFile` functions:

```
#ifndef _H_GLTFLOADER_
#define _H_GLTFLOADER_

#include "cgltf.h"
```

```
cgltf_data* LoadGLTFFile(const char* path);
void FreeGLTFFile(cgltf_data* handle);

#endif
```

2. Create a new file, GLTFLoader.cpp. This function takes a path and returns a cgltf_data pointer. Internally, the function calls cgltf_parse_file to load the glTF data from the file. cgltf_load_buffers is used to load any external buffer data. Finally, cgltf_validate makes sure that the glTF file that was just loaded was valid:

```
cgltf_data* LoadGLTFFile(const char* path) {
    cgltf_options options;
    memset(&options, 0, sizeof(cgltf_options));
    cgltf_data* data = NULL;
    cgltf_result result = cgltf_parse_file(&options,
                                           path, &data);
    if (result != cgltf_result_success) {
        cout << "Could not load: " << path << "\n";
        return 0;
    }
    result = cgltf_load_buffers(&options, data, path);
    if (result != cgltf_result_success) {
        cgltf_free(data);
        cout << "Could not load: " << path << "\n";
        return 0;
    }
    result = cgltf_validate(data);
    if (result != cgltf_result_success) {
        cgltf_free(data);
        cout << "Invalid file: " << path << "\n";
        return 0;
    }
    return data;
}
```

3. Implement the `FreeGLTFFile` function in `GLTFLoader.cpp` as well. This function is simple; it needs to call `cgltf_free` if the input pointer wasn't `null`:

```
void FreeGLTFFile(cgltf_data* data) {
    if (data == 0) {
        cout << "WARNING: Can't free null data\n";
    }
    else {
        cgltf_free(data);
    }
}
```

In later chapters, you will expand on the glTF `Loader` functions by introducing functions to load meshes, poses, and animations. In the next section, you will explore how glTF files can be exported from Blender3D.

Exploring the sample assets

The sample files you will be using throughout this book are CC0, public-domain-licensed assets from Quaternius. You can find additional assets in a similar style at `http://quaternius.com/assets.html`.

Additionally, later chapters also include screenshots of the open, three-dimensional Mannequin from GDQuest, available under an MIT license at `https://github.com/GDQuest/godot-3d-mannequin`.

Some assets already come in a glTF format, but some might be in `.blend`, `.fbx`, or some other format. When this happens, it's easy to import the model into Blender and export a glTF file. The next section will guide you through exporting glTF files from Blender.

Exporting from Blender

Blender is a free, three-dimensional content creation tool. You can download Blender from `https://www.blender.org/`. The following instructions are written for Blender 2.8 but they should work the same in newer versions as well.

If the model you are importing is already a `.blend` file, just double-click it and it should load up in Blender.

If the model is in a different format, such as `.DAE` or `.FBX`, you will need to import it. To do so, open Blender and you should see the default scene load up. This default scene has a cube, a light, and a camera:

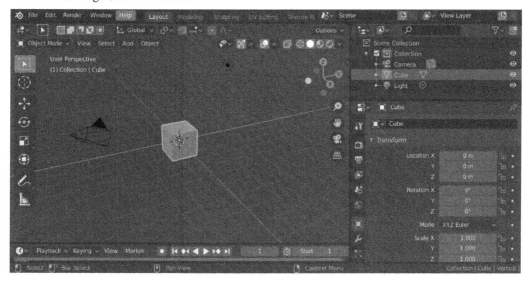

Figure 7.5: A default Blender3D scene

Select the cube by left-clicking on it, then hover over the three-dimensional viewport and hit the *Delete* key to delete the cube. Left-click on the camera to select it and delete it by hitting the *Delete* key. Do the same for the light.

You should now have an empty scene. From the **File** menu, select **File|Import** and select the appropriate model format to import. Find your file and double-click it to import it. Once a model is imported, select **File|Export glTF 2.0**. Set the export format to either glTF (text file) or glb (binary file).

Summary

In this chapter, you learned what glTF files are, what parts of the glTF format are useful for skinned animation, and how to use cglTF to load a glTF file. Don't worry if the format is still a bit confusing; it will make more sense as you start to parse various bits of data from cgltf files. Using cgltf will let you focus on converting glTF data into useful runtime structures without having to worry about manually parsing JSON files. In the next chapter, you will start implementing the building blocks of animation by implementing curves, frames, and tracks.

8
Creating Curves, Frames, and Tracks

In the early 2000s, it was common for games to take an animation that was authored in a 3D content creation tool such as Blender or Maya, play back the animation, and sample the transform of every joint in the animation at set intervals. Once the animation was sampled, the game's runtime linearly interpolated between the sampled frames.

While this works (and is doable with glTF files), it's not the most accurate way to play back animations. It wastes memory by including frames that don't actually need to exist. In a 3D content creation tool, animations are created using curves, such as the one shown in the following screenshot:

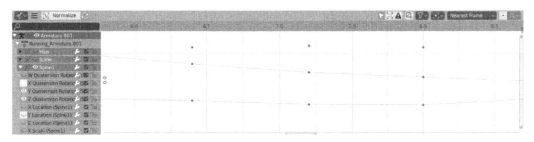

Figure 8.1: The Blender 3D curve editor

Modern games and animation systems evaluate these curves directly. Evaluating the animation curves directly saves memory, but curves are a bit more expensive in terms of processing power. By the end of this chapter, you should be able to do the following:

- Understand cubic Bézier splines and how to evaluate them
- Understand cubic Hermite splines and how to evaluate them
- Understand common interpolation methods
- Be able to create cubic, linear, and constant keyframes
- Understand how keyframes make up a cubic, linear, or constant track
- Be able to evaluate cubic, linear, and constant tracks
- Be able to combine three independent tracks into one transform track

Understanding cubic Bézier splines

To implement game animation, you need some understanding of curves. Let's start with the basics—a cubic Bézier spline. A Bézier spline has two points to interpolate between and two control points that help generate a curve. This is what a cubic Bézier spline looks like:

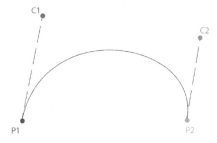

Figure 8.2: A cubic Bézier spline

Given the two points and the two controls, how is the curve generated? Let's explore interpolating the curve for a given time, **t**. Start by drawing a line from **P1** to **C1**, from **C1** to **C2**, and from **C2** to **P2**. Then, linearly interpolate along those lines with the value of **t**:

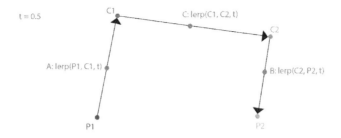

Figure 8.3: Linearly interpolating between points and control points

The interpolated points from **P1** to **C1** is **A**, from **C2** to **P2** is **B**, and from **C1** to **C2** is **C**. Next, you need to repeat this process, drawing lines and interpolating from **A** to **C** and from **C** to **B**. Let's call these newly interpolated points E and F:

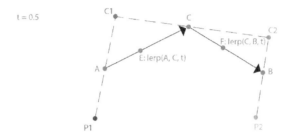

Figure 8.4: Linearly interpolating the results of figure 8.3

Repeat this one more time, drawing a line from **E** to **F** and interpolating along that line by **t** as well. Let's call the resulting point **R**. This point, **R**, is somewhere on the Bézier spline. If you were to calculate all points from $t=0$ to $t=1$, you could plot the curve:

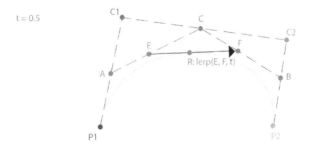

Figure 8.5: Linearly interpolating the results of figure 8.4

Let's explore the code required to draw a Bézier spline. Bézier splines will not be used anywhere else in this book, so implementing the following code is not required to follow along with the rest of this book:

1. First, you need to define what a Bézier spline is. Create a new templated class that contains two points and two control points:

```
template<typename T>
class Bezier {
public:
    T P1; // Point 1
    T C1; // Control 1
    T P2; // Point 2
    T C2; // Control 2
};
```

2. Next, implement the `Interpolate` function. This function takes a Bézier spline reference and a value, t, to interpolate the spline. It's assumed that t is greater than or equal to 0 and less than or equal to 1:

```
template<typename T>
inline T Interpolate(Bezier<T>& curve, float t) {
    T A = lerp(curve.P1, curve.C1, t);
    T B = lerp(curve.C2, curve.P2, t);
    T C = lerp(curve.C1, curve.C2, t);

    T D = lerp(A, C, t);
    T E = lerp(C, B, t);

    T R = lerp(D, E, t);
    return R;
}
```

The following code sample demonstrates how the Bezier class and the `Interpolate` function can be used to plot a Bézier spline:

1. First, you need to create the data that will be plotted:

```
Bezier<vec3> curve;
curve.P1 = vec3(-5, 0, 0);
curve.P2 = vec3(5, 0, 0);
curve.C1 = vec3(-2, 1, 0);
curve.C2 = vec3(2, 1, 0);

vec3 red = vec3(1, 0, 0);
```

```
vec3 green = vec3(0, 1, 0);
vec3 blue = vec3(0, 0, 1);
vec3 magenta = vec3(1, 0, 1);
```

2.   Next, draw the points and handles:

```
// Draw all relevant points
DrawPoint(curve.P1, red);
DrawPoint(curve.C1, green);
DrawPoint(curve.P2, red);
DrawPoint(curve.C2, green);

// Draw handles
DrawLine(curve.P1, curve.C1, blue);
DrawLine(curve.P2, curve.C2, blue);
```

3.   Finally, plot the spline:

```
// Draw the actual curve
// Resolution is 200 steps since last point is i + 1
for (int i = 0; i < 199; ++i) {
    float t0 = (float)i / 199.0f;
    float t1 = (float)(i + 1) / 199.0f;

    vec3 thisPoint = Interpolate(curve, t0);
    vec3 nextPoint = Interpolate(curve, t1);

    DrawLine(thisPoint, nextPoint, magenta);
}
```

In the preceding sample code, you can see that you can implement the Bézier `Interpolate` function by using six linear interpolations. To understand how Bézier splines work, you need to expand the `lerp` functions to what they actually are. Linear interpolation, `lerp(a, b, t)`, expands to `(1-t) * a + t * b`:

1.   Rewrite the `Interpolate` function so that all the `lerp` calls are expanded:

```
template<typename T>
inline T Interpolate(const Bezier<T>& curve, float t) {
    T A = curve.P1 * (1.0f - t) + curve.C1 * t;
    T B = curve.C2 * (1.0f - t) + curve.P2 * t;
    T C = curve.C1 * (1.0f - t) + curve.C2 * t;
    T D = A * (1.0f - t) + C * t;
    T E = C * (1.0f - t) + B * t;
    T R = D * (1.0f - t) + E * t;
```

```
        return R;
    }
```

2. Nothing has changed, but you no longer need to call the `lerp` function. This works for any data type, T, as long as `T operator*(const T& t, float f)` is defined. Let's try to simplify this in a mathematical sense. Instead of using the A, B, C, D, E, and R variables, expand these equations to the following:

```
((P1 * (1 - t) + C1 * t) * (1 - t) + (C1 * (1 - t)
+ C2 * t) * t) * (1 - t) + ((C1 * (1 - t) + C2 * t)
* (1 - t) + (C2 * (1 - t) + P2 * t) * t) * t
```

3. This is the equivalent of inlining all the `lerp` functions by hand. The resulting code is a little hard to read:

```
template<typename T>
inline T Interpolate(const Bezier<T>& c, float t) {
    return
        ((c.P1 * (1.0f - t) + c.C1 * t) * (1.0f - t) +
        (c.C1 * (1.0f - t) + c.C2 * t) * t) * (1.0f - t)
        + ((c.C1 * (1.0f - t) + c.C2 * t) * (1.0f - t) +
        (c.C2 * (1.0f - t) + c.P2 * t) * t) * t;
}
```

4. Why go through all this trouble? To start simplifying the math, let's start by combining like terms:

```
-P1t3 + 3P1t2 - 3P1t + P1 + 3C1t3 - 6C1t2 + 3C1t - 3C2t3
+ 3C2t2 + P2t3
```

5. Now that's starting to look like an equation! This simplified equation can be expressed in code as well:

```
template<typename T>
inline T Interpolate(const Bezier<T>& curve, float t) {
    return
        curve.P1 * (t * t * t) * -1.0f +
        curve.P1 * 3.0f * (t * t) -
        curve.P1 * 3.0f * t +
        curve.P1 +
        curve.C1 * 3.0f * (t * t * t) -
        curve.C1 * 6.0f * (t * t) +
        curve.C1 * 3.0f * t -
        curve.C2 * 3.0f * (t * t * t) +
```

```
        curve.C2 * 3.0f * (t * t) +
        curve.P2 * (t * t * t);
}
```

6. Take this simplification a bit further by isolating some of the terms:

```
P1( -t3 + 3t2 - 3t + 1) +
C1( 3t3 - 6t2 + 3t)+
C2(-3t3 + 3t2)+
P2(  t3)
```

7. In code, this is expressed as follows:

```
template<typename T>
inline T Interpolate(const Bezier<T>& c, float t) {
    float ttt = t * t * t;
    float tt = t * t;

    return
    c.P1 * (-1.0f * ttt + 3.0f * tt - 3.0f * t + 1.0f) +
    c.C1 * (3.0f * ttt - 6.0f * tt + 3.0f * t) +
    c.C2 * (-3.0f * ttt + 3.0f * tt) +
    c.P2 * ttt;
}
```

8. Simplify the function one more time:

```
P1((1-t)3) +
C1(3(1-t)2t) +
C2(3(1-t)t2) +
P2(t3)
```

9. The code for this final simplification looks as follows:

```
template<typename T>
inline T Interpolate(const Bezier<T>& curve, float t) {
    return curve.P1 * ((1 - t) * (1 - t) * (1 - t)) +
           curve.C1 * (3.0f * ((1 - t) * (1 - t)) * t) +
           curve.C2 * (3.0f * (1 - t) * (t * t)) +
           curve.P2 *(t * t * t);
}
```

If you plot these final equations out with *t* ranging from 0 to 1, you get the following graph:

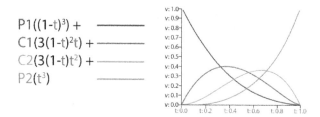

$$P1((1-t)^3) +$$
$$C1(3(1-t)^2 t) +$$
$$C2(3(1-t)t^2) +$$
$$P2(t^3)$$

Figure 8.6: The basis functions of a Bézier spline

These are the point basis functions of the cubic Bézier spline. They express how the value of the spline changes over time. For example, the influence of P1 drops over time; at *t=0*, the influence is full—it has a value of 1. However, by the time *t=1*, the influence of P1 is gone—it has a value of 0.

In this section, you went through the exercise of simplifying the Bézier spline evaluation function to arrive at the basis function of the spline. With Bézier splines, it's easy to follow this logic since you can start with an easy-to-understand implementation that just uses six lerp functions. With other curves, there is no easy place to start.

In the next section, we will explore another type of cubic spline—the cubic Hermite spline. Using the knowledge you learned in this section, you will be able to implement the Hermite evaluation function using only the basis function graph.

Understanding cubic Hermite splines

The most common spline type used in animation for games is a **cubic Hermite spline**. Unlike Bézier, a Hermite spline doesn't use points in space for its control; rather, it uses the tangents of points along the spline. You still have four values, as with a Bézier spline, but they are interpreted differently.

With the Hermite spline, you don't have two points and two control points; instead, you have two points and two slopes. The slopes are also referred to as tangents—throughout the rest of this chapter, the slope and tangent terms will be used interchangeably. The point basis functions for Hermite splines look as follows:

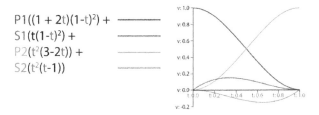

$$P1((1 + 2t)(1-t)^2) +$$
$$S1(t(1-t)^2) +$$
$$P2(t^2(3-2t)) +$$
$$S2(t^2(t-1))$$

Figure 8.7: The point basis functions of Hermite splines

When given the point basis functions, you can implement the spline evaluation function similar to how the Bézier interpolation function was implemented:

```
template<typename T>
T Hermite(float t, T& p1, T& s1, T& p2, T& s2) {
    return
        p1 * ((1.0f + 2.0f * t) * ((1.0f - t) * (1.0f - t))) +
        s1 * (t * ((1.0f - t) * (1.0f - t))) +
        p2 * ((t * t) * (3.0f - 2.0f * t)) +
        s2 * ((t * t) * (t - 1.0f));
}
```

It's possible to switch between Bézier and Hermite splines, but that's beyond the scope of what you need to know for animation. Some 3D content creation applications, such as Maya, let animators create animations using a Hermite spline, while others, such as Blender 3D, use Bézier curves.

It's useful to understand how these functions work, regardless of which one drives your animation system. There are, of course, more curve types, but Bézier and Hermite are the most common ones.

The glTF file format supports the constant, linear, and cubic interpolation types. You just learned how to do cubic interpolation, but you still need to implement both constant and linear interpolation.

Interpolation types

When defining an animation curve, generally, it follows one of three interpolation methods—constant, linear, or cubic. Cubic curves can be expressed using any cubic equation, such as Bézier curves (which is what Blender uses) or Hermite splines (which is what Maya uses). This book uses Hermite splines to represent cubic curves.

A **constant curve** keeps its value the same until the next keyframe. Sometimes, this type of curve is called a step curve. Visually, a constant curve looks as follows:

Figure 8.8: A constant curve

A **linear curve** interpolates between two frames in a linear fashion (that is, in a straight line). As you saw with the sampled curve approximation example earlier, if the samples of a linear track are close enough, it can start to approximate other types of curves as well. A linear curve looks as follows:

Figure 8.9: A linear curve

A **cubic curve** lets you define a curve in terms of values and tangents. The benefit of cubic curves is that you can express complex curves with little data. The downside is that interpolation becomes a bit more expensive. A cubic curve looks as follows (the tangents are the lines coming out of the keyframes):

Figure 8.10: A cubic curve

Interpolation types can be expressed as a simple enum class. Create a new file—`Interpolation.h`. Add header guards and add the following enum class declaration:

```
enum class Interpolation {
    Constant,
    Linear,
    Cubic
};
```

These are the three interpolation types that glTF supports as well. In the next section, you will start to implement animation tracks by creating a `Frame` structure to hold keyframe data.

Creating the Frame struct

What is a frame of data? That depends on the interpolation type. If the interpolation is constant (step) or linear, a frame is just a time and value. When the interpolation is cubic, you need to store the tangents as well.

A Hermite curve is made by connecting Hermite splines. Each control point consists of a time, a value, an incoming tangent, and an outgoing tangent. The incoming tangent is used if the control point is evaluated with the point that comes before it. The outgoing tangent is used if the control point is evaluated with the point that comes after it.

The time value stored in a frame is scalar, but what about the data and tangents? Should these values be scalar, a vector, or a quaternion? To make that decision, you have to think about how you might want to organize a collection of frames into a curve.

There are two strategies to choose from. You could create a scalar curve object, where the data and tangents are scalar values. Then, when you need a vector curve, you can combine several scalar curve objects into a vector curve object.

The advantage of having a scalar track and compositing higher-order tracks from it is that each component of a vector or quaternion curve can be interpolated differently. It can also save on memory since each component of the curve could have a different number of frames. The disadvantage is the additional effort of implementation.

The other strategy is to have specialized frame and curve types, such as a scalar frame, a vector frame, and a quaternion frame. Similarly, you could create separate classes to represent a scalar curve, a vector curve, and a quaternion curve.

The advantage of using specialized frames and curves is their ease of implementation. You can take advantage of using templates to avoid writing duplicate code. glTF files store animation tracks this way as well. The disadvantage is memory; every component of a curve is required to have the same number of keyframes.

In this book, you will implement explicit frames and curves (tracks). The Frame class will contain a time, a value, and both in and out tangents. If the interpolation type doesn't need tangents, you can simply ignore them. A frame can be an arbitrary size (such as scalar, vector 2, vector 3, quat, and so on). The time it contains will always be a scalar, but the value and tangent lengths can be anything:

1. Create a new file, Frame.h. Add the declaration of the Frame class to this new file. The Frame class needs arrays for the value and the in and out tangents, and a scalar for the time. Use a template to specify the size of each frame:

    ```
    template<unsigned int N>
    class Frame {
    ```

```
public:
    float mValue[N];
    float mIn[N];
    float mOut[N];
    float mTime;
};
```

2. Create the `typedef` data types for the common frame types:

```
typedef Frame<1> ScalarFrame;
typedef Frame<3> VectorFrame;
typedef Frame<4> QuaternionFrame;
```

The `Frame` class you just implemented is used to store keyframes in an animation track. An animation track is a collection of keyframes. In the next section, you will learn how to implement a `Track` class.

Creating the Track class

A `Track` class is a collection of frames. Interpolating a track returns the data type of the track; the result is the value along whatever curve the track defines at a specific point in time. A track must have at least two frames to interpolate between.

As mentioned in the *Creating the Frame struct* section, by following the examples in this book, you will implement explicit frame and track types. There will be separate classes for scalar, vector, and quaternion tracks. These classes are templated to avoid having to write duplicate code. A `vec3` track, for example, contains the `Frame<3>` type frames.

Because tracks have an explicit type, you can't make a keyframe in the X component of a `vec3` track without also adding a keyframe to the Y and Z components as well.

This can eat up more memory if you have a component that doesn't change. For example, notice how, in the following figure, the Z component has many frames, even though it's a straight line and two should be enough. This isn't a big trade-off; the additional memory that's taken is insignificant:

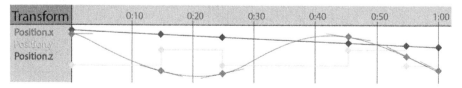

Figure 8.11: The components of a vec3 track

For skinned mesh rendering, animation tracks always animate joint transforms. However, animation tracks can be used to animate other values in a game as well, such as the intensity of a light or switching between two-dimensional sprites for a flipbook effect. In the next section, you will create a new header file and start declaring the actual Track class.

Declaring the Track class

A track is a collection of frames. The Frame class is templated, so the Track class needs to be templated as well. The Track class takes two template parameters—the first is the type (which is intended to be float, vec3, quat, and so on) and the other is the number of components that the type contains:

1. The Track class only needs two members—a vector of frames and an interpolation type. Create a new file, Track.h, and add the declaration of the Track class to this file:

```cpp
template<typename T, int N>
class Track {
protected:
    std::vector<Frame<N>> mFrames;
    Interpolation mInterpolation;
```

2. The Track class only needs a default constructor to initialize the mInterpolation variable. The generated copy constructor, assignment operator, and destructor are fine:

```cpp
public:
    Track();
```

3. Create getter and setter functions for the number of frames a track has, as well as its interpolation type and the start and end time:

```cpp
    void Resize(unsigned int size);
    unsigned int Size();
    Interpolation GetInterpolation();
    void SetInterpolation(Interpolation interp);
    float GetStartTime();
    float GetEndTime();
```

4. The `Track` class needs a way to sample the track when given a time. This `Sample` method should take a time value and whether the track is looping or not. Overload the `[] operator` to retrieve a reference to a frame:

```
T Sample(float time, bool looping);
Frame<N>& operator[](unsigned int index);
```

5. Next, you need to declare some helper functions. A track can be constant, linear, or cubic. There is only one `Sample` function that needs to handle all three of these cases. Rather than making a huge, hard-to-read function, create a helper function for each interpolation type:

```
protected:
    T SampleConstant(float time, bool looping);
    T SampleLinear(float time, bool looping);
    T SampleCubic(float time, bool looping);
```

6. Add a helper function to evaluate the Hermite splines:

```
T Hermite(float time, const T& p1, const T& s1,
          const T& p2, const T& s2);
```

7. Add a function to retrieve the frame index for a given time. This is the last frame right before the requested time. Also, add a helper function that takes an input time that is outside the range of the track and adjusts it to be a valid time on the track:

```
int FrameIndex(float time, bool looping);
float AdjustTimeToFitTrack(float t, bool loop);
```

8. You will need a way of casting an array of floats (the data inside a frame) to the templated type of the track. This function is specialized for each type of track:

```
    T Cast(float* value); // Will be specialized
};
```

9. As with the `Frame` class, add the `typedef` data types for the common `Track` types:

```
typedef Track<float, 1> ScalarTrack;
typedef Track<vec3, 3> VectorTrack;
typedef Track<quat, 4> QuaternionTrack;
```

The API of the `Track` class is small, which makes the class easy to work with. However, there is a lot of hidden complexity to the `Track` class; after all, this class is at the core of the animation system you are building. In the next section, you will start to implement the actual `Track` class.

Implementing the Track class

The `Track` class is templated, but it's not meant to be used outside of the animation system. Add template definitions for the `float`, `vec3`, and `quat` tracks to `Track.cpp`. This makes the compiler generate the code for these templates in the CPP file:

```
template Track<float, 1>;
template Track<vec3, 3>;
template Track<quat, 4>;
```

For character animation, the `vec3` and `quat` track types are all you need. If you need to add a new type of track, don't forget to add the template type to the `Track.cpp` file. In the following section, you will start to implement helper functions to load track data.

Implementing helper functions

The `Track` class is templated to avoid having to write duplicate code for all the track types. However, some functionality needs to be specific to the type of the `Track` class. Besides the `Cast` function, all type-specific functions reside in a new namespace—`TrackHelpers`.

These helper functions are not a part of the `Track` class; they rely on function overloading to make sure the right version of the helper function is called. One of the key responsibilities of these helper classes is to make sure quaternions are normalized and are in the right neighborhood. Because this code interpolates quaternions, neighborhooding is a concern:

1. For a track to be linearly interpolated, you need to create interpolation functions that work with each track type. Add the following helper functions to `Track.cpp` that provide the correct interpolation method for each of the data types that a track might contain. These functions belong in the `TrackHelpers` namespace:

    ```
    namespace TrackHelpers {
        inline float Interpolate(float a, float b, float t) {
            return a + (b - a) * t;
        }

        inline vec3 Interpolate(const vec3& a, const vec3& b,
    ```

```
                            float t) {
        return lerp(a, b, t);
    }

    inline quat Interpolate(const quat& a, const quat& b,
                            float t) {
        quat result = mix(a, b, t);
        if (dot(a, b) < 0) { // Neighborhood
            result = mix(a, -b, t);
        }
        return normalized(result); //NLerp, not slerp
    }
```

2. When a Hermite spline is interpolated, if the input type was a quaternion, the result needs to be normalized. Rather than providing a quaternion specification of the Hermite function, you can create helper functions that only normalize quaternions:

```
    inline float AdjustHermiteResult(float f) {
        return f;
    }

    inline vec3 AdjustHermiteResult(const vec3& v) {
        return v;
    }

    inline quat AdjustHermiteResult(const quat& q) {
        return normalized(q);
    }
```

3. There also needs to be a common Neighborhood operation that makes sure two quaternions are in the correct neighborhood. This function should do nothing for the other data types:

```
    inline void Neighborhood(const float& a, float& b){}
    inline void Neighborhood(const vec3& a, vec3& b){}

    inline void Neighborhood(const quat& a, quat& b) {
        if (dot(a, b) < 0) {
            b = -b;
        }
    }
}; // End Track Helpers namespace
```

The reason these helper functions exist is to avoid having to make specialized versions of the interpolation functions. Instead, the generic interpolation functions call these helper methods and function overloading makes sure the correct function is called. This does mean that you need to add new helper functions if you add a new type of track. In the next section, you will start implementing some of the `Track` functions.

Implementing the Track functions

In this section, you will start to implement the member functions of the `Track` class. The `Track` class has several unimportant functions that either need to call helper functions or are simply getter and setter functions. Begin implementing the `Track` class with these functions first:

1. The `Track` constructor needs to set the track's interpolation type. The getter and setter functions for the start and end times of the track are simple getter functions:

```
template<typename T, int N>
Track<T, N>::Track() {
    mInterpolation = Interpolation::Linear;
}


template<typename T, int N>
float Track<T, N>::GetStartTime() {
    return mFrames[0].mTime;
}

template<typename T, int N>
float Track<T, N>::GetEndTime() {
    return mFrames[mFrames.size() - 1].mTime;
}
```

2. The `Sample` function needs to call `SampleConstant`, `SampleLinear`, or `SampleCubic`, depending on the track type. The `[] operator` returns a reference to the specified frame:

```
template<typename T, int N>
T Track<T, N>::Sample(float time, bool looping) {
    if (mInterpolation == Interpolation::Constant) {
        return SampleConstant(time, looping);
    }
    else if (mInterpolation == Interpolation::Linear) {
        return SampleLinear(time, looping);
    }
```

```
        return SampleCubic(time, looping);
}

template<typename T, int N>
Frame<N>& Track<T, N>::operator[](unsigned int index) {
    return mFrames[index];
}
```

3. The `Resize` and `Size` functions are simple getter and setters around the size of the frames vector:

```
template<typename T, int N>
void Track<T, N>::Resize(unsigned int size) {
    mFrames.resize(size);
}

template<typename T, int N>
unsigned int Track<T, N>::Size() {
    return mFrames.size();
}
```

4. The interpolation type of the track also has simple getter and setter functions:

```
template<typename T, int N>
Interpolation Track<T, N>::GetInterpolation() {
    return mInterpolation;
}

template<typename T, int N>
void Track<T, N>::SetInterpolation(Interpolation
interpolation) {
    mInterpolation = interpolation;
}
```

5. The `Hermite` function implements the basic functions covered in the *Understanding cubic Hermite splines* section of this chapter. The second point might need to be negated by the `Neighborhood` helper function. Quaternions also need to be normalized. Both neighborhooding and normalization are carried out by helper functions:

```
template<typename T, int N>
T Track<T, N>::Hermite(float t, const T& p1, const T& s1,
                       const T& _p2, const T& s2) {
    float tt = t * t;
```

```
        float ttt = tt * t;

        T p2 = _p2;
        TrackHelpers::Neighborhood(p1, p2);

        float h1 = 2.0f * ttt - 3.0f * tt + 1.0f;
        float h2 = -2.0f * ttt + 3.0f * tt;
        float h3 = ttt - 2.0f * tt + t;
        float h4 = ttt - tt;

        T result = p1 * h1 + p2 * h2 + s1 * h3 + s2 * h4;
        return TrackHelpers::AdjustHermiteResult(result);
}
```

In the following sections, you will implement some of the more difficult functions of the
`Track` class, starting with the `FrameIndex` function.

Implementing the FrameIndex function

The `FrameIndex` function takes time as an argument; it should return the frame
immediately before that time (on the left). This behavior changes depending on whether
the track is intended to be sampled looping or not. Follow these steps to implement the
`FrameIndex` function:

1. If the track has one frame or less, it is invalid. If an invalid track is encountered,
    return `-1`:

    ```
    template<typename T, int N>
    int Track<T, N>::FrameIndex(float time, bool looping) {
        unsigned int size = (unsigned int)mFrames.size();
        if (size <= 1) {
            return -1;
        }
    ```

2. If the track is sampled as looping, the input time needs to be adjusted so that it falls
    between the start and end frames. This means you need to know the time at the first
    frame of the track, the time at the frame of the track, and the duration of the track:

    ```
        if (looping) {
            float startTime = mFrames[0].mTime;
            float endTime = mFrames[size - 1].mTime;
            float duration = endTime - startTime;
    ```

3. Since the track is looping, time needs to be adjusted so that it is within a valid range. To do this, make time relative to duration by subtracting the start time from it and modulo the result with duration. If time is negative, add the duration. Don't forget to add the start time back into time:

```
time = fmodf(time - startTime,
             endTime - startTime);
if (time < 0.0f) {
    time += endTime - startTime;
}
time = time + startTime;
}
```

4. If the track doesn't loop, any time value that is less than the start frame should clamp to 0 and any time value that is greater than the second-to-last frame should clamp to the second-to-last frame's index:

```
else {
    if (time <= mFrames[0].mTime) {
        return 0;
    }
    if (time >= mFrames[size - 2].mTime) {
        return (int)size - 2;
    }
}
```

5. Now that the time is in a valid range, loop through every frame. The frame that is closest to the time (but still less) is the frame whose index should be returned. This frame can be found by looping through the frames of the track backward and returning the first index whose time is less than the time that is looked up:

```
for (int i = (int)size - 1; i >= 0; --i) {
    if (time >= mFrames[i].mTime) {
        return i;
    }
}
// Invalid code, we should not reach here!
return -1;
} // End of FrameIndex
```

If a track does not loop and the time is greater than the last frame's time, the index of the second-to-last frame is used. Why the second-to-last frame and not the last frame? The Sample function always needs a current and next frame, and the next frame is found by adding 1 to the result of the FrameIndex function. When time equals the time of the last frame, the two frames that need to be interpolated are still the second-to-last frame and the last frame.

In the next section, you will implement the AdjustTimeToFitTrack function. This function is used to make sure any time that is sampled has a valid value. A valid value is any time between the start and end times of the track.

Implementing the AdjustTimeToFitTrack function

The next function to implement is AdjustTimeToFitTrack. When given a time, this function needs to adjust the time to be in the range of the start/end frames of the track. This is, of course, different depending on whether the track loops. Take the following steps to implement the AdjustTimeToFitTrack function:

1. If a track has less than one frame, the track is invalid. If an invalid track is used, return 0:

```
template<typename T, int N>
float Track<T, N>::AdjustTimeToFitTrack(float time,
                                        bool looping) {
    unsigned int size = (unsigned int)mFrames.size();
    if (size <= 1) {
        return 0.0f;
    }
```

2. Find the start time, end time, and duration of the track. The start time is the time of the first frame, the end time is the time of the last frame, and the duration is the difference between the two. If the track has a 0 duration, it is invalid—return 0:

```
    float startTime = mFrames[0].mTime;
    float endTime = mFrames[size - 1].mTime;
    float duration = endTime - startTime;
    if (duration <= 0.0f) {
        return 0.0f;
    }
```

3. If the track loops, adjust the time by the duration of the track:

```
if (looping) {
    time = fmodf(time - startTime,
                    endTime - startTime);
    if (time < 0.0f) {
        time += endTime - startTime;
    }
    time = time + startTime;
}
```

4. If the track does not loop, clamp the time to the first or last frame. Return the adjusted time:

```
else {
    if (time <= mFrames[0].mTime) {
        time = startTime;
    }
    if (time >= mFrames[size - 1].mTime) {
        time = endTime;
    }
}

return time;
}
```

The AdjustTimeToFitTrack function is useful because it keeps the animation sampling time in the range. This function is intended to be called when the playback time of an animation changes. Consider the following example:

```
Track<float, 1> t;
float mAnimTime = 0.0f;

void Update(float dt) { // dt: delta time of frame
    mAnimTime = t.AdjustTimeToFitTrack(mAnimTime + dt);
}
```

Any time the Update function is called in the example, the mAnimTime variable is incremented by deltaTime of the frame. However, because the incremented time is passed to AdjustTimeToFitTrack before it is assigned, it never has an invalid animation time value.

In the following section, you will implement the Cast function of the Track class. The Cast function is used to take an array of floats and cast it to whatever the templated type of the Track class is.

Implementing the Cast function

The Cast function is specialized; an implementation needs to be provided for every type of track. The Cast function takes a floating-point array and returns whatever the templated type, T, is of the Track class. The supported types are float, vec3, and quat:

```
template<> float Track<float, 1>::Cast(float* value) {
    return value[0];
}

template<> vec3 Track<vec3, 3>::Cast(float* value) {
    return vec3(value[0], value[1], value[2]);
}

template<> quat Track<quat, 4>::Cast(float* value) {
    quat r = quat(value[0], value[1], value[2], value[3]);
    return normalized(r);
}
```

This Cast function is important because it can cast a float array stored in a Frame class into the data type that the Frame class represents. For example, Frame<3> is cast to vec3. In the following sections, you will use the Cast function to return the correct data type when sampling a Track class.

Constant track sampling

In this section, you will implement the first of three sampling functions for a Track class—the **constant sampling** function. To do a constant (step) sample, find the frame based on the time with the FrameIndex helper. Make sure the frame is valid, then cast the value of that frame to the correct data type and return it:

```
template<typename T, int N>
T Track<T, N>::SampleConstant(float t, bool loop) {
    int frame = FrameIndex(t, loop);
    if (frame < 0 || frame >= (int)mFrames.size()) {
        return T();
    }

    return Cast(&mFrames[frame].mValue[0]);
}
```

Constant sampling is often used for things such as visibility flags, where it makes sense for the value of a variable to change from one frame to the next without any real interpolation. In the following section, you will learn how to implement linear track sampling. Linear sampling is very common; most content creation applications offer a "sampled" export option that exports linearly interpolated tracks.

Linear track sampling

The second type of sampling, **linear sampling**, interpolates between two frames. This function needs to find both the current and the next frames, then find the delta time between the two frames. Because of the `FrameIndex` function, you should never be in a situation where the current frame is the last frame of the track and the next frame is invalid.

Once you know the current frame, the next frame, and the delta time between them, you can interpolate. Call `AdjustTimeToFitTrack` to make sure the time is valid, subtract the time of the first frame from it, and divide the result by the frame delta. This results in the interpolation value, `t`.

Knowing the interpolation value, call the `TrackHelpers::Interpolate` function to do the interpolation:

```
template<typename T, int N>
T Track<T, N>::SampleLinear(float time, bool looping) {
    int thisFrame = FrameIndex(time, looping);
    if (thisFrame < 0 || thisFrame >= mFrames.size() - 1) {
        return T();
    }
    int nextFrame = thisFrame + 1;

    float trackTime = AdjustTimeToFitTrack(time, looping);
    float thisTime = mFrames[thisFrame].mTime;
    float frameDelta = mFrames[nextFrame].mTime - thisTime;

    if (frameDelta <= 0.0f) {
        return T();
    }
    float t = (trackTime - thisTime) / frameDelta;

    T start = Cast(&mFrames[thisFrame].mValue[0]);
    T end = Cast(&mFrames[nextFrame].mValue[0]);

    return TrackHelpers::Interpolate(start, end, t);
}
```

Linear sampling is common as many 3D content creation applications provide an option to approximate animation curves by sampling them at set intervals. In the following section, you will learn how to carry out the cubic interpolation of curves. Cubic interpolation stores less data than linear interpolation, but is more expensive to calculate.

Cubic track sampling

The final type of sampling, **cubic sampling**, finds the frames to sample and the interpolation time in the same way that linear sampling did. This function calls the `Hermite` helper function to do its interpolation.

If you imagine `time` as a play-head on a track, it is on the right of the first point and the left of the second point. Therefore, you need the out slope of the first point (because the play-head is moving away from it) and the in slope of the second point (because the play-head is moving toward it). Both slopes need to be scaled by the frame delta:

```
template<typename T, int N>
T Track<T, N>::SampleCubic(float time, bool looping) {
    int thisFrame = FrameIndex(time, looping);
    if (thisFrame < 0 || thisFrame >= mFrames.size() - 1) {
        return T();
    }
    int nextFrame = thisFrame + 1;

    float trackTime = AdjustTimeToFitTrack(time, looping);
    float thisTime = mFrames[thisFrame].mTime;
    float frameDelta = mFrames[nextFrame].mTime - thisTime;
    if (frameDelta <= 0.0f) {
        return T();
    }
    float t = (trackTime - thisTime) / frameDelta;
    size_t fltSize = sizeof(float);

    T point1 = Cast(&mFrames[thisFrame].mValue[0]);
    T slope1;// = mFrames[thisFrame].mOut * frameDelta;
    memcpy(&slope1, mFrames[thisFrame].mOut, N * fltSize);
    slope1 = slope1 * frameDelta;

    T point2 = Cast(&mFrames[nextFrame].mValue[0]);
    T slope2;// = mFrames[nextFrame].mIn[0] * frameDelta;
    memcpy(&slope2, mFrames[nextFrame].mIn, N * fltSize);
    slope2 = slope2 * frameDelta;
```

```
       return Hermite(t, point1, slope1, point2, slope2);
}
```

Why do the slopes use `memcpy` instead of the `Cast` function? This is because the `Cast` function normalizes quaternions, which is bad because slopes are not meant to be quaternions. Using `memcpy` instead of `Cast` copies the values directly, avoiding normalization.

In the next section, you will learn how to combine vector and quaternion tracks into a `TransformTrack`. The actual animation framework will work on the `TransformTrack` classes, which will not be templated.

Creating the TransformTrack class

For any animated transform, you don't want to maintain separate vector and quaternion tracks; instead, you build a higher-level structure—the transform track. A transform track encapsulates three tracks—one for the position, one for the rotation, and one for scale. You can sample the transform track at any point and get a full transform back, even if the component tracks are of different durations or start at different times.

One thing to consider is how you want to store these transform tracks in relation to an animated model. The skeleton of a model contains several bones. You can either store a vector of transform tracks—one for each bone—or you can add bone ID as a member of the transform track and only store as many as are needed.

This is important because a character can have a lot of bones, but not all animations will animate all of those bones. If you store one transform track for each bone, it wastes memory, but sampling an animation is faster. If you store only as many transform tracks as needed, sampling becomes a bit more expensive, but memory consumption goes down.

Implementation choices tend to always end up being memory versus speed. On modern systems, the delta on either axis should be trivial. In this section, you will add a bone ID to the transform tracks and only store as many tracks as needed.

Declaring the TransformTrack class

The `TransformTrack` class will need to hold an integer that represents which bone (joint) the track will affect. It also needs actual tracks for the position, rotation, and scale. These four pieces of information should together be enough to animate a joint's position, rotation, and scale.

As with the `Track` class, the `TransformTrack` class has getter and setter functions for the start and end times of the transform track. The start and end times of a transform track is dependent on its component tracks. Component tracks are the position, rotation, and scale tracks.

Out of the three tracks, the start time that is the lowest is used as the transform track's start time. The end time that is the largest of the three tracks is used as the transform track's end time.

Not all of the component tracks in a transform track need to be valid. For example, if only the position of a transform is animated, the rotation and scale component tracks can be left as invalid. A transform track is valid so long as at least one of its component tracks is valid.

Because not all of the component tracks are guaranteed to be valid, the `Sample` function of the `TransformTrack` class needs to take a reference transform. Take the following steps to declare the `TransformTrack` class:

1. Create a new file, `TransformTrack.h`, and start adding the `TransformTrack` definition to it by defining the member variables:

    ```
    class TransformTrack {
    protected:
        unsigned int mId;
        VectorTrack mPosition;
        QuaternionTrack mRotation;
        VectorTrack mScale;
    ```

2. The public API is straightforward. You need the default constructor to assign a default value to the joint ID of the track. You also need getter functions for the ID, the component tracks, and the start/end times, as well as the duration and validity. Only the ID needs a setter function; the component getter functions return mutable references:

    ```
    public:
        TransformTrack();
        unsigned int GetId();
        void SetId(unsigned int id);
        VectorTrack& GetPositionTrack();
        QuaternionTrack& GetRotationTrack();
        VectorTrack& GetScaleTrack();
        float GetStartTime();
        float GetEndTime();
        bool IsValid();
    ```

```
    Transform Sample(const Transform& ref, float time,
bool looping);
};
```

In the next section, you will start implementing the functions of TransfromTrack.

Implementing the TransformTrack class

Follow these steps to implement the TransformTrack class:

1. Create a new file, TransformTrack.cpp, to implement the TransformTrack class in. The constructor of the TransformTrack class is unimportant; assign a default value to the joint that the transform track represents. The getter and setter functions for the track ID are also trivial:

```cpp
TransformTrack::TransformTrack() {
    mId = 0;
}

unsigned int TransformTrack::GetId() {
    return mId;
}

void TransformTrack::SetId(unsigned int id) {
    mId = id;
}
```

2. Next, implement functions to access the different component tracks stored in the transform track. These functions need to return a reference so that you can mutate the returned tracks:

```cpp
VectorTrack& TransformTrack::GetPositionTrack() {
    return mPosition;
}

QuaternionTrack& TransformTrack::GetRotationTrack() {
    return mRotation;
}

VectorTrack& TransformTrack::GetScaleTrack() {
    return mScale;
}
```

3. The `IsValid` helper function should only return `true` if at least one of the component tracks stored in the `TransformTrack` class is valid. For a track to be valid, it needs to have two or more frames:

```
bool TransformTrack::IsValid() {
    return mPosition.Size() > 1 ||
            mRotation.Size() > 1 ||
            mScale.Size() > 1;
}
```

4. The `GetStartTime` function should return the smallest start time of the three component tracks. If none of the components are valid (that is, they all have one or no frames), then `TransformTrack` isn't valid. In this case, just return 0:

```
float TransformTrack::GetStartTime() {
    float result = 0.0f;
    bool isSet = false;

    if (mPosition.Size() > 1) {
        result = mPosition.GetStartTime();
        isSet = true;
    }
    if (mRotation.Size() > 1) {
        float rotationStart = mRotation.GetStartTime();
        if (rotationStart < result || !isSet) {
            result = rotationStart;
            isSet = true;
        }
    }
    if (mScale.Size() > 1) {
        float scaleStart = mScale.GetStartTime();
        if (scaleStart < result || !isSet) {
            result = scaleStart;
            isSet = true;
        }
    }

    return result;
}
```

5. The `GetEndTime` function is similar to the `GetStartTime` function. The only difference is that this function looks for the greatest track end time:

```
float TransformTrack::GetEndTime() {
    float result = 0.0f;
    bool isSet = false;

    if (mPosition.Size() > 1) {
        result = mPosition.GetEndTime();
        isSet = true;
    }
    if (mRotation.Size() > 1) {
        float rotationEnd = mRotation.GetEndTime();
        if (rotationEnd > result || !isSet) {
            result = rotationEnd;
            isSet = true;
        }
    }
    if (mScale.Size() > 1) {
        float scaleEnd = mScale.GetEndTime();
        if (scaleEnd > result || !isSet) {
            result = scaleEnd;
            isSet = true;
        }
    }

    return result;
}
```

6. The `Sample` function only samples one of its component tracks if that track has two or more frames. Since a `TransformTrack` class can animate only one component, such as the position, this function needs to take a reference transform as an argument. If one of the transform components isn't animated by the transform track, the value of the reference transform is used:

```
Transform TransformTrack::Sample(const Transform& ref,
                                 float time, bool loop) {
    Transform result = ref; // Assign default values
    if (mPosition.Size() > 1) { // Only if valid
        result.position = mPosition.Sample(time, loop);
    }
    if (mRotation.Size() > 1) { // Only if valid
        result.rotation = mRotation.Sample(time, loop);
    }
```

```
        if (mScale.Size() > 1) { // Only if valid
            result.scale = mScale.Sample(time, loop);
        }
        return result;
}
```

Because not all animations contain the same tracks, it's important to reset the pose that you are sampling any time the animation that you are sampling switches. This ensures that the reference transform is always correct. To reset the pose, assign it to be the same as the rest pose.

Summary

In this chapter, you learned about the building blocks of animation, what is in one frame of data, how several frames can make a track, and how a few tracks can animate a transform. You explored the different interpolation methods for interpolating an animation track and made these methods work for scalar, vector, and quaternion tracks.

The classes you built in this chapter will be used as the building blocks for creating animation clips in the next chapter. In the next chapter, you will implement animation clips and poses. The animation clips will be made of the `TransformTrack` objects. These tracks are at the core of a modern animation system.

There are two samples in the `Chapter08` folder of the downloadable content for this book. `Sample00` contains all the code used up to this point in the book and `Sample01` creates several tracks and plots them all on screen. Visually plotting tracks is a good idea as it can help prevent debug problems early on.

9
Implementing Animation Clips

An animation clip is a collection of the `TransformTrack` objects. An animation clip animates a collection of transforms over time and the collection of transforms that is animated is called a pose. Think of a pose as the skeleton of an animated character at a specific point in time. A pose is a hierarchy of transforms. The value of each transform affects all of its children.

Let's walk through what it takes to generate the pose for one frame of a game's character animation. When an animation clip is sampled, the result is a pose. An animation clip is made up of animation tracks and each animation track is made up of one or more frames. This relationship looks something like this:

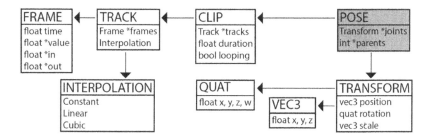

Figure 9.1: The dependencies of generating a pose

By the end of this chapter, you should be able to load animation clips from glTF files and sample those clips into a pose.

Implementing poses

To store a parent-child hierarchy between transforms, you need to maintain two parallel vectors—one filled with transforms and one filled with integers. The integer array contains the index of the parent transform for each joint. Not all joints have parents; if a joint doesn't have a parent, its parent value is negative.

When thinking about a skeleton or pose, it's easy to think of a hierarchy that has one root node and many nodes that branch off it. In practice, it's not uncommon to have two or three root nodes. Sometimes, file formats store models in a way that the first node of the skeleton is a root node, but there is also a root node that all the skinned meshes are children of. These hierarchies tend to look like this:

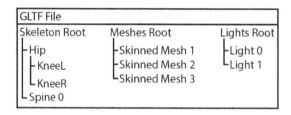

Figure 9.2: Multiple root nodes in one file

There are three common poses for an animated character—the current pose, the bind pose, and the rest pose. The rest pose is the default configuration of all the bones. The animation describes the transformation of each bone over time. Sampling an animation in time results in the current pose that is used to skin a character. The bind pose is covered in the next chapter.

Not all animations affect every bone or joint of a character; this means that some animations might not change the value of a joint. Remember, in this context a joint is expressed as a `Transform` object. What happens if animation **A** animates the joint at index 1 but animation **B** doesn't? The following list shows you the result:

- If you only play **A** or **B**, everything is fine.
- If you play **B** and then **A**, everything is fine.
- If you play **A** and then **B**, things get a bit wonky.

In the last example, where you play animation **A** first and **B** second, the joint at index 1 maintains its last modified transform from animation **A**. Because of this, you must reset the current pose so that it is the same as the rest pose whenever you switch between animations. In the following section, you will begin declaring the Pose class.

Declaring the Pose class

The Pose class needs to keep track of the transformation of every joint in the skeleton of the character that you are animating. It also needs to keep track of the parent joint of every joint. This data is kept in two parallel vectors.

Before a new animation clip is sampled, the pose of the current character needs to be reset to the rest pose. The Pose class implements a copy constructor and assignment operator to make copying poses as fast as possible. Follow these steps to declare the Pose class:

1. Create a new header file, Pose.h. Add the definition of the Pose class to this file, starting with the parallel vectors for joint transforms and their parents:

```cpp
class Pose {
protected:
    std::vector<Transform> mJoints;
    std::vector<int> mParents;
```

2. Add a default constructor and a copy constructor and overload the assignment operator. The Pose class also has a convenience constructor that takes the number of joints the pose will have as arguments:

```cpp
public:
    Pose();
    Pose(const Pose& p);
    Pose& operator=(const Pose& p);
    Pose(unsigned int numJoints);
```

3. Add a getter and setter function for the number of joints in the pose. When the setter function is used, both the mJoints and mParents vectors need to be resized:

```cpp
    void Resize(unsigned int size);
    unsigned int Size();
```

4. Add getter and setter functions for the parent of a joint. Both of these functions need to take the index of the joint as an argument:

```cpp
    int GetParent(unsigned int index);
    void SetParent(unsigned int index, int parent);
```

5. The `Pose` class needs to provide a way to get and set the local transform of a joint, as well as to retrieve the global transform of a joint. Overload `[] operator` to return the global transform of a joint:

```
Transform GetLocalTransform(unsigned int index);
void SetLocalTransform(unsigned int index,
                            const Transform& transform);
Transform GetGlobalTransform(unsigned int index);
Transform operator[](unsigned int index);
```

6. For a `Pose` class to be passed to OpenGL, it needs to be converted into a linear array of matrices. The `GetMatrixPalette` function carries out this conversion. The function takes a reference to a vector of matrices and fills it out with the global transform matrix of each joint in the pose:

```
void GetMatrixPalette(std::vector<mat4>& out);
```

7. Finish setting up the `Pose` class by overloading the equality and inequality operators:

```
bool operator==(const Pose& other);
bool operator!=(const Pose& other);
};
```

The `Pose` class is used to hold the transformation of every bone in an animated hierarchy. Think of it as a frame in an animation; the `Pose` class represents the state of an animation at a given time. In the following section, you will implement the `Pose` class.

Implementing the Pose class

Create a new file, `Pose.cpp`. You will implement the `Pose` class in this file. Take the following steps to implement the `Pose` class:

1. The default constructor doesn't have to do anything. The copy constructor calls the assignment operator. The convenience constructor calls the `Resize` method:

```
Pose::Pose() { }

Pose::Pose(unsigned int numJoints) {
    Resize(numJoints);
}

Pose::Pose(const Pose& p) {
    *this = p;
}
```

2. The assignment operator needs to copy the pose as fast as possible. You need to make sure the pose isn't assigned to itself. Next, make sure that the pose has the correct number of joints and parents. Then, carry out a mem-copy to fast-copy all of the parent and pose data:

```
Pose& Pose::operator=(const Pose& p) {
    if (&p == this) {
        return *this;
    }

    if (mParents.size() != p.mParents.size()) {
        mParents.resize(p.mParents.size());
    }
    if (mJoints.size() != p.mJoints.size()) {
        mJoints.resize(p.mJoints.size());
    }

    if (mParents.size() != 0) {
        memcpy(&mParents[0], &p.mParents[0],
                sizeof(int) * mParents.size());
    }
    if (mJoints.size() != 0) {
        memcpy(&mJoints[0], &p.mJoints[0],
                sizeof(Transform) * mJoints.size());
    }

    return *this;
}
```

3. Since the parent and joint vectors are parallel, the `Resize` function needs to set the size of both. The `size` getter function can return the size of either vector:

```
void Pose::Resize(unsigned int size) {
    mParents.resize(size);
    mJoints.resize(size);
}

unsigned int Pose::Size() {
    return mJoints.size();
}
```

4. The getter and setter methods for the local transforms are simple:

```
Transform Pose::GetLocalTransform(unsigned int index) {
    return mJoints[index];
}

void Pose::SetLocalTransform(unsigned int index, const
Transform& transform) {
    mJoints[index] = transform;
}
```

5. Starting from the current transform, the GetGlobalTransform method needs to combine all the transforms up the parent chain until it reaches the root bone. Remember, transform concatenation is carried out from right to left. The overloaded [] operator should be treated as an alias for GetGlobalTransform:

```
Transform Pose::GetGlobalTransform(unsigned int i) {
    Transform result = mJoints[i];
    for (int p = mParents[i]; p >= 0; p = mParents[p]) {
        result = combine(mJoints[p], result);
    }

    return result;
}

Transform Pose::operator[](unsigned int index) {
    return GetGlobalTransform(index);
}
```

6. To convert a Pose class into a vector of matrices, loop through every transform in the pose. For every transform, find the global transform, convert it into a matrix, and store the result in the vector of matrices. This function isn't optimized yet; you will optimize it in a later chapter:

```
void Pose::GetMatrixPalette(std::vector<mat4>& out) {
    unsigned int size = Size();
    if (out.size() != size) {
        out.resize(size);
    }

    for (unsigned int i = 0; i < size; ++i) {
        Transform t = GetGlobalTransform(i);
```

```
            out[i] = transformToMat4(t);
        }
    }
```

7. The getter and setter methods for the parent joint indices are simple:

```
int Pose::GetParent(unsigned int index) {
    return mParents[index];
}

void Pose::SetParent(unsigned int index, int parent) {
    mParents[index] = parent;
}
```

8. When comparing two poses, you need to make sure that all of the joint transforms and parent indices are identical in both poses:

```
bool Pose::operator==(const Pose& other) {
    if (mJoints.size() != other.mJoints.size()) {
        return false;
    }
    if (mParents.size() != other.mParents.size()) {
        return false;
    }
    unsigned int size = (unsigned int)mJoints.size();
    for (unsigned int i = 0; i < size; ++i) {
        Transform thisLocal = mJoints[i];
        Transform otherLocal = other.mJoints[i];
        int thisParent = mParents[i];
        int otherParent = other.mParents[i];

        if (thisParent != otherParent) { return false; }
        if (thisLocal.position != otherLocal.position) {
        return false; }
        if (thisLocal.rotation != otherLocal.rotation {
        return false; }
        if (thisLocal.scale != otherLocal.scale {
        return false; }
    }
    return true;
}

bool Pose::operator!=(const Pose& other) {
    return !(*this == other);
}
```

It's not uncommon for one animated character to have multiple active poses. Consider a case where a character runs and shoots a gun at the same time. Two animations will likely play—one that affects the lower body, the **run** animation, and one that affects the upper body, the **shoot** animation. These poses blend together into a final pose that is used to display the animated character. This type of animation blending is covered in *Chapter 12, Blending between Animations*.

In the following section, you will implement animation clips. An animation clip contains the animation for all the animated joints in a pose over time. The Clip class is used to sample animations and generate poses to display.

Implementing clips

An animation clip is a collection of animation tracks; each track describes the motion of one joint over time and all of the tracks combined describe the motion of the animated model over time. If you sample an animation clip, you get a pose that describes the configuration of each joint in the animation clip at the specified time.

For a basic clip class, all you need is a vector of **transform tracks**. Because transform tracks contain the ID of the joint that they affect, you can have a minimal number of tracks per clip. The Clip class should also keep track of metadata, such as the name of the clip, whether the clip is looping, and information about the time or duration of the clip.

Declaring the Clip class

The Clip class needs to maintain a vector of transform tracks. This is the most important data that the clip contains. Other than the tracks, a clip has a name, a start time, and an end time, and the clip should know whether it's looping or not.

The looping attribute of the Clip class could be offloaded to a construct that's further down the pipeline (such as an animation component or something similar). However, when implementing a bare-bones animation system, this is a good place to put the looping property:

1. Create a new file, Clip.h, and start the declaration of the Clip class:

```
class Clip {
protected:
    std::vector<TransformTrack> mTracks;
    std::string mName;
    float mStartTime;
    float mEndTime;
    bool mLooping;
```

2. Clips are sampled in the same way that tracks are sampled. The provided sample time might be outside the range of the clip. To deal with this, you need to implement a helper function that adjusts the provided sample time so that it is within the range of the current animation clip:

```
protected:
    float AdjustTimeToFitRange(float inTime);
```

3. The Clip class needs a default constructor to assign default values to some of its members. The compiler-generated destructor, the copy constructor, and the assignment operator should be fine here:

```
public:
    Clip();
```

4. The Clip class should provide a way to get the number of joints a clip contains, as well as the joint ID for a specific track index. You also need to have a joint ID setter that's based on the index of the joint in the clip:

```
unsigned int GetIdAtIndex(unsigned int index);
void SetIdAtIndex(unsigned int idx, unsigned int id);
unsigned int Size();
```

5. Retrieving data from a clip can be done in one of two ways. The [] operator returns a transform track for the specified joint. If no track exists for the specified joint, one is created and returned. The Sample function takes a Posereference and a time and returns a float value that is also a time. This function samples the animation clip at the provided time into the Pose reference:

```
float Sample(Pose& outPose, float inTime);
TransformTrack& operator[](unsigned int index);
```

6. We need a public helper function to figure out the start and end times of the animation clip. The RecalculateDuration function loops through all the TransformTrack objects and sets the start/end time of the animation clip based on the tracks that make up the clip. This function is intended to be called by the code that loads the animation clip from a file format.

```
void RecalculateDuration();
```

7. Finally, the `Clip` class takes simple getter and setter functions:

```
std::string& GetName();
void SetName(const std::string& inNewName);
float GetDuration();
float GetStartTime();
float GetEndTime();
bool GetLooping();
void SetLooping(bool inLooping);
};
```

The `Clip` class implemented here can be used to animate anything; don't feel like you are limited to humans and humanoid animations. In the following section, you will implement the `Clip` class.

Implementing the Clip class

Create a new file, `Clip.cpp`. You will implement the `Clip` class in this new file. Follow these steps to implement the `Clip` class:

1. The default constructor needs to assign some default values to the members of the `Clip` class:

```
Clip::Clip() {
    mName = "No name given";
    mStartTime = 0.0f;
    mEndTime = 0.0f;
    mLooping = true;
}
```

2. To implement the `Sample` function, make sure the clip is valid and that the time is in the range of the clip. Then, loop through all of the tracks. Get the joint ID of the track, sample the track, and assign the sampled value back to the `Pose` reference. If a component of a transform isn't animated, the reference components are used to provide default values. The function then returns the adjusted time:

```
float Clip::Sample(Pose& outPose, float time) {
    if (GetDuration() == 0.0f) {
        return 0.0f;
    }
    time= AdjustTimeToFitRange(time);

    unsigned int size = mTracks.size();
    for (unsigned int i = 0; i < size; ++i) {
```

```
            unsigned int j = mTracks[i].GetId(); // Joint
            Transform local = outPose.GetLocalTransform(j);
            Transform animated = mTracks[i].Sample(
                            local, time, mLooping);
            outPose.SetLocalTransform(j, animated);
        }
        return time;
    }
```

3. The `AdjustTimeToFitRange` function that should loop has the same logic
    as the `AdjustTimeToFitTrack` function you implemented for the templated
    `Track` class:

```
float Clip::AdjustTimeToFitRange(float inTime) {
    if (mLooping) {
        float duration = mEndTime - mStartTime;
        if (duration <= 0) { 0.0f; }
        inTime = fmodf(inTime - mStartTime,
                    mEndTime - mStartTime);
        if (inTime < 0.0f) {
            inTime += mEndTime - mStartTime;
        }
        inTime = inTime + mStartTime;
    }
    else {
        if (inTime < mStartTime) {
            inTime = mStartTime;
        }
        if (inTime > mEndTime) {
            inTime = mEndTime;
        }
    }
    return inTime;
}
```

4. The `RecalculateDuration` function sets `mStartTime` and `mEndTime` to
    default values of 0. Next, these functions loop through every `TransformTrack`
    object in the animation clip. If the track is valid, the start and end times of the track
    are retrieved. The smallest start time and the largest end time are stored. The start
    time of a clip might not be 0; it's possible to have a clip that starts at an arbitrary
    point in time:

```
void Clip::RecalculateDuration() {
    mStartTime = 0.0f;
```

```
    mEndTime = 0.0f;
    bool startSet = false;
    bool endSet = false;
    unsigned int tracksSize = mTracks.size();
    for (unsigned int i = 0; i < tracksSize; ++i) {
        if (mTracks[i].IsValid()) {
            float startTime = mTracks[i].GetStartTime();
            float endTime = mTracks[i].GetEndTime();

            if (startTime < mStartTime || !startSet) {
                mStartTime = startTime;
                startSet = true;
            }

            if (endTime > mEndTime || !endSet) {
                mEndTime = endTime;
                endSet = true;
            }
        }
    }
}
```

5. `[]` `operator` is meant to retrieve the `TransformTrack` object for a specific joint in the clip. This function is mainly used by whatever code loads the animation clip from a file. The function performs a linear search through all of the tracks to see whether any of them targets the specified joint. If a qualifying track is found, a reference to it is returned. If no qualifying track is found, a new one is created and returned:

```
TransformTrack& Clip::operator[](unsigned int joint) {
    for (int i = 0, s = mTracks.size(); i < s; ++i) {
        if (mTracks[i].GetId() == joint) {
            return mTracks[i];
        }
    }

    mTracks.push_back(TransformTrack());
    mTracks[mTracks.size() - 1].SetId(joint);
    return mTracks[mTracks.size() - 1];
}
```

6. The remaining getter functions of the `Clip` class are simple:

```cpp
std::string& Clip::GetName() {
    return mName;
}
unsigned int Clip::GetIdAtIndex(unsigned int index) {
    return mTracks[index].GetId();
}
unsigned int Clip::Size() {
    return (unsigned int)mTracks.size();
}
float Clip::GetDuration() {
    return mEndTime - mStartTime;
}
float Clip::GetStartTime() {
    return mStartTime;
}
float Clip::GetEndTime() {
    return mEndTime;
}
bool Clip::GetLooping() {
    return mLooping;
}
```

7. Similarly, the remaining setter functions of the `Clip` class are simple:

```cpp
void Clip::SetName(const std::string& inNewName) {
    mName = inNewName;
}
void Clip::SetIdAtIndex(unsigned int index, unsigned int
id) {
    return mTracks[index].SetId(id);
}
void Clip::SetLooping(bool inLooping) {
    mLooping = inLooping;
}
```

An animation clip always modifies the same joints. There is no need to re-set the pose that is sampled into so that it is the bind pose every frame. However, when switching animations, there is no guarantee that two clips will animate the same tracks. It's a good idea to reset the pose that is sampled into so that it is the bind pose whenever we switch animation clips!

In the following section, you will learn how to load the rest pose of a character from a glTF file. The rest pose is important; it's the pose that a character is in when it's not animated.

glTF – loading the rest pose

In this book, we will assume that a glTF file only contains one animated character. It's safe to assume that the entire hierarchy of the glTF file can be treated as the skeleton of the model. This makes loading the rest pose easy as the rest pose becomes the hierarchy in its initial configuration.

Before loading the rest pose, you need to create several helper functions. These functions are internal to the glTF loader and should not be exposed in the header file. Create a new namespace in `GLTFLoader.cpp` and call it `GLTFHelpers`. All the helper functions are created in this namespace.

Follow these steps to implement the helper functions that are needed to load the rest pose from a glTF file:

1. First, implement a helper function to get the local transform of `cgltf_node`. A node can store its transform either as a matrix or as a separate position, rotation, and scale components. If the node stores its transformation as a matrix, use the `mat4ToTransform` decomposition function; otherwise, create the components as needed:

```cpp
// Inside the GLTFHelpers namespace
Transform GLTFHelpers::GetLocalTransform(cgltf_node& n){
    Transform result;

    if (n.has_matrix) {
        mat4 mat(&n.matrix[0]);
        result = mat4ToTransform(mat);
    }

    if (n.has_translation) {
        result.position = vec3(n.translation[0],
            n.translation[1], n.translation[2]);
    }

    if (n.has_rotation) {
        result.rotation = quat(n.rotation[0],
          n.rotation[1], n.rotation[2], n.rotation[3]);
    }
```

```
    if (n.has_scale) {
        result.scale = vec3(n.scale[0], n.scale[1],
                                n.scale[2]);
    }

    return result;
}
```

2. Next, implement a helper function to get the index of `cgltf_node` from an array. The `GLTFNodeIndex` function can perform a simple linear lookup by looping through all the nodes in a `.gltf` file and returning the index of the node that you are searching for. If the index is not found, return `-1` to signal an invalid index:

```
// Inside the GLTFHelpers namespace
int GLTFHelpers::GetNodeIndex(cgltf_node* target,
    cgltf_node* allNodes, unsigned int numNodes) {
    if (target == 0) {
        return -1;
    }
    for (unsigned int i = 0; i < numNodes; ++i) {
        if (target == &allNodes[i]) {
            return (int)i;
        }
    }
    return -1;
}
```

3. With these helper functions, loading the rest pose takes very little work. Loop through all the nodes in the current glTF file. For each node, assign the local transform to the pose that will be returned. You can find the parent of a node using the `GetNodeIndex` helper function, which returns `-1` if a node has no parent:

```
Pose LoadRestPose(cgltf_data* data) {
    unsigned int boneCount = data->nodes_count;
    Pose result(boneCount);

    for (unsigned int i = 0; i < boneCount; ++i) {
        cgltf_node* node = &(data->nodes[i]);

        Transform transform =
        GLTFHelpers::GetLocalTransform(data->nodes[i]);
        result.SetLocalTransform(i, transform);
```

```
                int parent = GLTFHelpers::GetNodeIndex(
                        node->parent, data->nodes,
                        boneCount);
            result.SetParent(i, parent);
        }

        return result;
    }
```

In the following section, you will learn how to load joint names from a glTF file. These joint names appear in the same order as the rest pose joints. Knowing the joint names can be helpful to debug what a skeleton looks like. Joint names can also be used to retrieve a joint by something other than an index. The animation system you will build in this book does not support joint lookup by name, only index.

glTF – loading joint names

At some point, you might want to know the name assigned to each joint that is loaded. This can help make debugging or building tools easier. To load the names of every joint in the same order that you loaded the joints for the rest pose in, loop through the joints and use the name accessor.

Implement the `LoadJointNames` function in `GLTFLoader.cpp`. Don't forget to add the function declaration to `GLTFLoader.h`:

```
std::vector<std::string> LoadJointNames(cgltf_data* data) {
    unsigned int boneCount = (unsigned int)data->nodes_count;
    std::vector<std::string> result(boneCount, "Not Set");

    for (unsigned int i = 0; i < boneCount; ++i) {
        cgltf_node* node = &(data->nodes[i]);

        if (node->name == 0) {
            result[i] = "EMPTY NODE";
        }
        else {
            result[i] = node->name;
        }
    }

    return result;
}
```

Joint names are extremely useful for debugging. They let you associate the index of a joint with a name, so you know what the data represents. In the following section, you will learn how to load animation clips from glTF files.

glTF – loading animation clips

To generate pose data at runtime, you need to be able to load animation clips. As with the rest pose, this requires a few helper functions.

The first helper function you need to implement, GetScalarValues, reads the floating-point values of a gltf accessor. This can be done with the cgltf_accessor_read_float helper function.

The next helper function, TrackFromChannel, does most of the heavy lifting. It converts a glTF animation channel into a VectorTrack or a QuaternionTrack. glTF animation channels are documented at https://github.com/KhronosGroup/glTF-Tutorials/blob/master/gltfTutorial/gltfTutorial_007_Animations.md.

The LoadAnimationClips function should return a vector of clips objects. This isn't optimal; it's done to make the loading API easier to use. If performance is a concern, consider passing the result vector as a reference.

Follow these steps to load animations from a glTF file:

1. Implement the GetScalarValues helper function in GLTFLoader.cpp in the GLTFHelpers namespace:

```cpp
// Inside the GLTFHelpers namespace
void GLTFHelpers::GetScalarValues( vector<float>& out,
                  unsigned int compCount,
                  const cgltf_accessor& inAccessor) {
    out.resize(inAccessor.count * compCount);
    for (cgltf_size i = 0; i < inAccessor.count; ++i) {
        cgltf_accessor_read_float(&inAccessor, i,
                                  &out[i * compCount],
                                  compCount);
    }
}
```

2. Implement the `TrackFromChannel` helper function in `GLTFLoader.cpp`.
    Start the function implementation by setting the `Track` interpolation. To do
    this, make sure the `Interpolation` type of the track matches the `cgltf_`
    `interpolation_type` type of the sampler:

```cpp
// Inside the GLTFHelpers namespace
template<typename T, int N>
void GLTFHelpers::TrackFromChannel(Track<T, N>& result,
            const cgltf_animation_channel& channel) {
    cgltf_animation_sampler& sampler = *channel.sampler;

    Interpolation interpolation =
                    Interpolation::Constant;
    if (sampler.interpolation ==
        cgltf_interpolation_type_linear) {
        interpolation = Interpolation::Linear;
    }
    else if (sampler.interpolation ==
            cgltf_interpolation_type_cubic_spline) {
        interpolation = Interpolation::Cubic;
    }
    bool isSamplerCubic = interpolation ==
                        Interpolation::Cubic;
    result.SetInterpolation(interpolation);
```

3. The sampler input is an accessor to the animation timeline. The sampler output
    is an accessor to the animation values. Use `GetScalarValues` to convert these
    accessors into linear arrays of floating-point numbers. The number of frames the
    number of elements in the sampler input. The number of components per frame
    (`vec3` or `quat`) is the number of value elements divided by the number of timeline
    elements. Resize the track to have enough room to store all the frames:

```cpp
std::vector<float> time; // times
GetScalarValues(time, 1, *sampler.input);

std::vector<float> val; // values
GetScalarValues(val, N, *sampler.output);

unsigned int numFrames = sampler.input->count;
unsigned int compCount = val.size() / time.size();
result.Resize(numFrames);
```

4. To parse the `time` and `value` arrays into frame structures, loop through every frame in the sampler. For each frame, set the time, then read the input tangent, the value, then the output tangent. Input and output tangents are only available if the sampler is cubic; if it is not, these should default to 0. A local `offset` variable needs to be used to deal with cubic tracks since the input and output tangents are as large as the number of components:

```
for (unsigned int i = 0; i < numFrames; ++i) {
    int baseIndex = i * compCount;
    Frame<N>& frame = result[i];
    int offset = 0;

    frame.mTime = time[i];

    for (int comp = 0; comp < N; ++comp) {
        frame.mIn[comp] = isSamplerCubic ?
            val[baseIndex + offset++] : 0.0f;
    }

    for (int comp = 0; comp < N; ++comp) {
        frame.mValue[comp] = val[baseIndex +
                                offset++];
    }

    for (int comp = 0; comp < N; ++comp) {
        frame.mOut[comp] = isSamplerCubic ?
            val[baseIndex + offset++] : 0.0f;
    }
}
} // End of TrackFromChannel function
```

5. Implement the `LoadAnimationClips` function in `GLTFLoader.cpp`; don't forget to add the declaration of the function to `GLTFLoader.h`. Loop through all the clips in the provided `gltf_data`. For every clip, set its name. Loop through all of the channels in the clip and find the index of the node that the current channel affects:

```
std::vector<Clip> LoadAnimationClips(cgltf_data* data) {
    unsigned int numClips = data->animations_count;
    unsigned int numNodes = data->nodes_count;

    std::vector<Clip> result;
    result.resize(numClips);
```

```
for (unsigned int i = 0; i < numClips; ++i) {
    result[i].SetName(data->animations[i].name);

    unsigned int numChannels =
            data->animations[i].channels_count;
    for (unsigned int j = 0; j < numChannels; ++j){
        cgltf_animation_channel& channel =
                data->animations[i].channels[j];
        cgltf_node* target = channel.target_node;
        int nodeId = GLTFHelpers::GetNodeIndex(
                target, data->nodes, numNodes);
```

6. Each channel of a glTF file is an animation track. Some nodes might only animate their position, while others might animate the position, rotation, and scale. Check the type of channel that is parsed and call the TrackFromChannel helper function to convert it into an animation track. The [] operator of the Track class either retrieves the current track or creates a new one. This means the TransformTrack function for the node that you are parsing is always valid:

```
if (channel.target_path ==
    cgltf_animation_path_type_translation){
    VectorTrack& track =
        result[i][nodeId].GetPositionTrack();
    GLTFHelpers::TrackFromChannel<vec3, 3>
                    (track, channel);
}
else if (channel.target_path ==
        cgltf_animation_path_type_scale) {
    VectorTrack& track =
            result[i][nodeId].GetScaleTrack();
    GLTFHelpers::TrackFromChannel<vec3, 3>
                    (track, channel);
}
else if (channel.target_path ==
        cgltf_animation_path_type_rotation) {
    QuaternionTrack& track =
            result[i][nodeId].GetRotationTrack();
    GLTFHelpers::TrackFromChannel<quat, 4>
                    (track, channel);
}
} // End num channels loop
```

7. After all the tracks in a clip have been populated, call the `ReclaculateDuration` function of the clip. This ensures that the playback happens in the proper time range:

```
        result[i].RecalculateDuration();
    } // End num clips loop

    return result;
} // End of LoadAnimationClips function
```

Being able to load animation clips and sample them into poses is about half of the work involved in animation programming. You can load an animation clip, sample it as the application updates, and use debug lines to draw the pose. The result is an animated skeleton. In the next chapter, you will learn how to use this animated skeleton to deform a mesh.

Summary

In this chapter, you implemented the `Pose` and `Clip` classes. You learned how to load the rest pose out of a glTF file, as well as how to load animation clips. You also learned how to sample an animation clip to produce a pose.

The downloadable content for this book can be found on GitHub at `https://github.com/PacktPublishing/Game-Animation-Programming`. The sample in `Chapter09/Sample01` loads a glTF file and uses the `DebugDraw` functions to draw both the rest pose and the currently animated pose. To draw a bone using debug lines, draw a line from the position of the joint to the position of its parent.

Keep in mind that not all clips animate every joint of a pose. Any time the animation clip that you are sampling changes, the post it is sampled into needs to be reset. Resetting a pose is easy—assign to it the value of the rest pose. This is demonstrated in the code samples for this chapter.

In the next chapter, you will learn how to skin an animated mesh. Once you know how to skin a mesh, you will be able to display an animated model.

10
Mesh Skinning

Deforming a mesh to match an animated pose is called skinning. In order to implement skinning, you first need to declare a mesh class. Once you have declared a mesh class, it can be deformed using a shader (GPU skinning) or just with C++ code (CPU skinning). Both of these skinning methods are covered in this chapter. By the end of this chapter, you should be able to do the following:

- Understand how a skinned mesh is different from a non-skinned mesh
- Understand the entire skinning pipeline
- Implement a skeleton class
- Load the bind pose of a skeleton from a glTF file
- Implement a skinned mesh class
- Load skinned meshes from a gLTF file
- Implement CPU skinning
- Implement GPU skinning

Exploring meshes

A mesh is made up of several vertices. Normally, each vertex has at least a position, a normal, and maybe a texture coordinate. This is the definition of a vertex for a simple static mesh. This definition has the following vertex components:

- The position (vec3)
- The normal (vec3)
- The texture coordinate (vec2)

> **Important information:**
>
> The model used to demonstrate skinning in this chapter is the Godot mannequin from GDQuest. It's an MIT-licensed model and you can find it on GitHub at `https://github.com/GDQuest/godot-3d-mannequin`.

When a mesh is modeled, it's modeled in a certain pose. For characters, this is often a *T* pose or an *A* pose. The modeled mesh is static. The following figure shows the *T* pose for the Godot mannequin:

Figure 10.1: The Godot mannequin's T pose

Once a mesh is modeled, a skeleton is created in the mesh. Each vertex in the mesh is assigned to one or more bones of the skeleton. This process is called rigging. The skeleton is created in a pose that fits inside the mesh; this is the **bind pose** of the model.

Figure 10.2: Visualizing the bind pose of the mesh and skeleton

The bind pose and the rest pose are usually the same, but that is not always the case. In this book, we will treat the two as separate poses. The preceding figure shows the bind pose of the skeleton rendered on top of the character mesh. In the next section, you will explore how a mesh such as this can be skinned.

Understanding skinning

Skinning is the process of specifying which vertex should be deformed by which bone. One vertex can be influenced by multiple bones. Rigid skinning refers to associating each vertex with exactly one bone. Smooth skinning associates vertices with multiple bones.

Typically, the vertex-to-bone mapping is done per vertex. This means each vertex knows which bones it belongs to. Some file formats, store this relationship in reverse, where each bone contains a list of vertices it affects. Both approaches are valid; throughout the rest of this book, the mapping is done per vertex.

To (rigid) skin a mesh, assign each vertex to a bone. To assign a joint to a vertex in code, add a new attribute to each vertex. This attribute is just an integer that holds the index of the bone that deforms the vertex. In the following figure, all the triangles that should be assigned to the lower-left arm bone are colored darker than the rest of the mesh:

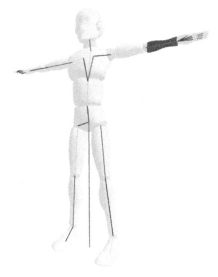

Figure 10.3: Isolating the lower arm

Let's take a second to review the vertex transformation pipeline in a little more detail. Here, the concept of **space** is introduced. Space refers to transforming a vertex by a matrix. For example, if you have a projection matrix, it would transform a vertex into NDC space. The vertex transformation pipeline is as follows:

- When a mesh is created, all its vertices are in what is called model space.

- A model space vertex is multiplied by the model matrix, which puts it into world space.

- A world space vertex is multiplied by the view matrix to put it into camera space.

- A camera space vertex is multiplied by the projection matrix to move it into NDC space.

To skin a mesh, a new skinning step needs to be added to the vertex transformation pipeline. The skinning step moves the vertex from skin space to model space. This means the new step comes before any other steps in the transformation pipeline.

Skin space vertices can be moved back into model space if they are multiplied by the current animation pose. This transformation is covered in detail in the *Implementing CPU skinning* section of this chapter. Once the vertex is back in model space, it should already be animated. The animation pose matrix transformation does the actual animation. An animated vertex transformation pipeline works like this:

- A mesh is loaded—all of its vertices are in model space.

- A model space vertex is multiplied by the skin matrix to move it into skin space.

- A kin space vertex is multiplied by the pose matrix to move it back into model space.

- A model space vertex is multiplied by the model matrix, which puts it into world space.

- A world space vertex is multiplied by the view matrix to put it into camera space.

- A camera space vertex is multiplied by the projection matrix to move it into NDC space.

To skin a mesh, each vertex needs to be transformed into skin space. When a vertex in skin space is transformed by the world transform of the joint it belongs to, the vertex should end up in model space, assuming the pose that is used is the bind pose.

In the following section, you will explore the skinning pipeline with practical examples.

Exploring rigid skinning

To skin a mesh, each vertex needs to be multiplied by the inverse bind pose transform of the joint it belongs to. To find the inverse bind pose transform of a joint, find the world transform of the joint, then invert it. When a matrix (or transform) is multiplied by its inverse, the result is always identity.

Multiplying the vertices of a skin space mesh by the world space transformation of a joint in bind pose undoes the original inverse bind pose multiplication, `inverse bind pose * bind pose = identity`. However, multiplying by a different pose results in the vertices being offset from the bind pose by the delta between the two poses.

Let's explore how a vertex is moved into skin space visually. For example, multiplying all the vertices in the Godot mannequin forearm by the inverse bind pose of the forearm bone puts only the forearm triangles into skin space. This leaves the mesh looking as it does in the following figure:

Figure 10.4: The lower-arm mesh transformed by the inverse bind pose

To transform the vertices from skin space back to model space, apply the transformation of each bone in the pose sequentially until the target bone is reached. The following figure demonstrates the six steps that need to be taken from the root bone to the forearm bone:

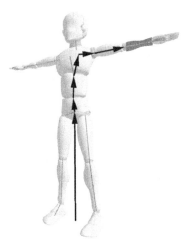

Figure 10.5: Visualizing the transform chain to the lower arm

In code, all the transforms that need to be taken to reach a bone can be accumulated using matrix multiplication. Alternatively, if you use the Transform structs, you can use the combine method. Moving the vertex back into model space is done only once with the accumulated matrix or transform.

Transforming the mesh into skin space is done by multiplying each vertex by the inverse bind pose of the joint it belongs to. How can you get the inverse bind pose matrix of a bone? Using the bind pose, find the world transform of the bone, turn it into a matrix, and invert the matrix.

The following figure shows the Godot mannequin in skin space. Seeing a mesh such as this indicates an error in the skinning pipeline. The most common reason for seeing a mesh such as this is that there has been an error in the multiplication order of the inverse bind pose and animated pose:

Figure 10.6: The full mesh multiplied by the inverse bind pose

The skinning implementation discussed so far is called rigid skinning. With rigid skinning, each vertex is influenced by only one bone. In the following section, you will begin to explore smooth skinning, which makes skinned meshes look better by assigning multiple bone influences to a single vertex.

The rigid skinning pipeline

Let's explore the pipeline that each vertex must go through. The following figure shows the transformation pipeline of a static mesh compared to a rigid skinned mesh. The order of steps in the following diagram is left to right, following the arrows:

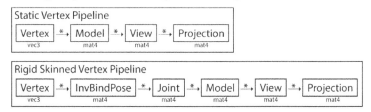

Figure 10.7: The vertex skinning pipelines

The **rigid skinned vertex pipeline** shown in the preceding figure works as follows:

- Move the vertex into skin space by multiplying it by the inverse bind pose matrix of the joint it is assigned to.

- Multiply the skinned vertex by the animated joint's world matrix. This results in the vertex being in local space again, but it is deformed to the animated pose.

- Once the vertex is in the animated local position, put it through the normal model view projection transformation.

- Exploring smooth skinning

The problem with rigid skinning is bending joints. Since each vertex belongs to one bone, vertices that are in joints such as the elbow do not bend naturally. Breaks in a mesh at joints such as in the elbow can be avoided by assigning different vertices of a triangle to different bones. The resulting mesh doesn't maintain its volume well and looks awkward.

Rigid skinning isn't free; it introduces additional matrix multiplications to each vertex. This can be optimized down to just one additional multiplication, which is covered in the next chapter. In the following section, you will explore smooth skinning.

Exploring smooth skinning

The primary problem with rigid skinning is that it can create visual breaks in a mesh, as shown in the following figure. Even if these artifacts are addressed, deformation around bendable joints does not look good when smooth-skinned:

Figure 10.8: A visible artifact of rigid skinning

Smooth skinning has fewer artifacts and maintains its volume better than rigid skinning. The idea behind smooth skinning is that more than one bone can influence a vertex. Each influence also has a weight. The weight is used to blend the skinned vertices into a combined, final vertex. All weights must add up to 1.

Think of smooth skinning as skinning a mesh multiple times and blending the results. How many influences a bone can have has a big impact here. Generally, after four bones, the influence of each additional bone is not visible. This is convenient as it lets you use the `ivec4` and `vec4` structs to add influences and weights to vertices.

The following figure shows a mesh that is skinned with the middle vertices attached to the top bone on the left and the bottom bone on the right. These are the two skinned positions that need to be blended. If each pose has a weight of 0.5, the final interpolated vertex position will be halfway between the vertices. This is shown in the middle diagram of the following figure:

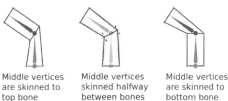

Figure 10.9: Assigning multiple joints to a vertex

Averaging joint influences on a vertex is called smooth skinning, or **linear blend skinning** (**LBS**). It has a few artifacts, but it's the standard way to skin characters. Currently, LBS is the most popular way to implement skinned animations.

After adding support for smooth skinning, the final vertex structure now looks like this:

- The position (`vec3`)

- The normal (`vec3`)

- The texture coordinate (`vec2`)

- The joint influences (`ivec4`)

- The influence weights (`vec4`)

> **Important information**
>
> glTF supports attaching skinned meshes to arbitrary nodes and those nodes can be animated. This adds an extra step to calculating the skin matrix. To avoid this extra step, we will ignore the mesh pivot and assume that all the mesh node global transforms are at the origin. This is a safe assumption to make so long as a single glTF file is assumed to only contain one skinned mesh.

Smooth skinning is currently the standard form used in game animation. Most games use four bones per vertex and work similarly to what you will implement in this chapter. In the following section, you will implement a `Skeleton` class to help keep track of some of the different data needed to skin a mesh.

Implementing skeletons

When animating a model, there are several things to keep track of, such as the animated pose or inverse bind pose. The concept of a skeleton is to combine data that is shared between animated models into a single structure.

Both the bind pose and inverse bind pose are shared among all instances of a character. That is, if there are 15 characters on screen, each of them has a unique animated pose, but they all share the same rest pose, bind pose, inverse bind pose, and joint names.

In the following sections, you will implement a new class—the `Skeleton` class. This `Skeleton` class contains all the shared data that two animated meshes might need. It also keeps track of the rest pose, bind pose, inverse bind pose, and joint names. Some engines call the skeleton an armature or a rig.

The Skeleton class declaration

The `Skeleton` class contains the rest pose and bind pose of a character, the name for every joint of the character, and—most importantly—the inverse bind pose. Since the inverse bind pose involves inverting matrices, it should only be calculated once. Follow these steps to declare the new `Skeleton` class:

1. Create a new file, `Skeleton.h`. Declare the `Skeleton` class in this file. Add a rest pose, a bind pose, the inverse bind pose, and the joint names for the current animated model to the `Skeleton` class. The inverse bind pose should be implemented as a vector of matrices:

```
class Skeleton {
protected:
    Pose mRestPose;
    Pose mBindPose;
    std::vector<mat4> mInvBindPose;
    std::vector<std::string> mJointNames;
```

2. Add a helper function, `UpdateInverseBindPose`. This function updates the inverse bind pose matrix any time that the bind pose is set:

```
protected:
    void UpdateInverseBindPose();
```

3. Declare a default constructor and a convenience constructor. Also, declare methods to set the rest pose, bind pose, and joint names of the skeleton and helper functions to retrieve references to all the variables of the skeleton:

```
public:
    Skeleton();
    Skeleton(const Pose& rest, const Pose& bind,
             const std::vector<std::string>& names);

    void Set(const Pose& rest, const Pose& bind,
             const std::vector<std::string>& names);

    Pose& GetBindPose();
    Pose& GetRestPose();
    std::vector<mat4>& GetInvBindPose();
    std::vector<std::string>& GetJointNames();
    std::string& GetJointName(unsigned int index);
}; // End Skeleton class
```

Think of the `Skeleton` class as a helper class—it puts the bind pose, inverse bind pose, rest pose, and joint names into an easy-to-manage object. The skeleton is shared; you can have many characters, each with a unique animated pose, but they can all share the same skeleton. In the following section, you will implement the `Skeleton` class.

The Skeleton class implementation

The inverse bind pose is stored in the skeleton as an array of matrices. Any time the bind pose of the skeleton is updated, the inverse bind pose should be re-calculated as well. To find the inverse bind pose, find the world space matrix of every joint in the skeleton, then invert the world space joint matrix. Create a new file, Skeleton.cpp. Then, implement the skeleton constructors. Take the following steps to do so:

1. Create two constructors—the default constructor does not do anything. The other convenience constructor takes a rest pose, a bind pose, and the joint names. It calls the Set method:

```
Skeleton::Skeleton() { }

Skeleton::Skeleton(const Pose& rest, const Pose& bind,
              const std::vector<std::string>& names) {
    Set(rest, bind, names);
}
```

2. Create the Set method, which should set the internal pose, bind pose, and joint names of the skeleton. Once the bind pose is set, call the UpdateInverseBindPose function to populate the inverse bind pose matrix palette:

```
void Skeleton::Set(const Pose& rest, const Pose& bind,
              const std::vector<std::string>& names) {
    mRestPose = rest;
    mBindPose = bind;
    mJointNames = names;
    UpdateInverseBindPose();
}
```

3. Implement the UpdateInverseBindPose function next. Make sure that the matrix vector has the right size, then loop through all of the joints in the bind pose. Get the world space transform of each joint, convert it into a matrix, and invert the matrix. This inverted matrix is the inverse bind pose matrix for the joint:

```
void Skeleton::UpdateInverseBindPose() {
    unsigned int size = mBindPose.Size();
    mInvBindPose.resize(size);

    for (unsigned int i = 0; i < size; ++i) {
        Transform world = mBindPose.GetGlobalTransform(i);
        mInvBindPose[i] = inverse(transformToMat4(world));
```

```
            }
        }
```

4. Implement the simple getter and setter functions in the Skeleton class:

```cpp
Pose& Skeleton::GetBindPose() {
    return mBindPose;
}

Pose& Skeleton::GetRestPose() {
    return mRestPose;
}

std::vector<mat4>& Skeleton::GetInvBindPose() {
    return mInvBindPose;
}

std::vector<std::string>& Skeleton::GetJointNames() {
    return mJointNames;
}

std::string& Skeleton::GetJointName(unsigned int idx) {
    return mJointNames[idx];
}
```

It is possible to get around returning references by providing explicit getter functions, such as Transform GetBindPoseTransform(unsigned int index). This makes more sense to do after you have worked through the next chapter, where you learn how to optimize the animation data. For now, it's more valuable to have access to these references and not modify them.

To generate an inverse bind pose matrix, you don't have to convert the transform into a matrix and then invert it; you could invert the transform and then convert it into a matrix. The performance delta between the two is minimal.

The Skeleton class keeps track of the bind pose, inverse bind pose, and joint names of an animated model. This data can be shared between all the animated instances of a model. In the next section, you will implement bind pose loading from glTF files. The glTF format does not store the actual bind pose.

glTF – loading the bind pose

You are now ready to load the bind pose from a glTF file, but there is a problem. glTF files don't store the bind pose. Instead, for each skin that a glTF file contains, it stores a matrix array that holds the inverse bind pose matrix for each joint that affects the skin.

Storing the inverse bind pose matrices like this is good for optimization, which will make more sense in the next chapter, but for now, it is something we have to deal with. So, how do you get the bind pose?

To get the bind pose, load the rest pose and convert each transform in the rest pose into a world space transform. This makes sure that if a skin didn't provide an inverse bind pose matrix for a joint, a good default value is available.

Next, loop through each skinned mesh in the .gltf file. For each skinned mesh, invert the inverse bind pose matrix of each joint. Inverting the inverse bind pose matrix results in the bind pose matrix. Convert the bind pose matrix into a transform that can be used in the bind pose.

This works, but all the joint transforms are in world space. You need to convert each joint so that it is local to the parent of the joint. Take the following steps to implement the LoadBindPose function in GLTFLoader.cpp:

1. Start implementing the LoadBindPose function by building a vector of transforms. Populate the vector of transforms with the global transform of each joint in the rest pose:

```
Pose LoadBindPose(cgltf_data* data) {
    Pose restPose = LoadRestPose(data);
    unsigned int numBones = restPose.Size();
    std::vector<Transform> worldBindPose(numBones);
    for (unsigned int i = 0; i < numBones; ++i) {
      worldBindPose[i] = restPose.GetGlobalTransform(i);
    }
```

2. Loop through every skinned mesh in the glTF file. Read the inverse_bind_matrices accessor into a large vector of float values. The vector needs to contain the contain numJoints * 16 elements since each matrix is a 4x4 matrix:

```
    unsigned int numSkins = data->skins_count;
    for (unsigned int i = 0; i < numSkins; ++i) {
        cgltf_skin* skin = &(data->skins[i]);
        std::vector<float> invBindAccessor;
        GLTFHelpers::GetScalarValues(invBindAccessor,
                    16, *skin->inverse_bind_matrices);
```

3. For each joint in the skin, get the inverse bind matrix. Invert the inverse bind pose matrix to get the bind pose matrix. Convert the bind pose matrix into a transform. Store this world space transform in the `worldBindPose` vector:

```
unsigned int numJoints = skin->joints_count;
for (int j = 0; j < numJoints; ++j) {
    // Read the ivnerse bind matrix of the joint
    float* matrix = &(invBindAccessor[j * 16]);
    mat4 invBindMatrix = mat4(matrix);
    // invert, convert to transform
    mat4 bindMatrix = inverse(invBindMatrix);
    Transform bindTransform =
                    mat4ToTransform(bindMatrix);
    // Set that transform in the worldBindPose.
    cgltf_node* jointNode = skin->joints[j];
    int jointIndex = GLTFHelpers::GetNodeIndex(
            jointNode, data->nodes, numBones);
    worldBindPose[jointIndex] = bindTransform;
} // end for each joint
} // end for each skin
```

4. Convert each joint so that it is relative to its parent. To move a joint into the space of another joint—that is, to make it relative to another joint—combine the world transform of the joint with the inverse world transform of its parent:

```
//Convert the world bind pose to a regular bind pose
Pose bindPose = restPose;
for (unsigned int i = 0; i < numBones; ++i) {
    Transform current = worldBindPose[i];
    int p = bindPose.GetParent(i);
    if (p >= 0) { // Bring into parent space
        Transform parent = worldBindPose[p];
        current = combine(inverse(parent), current);
    }
    bindPose.SetLocalTransform(i, current);
}

    return bindPose;
} // End LoadBindPose function
```

Reconstructing the bind pose is not ideal, but it is a quirk of glTF that you have to deal with. By using the rest pose as the default joint values, any joint that does not have an inverse bind pose matrix still has a valid default orientation and size.

In this section, you learned how to load the bind pose of an animated mesh from a glTF file. In the next section, you will create a convenience function to load a skeleton from a glTF file with only one function call.

glTF – loading a skeleton

We need to implement one more loading function—the `LoadSkeleton` function. This is a convenience function that loads a skeleton without having to call three separate functions.

Implement the `LoadSkeleton` function in `GLTFLoader.cpp`. Don't forget to add the function declaration to `GLTFLoader.h`. The function returns a new skeleton by calling the existing `LoadPose`, `LoadBindPose`, and `LoadJointNames` functions:

```
Skeleton LoadSkeleton(cgltf_data* data) {
    return Skeleton(
        LoadRestPose(data),
        LoadBindPose(data),
        LoadJointNames(data)
    );
}
```

The `LoadSkeleton` function is just a helper function that allows you to initialize a skeleton with a single function call. In the next section, you will implement a `Mesh` class, which will let you display animated meshes.

Implementing meshes

The definition of a mesh is dependent on the game (or engine) that implements it. It's beyond the scope of this book to implement a comprehensive mesh class. Instead, in this section, you will declare a naive version of a mesh that stores some data on the CPU and the GPU and provides a way to sync the two together.

The Mesh class declaration

What is the most basic implementation of a mesh? Each vertex has a position, a normal, and some texture coordinates. To skin the mesh, each vertex also has four bones that might influence it and weights to determine how much each bone influences the vertex by. Meshes usually use an index array, but this is optional.

In this section, you will implement both CPU and GPU skinning. To skin a mesh on the CPU, you need to keep an additional copy of the pose and normal data, as well as a matrix palette to use for skinning.

Create a new file, `Mesh.h`, to declare the `Mesh` class in. Follow these steps to declare the new `Mesh` class:

1. Start declaring the `Mesh` class. It should maintain a copy of the mesh data on the CPU as well as on the GPU. Store vectors for the position, normal, tex coordinates, weights, and influences that define each vertex. Include an optional vector for indices:

    ```
    class Mesh {
    protected:
        std::vector<vec3> mPosition;
        std::vector<vec3> mNormal;
        std::vector<vec2> mTexCoord;
        std::vector<vec4> mWeights;
        std::vector<ivec4> mInfluences;
        std::vector<unsigned int> mIndices;
    ```

2. Each of the vectors listed in the preceding code also needs to be set appropriate attributes. Create `Attribute` pointers for each one, as well as an index buffer pointer:

    ```
    protected:
        Attribute<vec3>* mPosAttrib;
        Attribute<vec3>* mNormAttrib;
        Attribute<vec2>* mUvAttrib;
        Attribute<vec4>* mWeightAttrib;
        Attribute<ivec4>* mInfluenceAttrib;
        IndexBuffer* mIndexBuffer;
    ```

3. Add an additional copy of the pose and normal data, as well as a matrix palette to use for CPU skinning:

    ```
    protected:
        std::vector<vec3> mSkinnedPosition;
        std::vector<vec3> mSkinnedNormal;
        std::vector<mat4> mPosePalette;
    ```

4. Add declarations for the constructor, copy constructor, and assignment operator, as well as the destructor:

```
public:
    Mesh();
    Mesh(const Mesh&);
    Mesh& operator=(const Mesh&);
    ~Mesh();
```

5. Declare getter functions for all the attributes that the mesh contains. These functions return the vector references. The vector references are not read-only; you use these when loading meshes to populate the mesh data:

```
std::vector<vec3>& GetPosition();
std::vector<vec3>& GetNormal();
std::vector<vec2>& GetTexCoord();
std::vector<vec4>& GetWeights();
std::vector<ivec4>& GetInfluences();
std::vector<unsigned int>& GetIndices();
```

6. Declare the CPUSkin function, which applies CPU mesh-skinning. To skin a mesh, you need both a skeleton and an animated pose. Declare the UpdateOpenGLBuffers function, which syncs the vectors holding data to the GPU:

```
void CPUSkin(Skeleton& skeleton, Pose& pose);
void UpdateOpenGLBuffers();
void Bind(int position, int normal, int texCoord,
          int weight, int influence);
```

7. Declare functions to bind, draw, and unbind the mesh:

```
void Draw();
void DrawInstanced(unsigned int numInstances);
void UnBind(int position, int normal, int texCoord,
            int weight, int influence);

};
```

This Mesh class is not production-ready, but it's easy to work with and will work for the rest of this book. In the next section, you will start implementing the Mesh class.

The Mesh class implementation

The Mesh class contains two copies of the same data. It keeps all the vertex data on the CPU side in vectors and on the GPU side in vertex buffer objects. The intended use of this class is to edit the CPU-side vertices, then sync the changes to the GPU with the UpdateOpenGLBuffers functions.

Create a new file, Mesh.cpp; you will implement the Mesh class in this file. Follow these steps to implement the Mesh class:

1. Implement the default constructor, which needs to make sure all the attributes (and the index buffer) are allocated:

```
Mesh::Mesh() {
    mPosAttrib = new Attribute<vec3>();
    mNormAttrib = new Attribute<vec3>();
    mUvAttrib = new Attribute<vec2>();
    mWeightAttrib = new Attribute<vec4>();
    mInfluenceAttrib = new Attribute<ivec4>();
    mIndexBuffer = new IndexBuffer();
}
```

2. Implement the copy constructor. Create the buffers in the same way that you did for the constructor, then call the assignment operator:

```
Mesh::Mesh(const Mesh& other) {
    mPosAttrib = new Attribute<vec3>();
    mNormAttrib = new Attribute<vec3>();
    mUvAttrib = new Attribute<vec2>();
    mWeightAttrib = new Attribute<vec4>();
    mInfluenceAttrib = new Attribute<ivec4>();
    mIndexBuffer = new IndexBuffer();
    *this = other;
}
```

3. Implement the assignment operator, which will copy out the CPU-side members (all of the vectors) and then call the UpdateOpenGLBuffers function to upload the attribute data to the GPU:

```
Mesh& Mesh::operator=(const Mesh& other) {
    if (this == &other) {
        return *this;
    }
    mPosition = other.mPosition;
    mNormal = other.mNormal;
```

```
        mTexCoord = other.mTexCoord;
        mWeights = other.mWeights;
        mInfluences = other.mInfluences;
        mIndices = other.mIndices;
        UpdateOpenGLBuffers();
        return *this;
}
```

4. Implement the destructor, making sure you delete all the data that the constructors had allocated:

```
Mesh::~Mesh() {
        delete mPosAttrib;
        delete mNormAttrib;
        delete mUvAttrib;
        delete mWeightAttrib;
        delete mInfluenceAttrib;
        delete mIndexBuffer;
}
```

5. Implement the Mesh getter functions. These functions return references to vectors. The references are expected to be edited after they are returned:

```
std::vector<vec3>& Mesh::GetPosition() {
        return mPosition;
}
std::vector<vec3>& Mesh::GetNormal() {
        return mNormal;
}
std::vector<vec2>& Mesh::GetTexCoord() {
        return mTexCoord;
}
std::vector<vec4>& Mesh::GetWeights() {
        return mWeights;
}
std::vector<ivec4>& Mesh::GetInfluences() {
        return mInfluences;
}
std::vector<unsigned int>& Mesh::GetIndices() {
        return mIndices;
}
```

6. Implement the `UpdateOpenGLBuffers` function by calling `Set` on each of the attribute objects. If one of the CPU-side vectors has a size of `0`, then there is nothing to set:

```
void Mesh::UpdateOpenGLBuffers() {
    if (mPosition.size() > 0) {
        mPosAttrib->Set(mPosition);
    }
    if (mNormal.size() > 0) {
        mNormAttrib->Set(mNormal);
    }
    if (mTexCoord.size() > 0) {
        mUvAttrib->Set(mTexCoord);
    }
    if (mWeights.size() > 0) {
        mWeightAttrib->Set(mWeights);
    }
    if (mInfluences.size() > 0) {
        mInfluenceAttrib->Set(mInfluences);
    }
    if (mIndices.size() > 0) {
        mIndexBuffer->Set(mIndices);
    }
}
```

7. Implement the `Bind` function. This takes integers that are bind slot indices. If the bind slot is valid (that is, it's `0` or greater), the `BindTo` function of the attribute is called:

```
void Mesh::Bind(int position, int normal, int texCoord,
                int weight, int influence) {
    if (position >= 0) {
        mPosAttrib->BindTo(position);
    }
    if (normal >= 0) {
        mNormAttrib->BindTo(normal);
    }
    if (texCoord >= 0) {
        mUvAttrib->BindTo(texCoord);
    }
    if (weight >= 0) {
        mWeightAttrib->BindTo(weight);
    }
    if (influence >= 0) {
```

```
        mInfluenceAttrib->BindTo(influence);
    }
}
```

8. Implement the `Draw` and `DrawInstanced` functions, which call the appropriate global `::Draw` and `::DrawInstanced` functions:

```cpp
void Mesh::Draw() {
    if (mIndices.size() > 0) {
        ::Draw(*mIndexBuffer, DrawMode::Triangles);
    }
    else {
        ::Draw(mPosition.size(), DrawMode::Triangles);
    }
}

void Mesh::DrawInstanced(unsigned int numInstances) {
    if (mIndices.size() > 0) {
        ::DrawInstanced(*mIndexBuffer,
          DrawMode::Triangles, numInstances);
    }
    else {
        ::DrawInstanced(mPosition.size(),
          DrawMode::Triangles, numInstances);
    }
}
```

9. Implement the `UnBind` function, which also takes integer bind slots for arguments but calls `UnBindFrom` on the attribute objects:

```cpp
void Mesh::UnBind(int position, int normal, int texCoord,
                  int weight, int influence) {
    if (position >= 0) {
        mPosAttrib->UnBindFrom(position);
    }
    if (normal >= 0) {
        mNormAttrib->UnBindFrom(normal);
    }
    if (texCoord >= 0) {
        mUvAttrib->UnBindFrom(texCoord);
    }
    if (weight >= 0) {
        mWeightAttrib->UnBindFrom(weight);
    }
    if (influence >= 0) {
```

```
                     mInfluenceAttrib->UnBindFrom(influence);
        }
    }
```

The Mesh class contains vectors to hold the CPU data and attributes to copy that data to the GPU. It provides a simple interface to render an entire mesh. In the following section, you will learn how to implement CPU skinning to animate a mesh.

Implementing CPU skinning

It is easier to understand skinning by implementing it on the CPU first, without having to worry about shaders. In this section, you will create a CPU-skinning reference implementation. GPU skinning is covered later on in this chapter.

> **Important information:**
> CPU skinning is useful if the platform you are developing for has a limited number of uniform registers or a small uniform buffer.

When implementing CPU skinning, you need to keep two copies of the animated mesh. The mPosition and mNormal vectors do not change. The result of the skinned positions and normals is stored in mSkinnedPosition and mSkinnedNormal. These vectors are then synced to the position and normal attributes to draw.

To skin a vertex, you need to calculate the skin transform. The skin transform needs to transform the vertex by the inverse bind pose, then by the current animated pose. You can do this by calling the inverse function on the bind pose transform, then combine it with the pose transform.

For each vertex, ivec4 in the mInfluences vector contains the joint IDs that affect the vertex. You need to transform the vertex by all four joints, which means you skin the mesh four times—once to each bone that influences the vertex.

Not every joint contributes in the same way to the final vertex. For each vertex, vec4 stored in mWeights contains a scalar value of 0 to 1. These values are used to blend the skinned vertices together. If a joint does not influence the vertex, its weight is 0 and it has no effect on the final skinned mesh.

The content of the weights is expected to be normalized in a way that if all the weights are added together, they equal 1. This way, the weights can be used to blend, since they all add up to an influence of 1. For example, (0.5, 0.5, 0, 0) would be valid, but (0.6, 0.5, 0, 0) would not.

Follow these steps to implement CPU skinning:

1. Start implementing the CPUSkin function. Make sure the skinned vectors have enough storage space and get the bind pose from the skeleton. Next, loop through each vertex:

```
void Mesh::CPUSkin(Skeleton& skeleton, Pose& pose) {
    unsigned int numVerts = mPosition.size();
    if (numVerts == 0) { return;  }

    mSkinnedPosition.resize(numVerts);
    mSkinnedNormal.resize(numVerts);
    Pose& bindPose = skeleton.GetBindPose();

    for (unsigned int i = 0; i < numVerts; ++i) {
        ivec4& joint = mInfluences[i];
        vec4& weight = mWeights[i];
```

2. Calculate the skin transform. Transform both the first vertex and normal influences:

```
        Transform skin0 = combine(pose[joint.x],
                            inverse(bindPose[joint.x]));
        vec3 p0 = transformPoint(skin0, mPosition[i]);
        vec3 n0 = transformVector(skin0, mNormal[i]);
```

3. Repeat this process for the other three joints that might influence the current vertex:

```
        Transform skin1 = combine(pose[joint.y],
                            inverse(bindPose[joint.y]));
        vec3 p1 = transformPoint(skin1, mPosition[i]);
        vec3 n1 = transformVector(skin1, mNormal[i]);

        Transform skin2 = combine(pose[joint.z],
                            inverse(bindPose[joint.z]));
        vec3 p2 = transformPoint(skin2, mPosition[i]);
        vec3 n2 = transformVector(skin2, mNormal[i]);

        Transform skin3 = combine(pose[joint.w],
                            inverse(bindPose[joint.w]));
        vec3 p3 = transformPoint(skin3, mPosition[i]);
        vec3 n3 = transformVector(skin3, mNormal[i]);
```

4. By this point, you have skinned the vertex four times—once to each bone that influences it. Next, you need to combine these into the final vertex.

5. Blend the skinned positions and normal using `mWeights`. Set the position and normal attributes as the newly updated skinned positions and normals:

```
            mSkinnedPosition[i] = p0 * weight.x +
                                  p1 * weight.y +
                                  p2 * weight.z +
                                  p3 * weight.w;
            mSkinnedNormal[i] = n0 * weight.x +
                                n1 * weight.y +
                                n2 * weight.z +
                                n3 * weight.w;
        }

    mPosAttrib->Set(mSkinnedPosition);
    mNormAttrib->Set(mSkinnedNormal);
}
```

Let's unpack what's happening here. This is the basic skinning algorithm. Every vertex has a `vec4` value called weights and an `ivec4` value called influences. Each vertex has four joints that influence it and four weights. A weight could be `0` if the joint has no influence on the vertex.

The x, y, z, and w components of the `ivec4` influences are indices in the animated pose and inverse bind pose matrix arrays. The x, y, z, and w components of the `vec4` weights are scalar weights to apply to the same component of the `ivec4` influences.

Loop through all the vertices. For each vertex, transform the position and the normal of the vertex by the skin transform of each joint that affects the vertex. The skin transform is the combination of the inverse bind pose and the pose transformations. This means you will end up skinning the vertex four times. Scale each transformed position or normal by the weight of the joint it belongs to and add all four values together. The resulting sum is the skinned position or normal.

This is the skinning algorithm; it stays the same no matter how it is expressed. There are several ways to represent the joint transformations, such as using `Transform` objects, matrices, and dual quaternions. No matter what the representation is, the algorithm stays the same. In the following section, you will learn how to implement the skinning algorithm using matrices instead of `Transform` objects.

Skinning with matrices

The common way to skin a vertex is to linearly blend matrices into a single skin matrix, then transform the vertex by this skin matrix. To do this, use the inverse bind pose stored in the skeleton and get the matrix palette from the pose.

To build a skin matrix, multiply the pose matrix by the inverse bind pose. Remember, the vertex should be transformed by the inverse bind pose first, then the animated pose. With right-to-left multiplication, this puts the inverse bind pose on the right side.

Multiply the matrices together for each joint that affects the current vertex, then scale the resulting matrix by the weight of the vertex. Once all the matrices are scaled, add them together. The resulting matrix is the skin matrix that can be used to transform both the vertex position and normal.

The following code re-implements the CPUSkin function using matrix palette skinning. This code is very similar to the shader code that you will need to implement to run skinning on the GPU:

```cpp
void Mesh::CPUSkin(Skeleton& skeleton, Pose& pose) {
    unsigned int numVerts = (unsigned int)mPosition.size();
    if (numVerts == 0) { return; }

    mSkinnedPosition.resize(numVerts);
    mSkinnedNormal.resize(numVerts);

    pose.GetMatrixPalette(mPosePalette);
    vector<mat4> invPosePalette = skeleton.GetInvBindPose();

    for (unsigned int i = 0; i < numVerts; ++i) {
        ivec4& j = mInfluences[i];
        vec4& w = mWeights[i];

        mat4 m0=(mPosePalette[j.x]*invPosePalette[j.x])*w.x;
        mat4 m1=(mPosePalette[j.y]*invPosePalette[j.y])*w.y;
        mat4 m2=(mPosePalette[j.z]*invPosePalette[j.z])*w.z;
        mat4 m3=(mPosePalette[j.w]*invPosePalette[j.w])*w.w;

        mat4 skin = m0 + m1 + m2 + m3;

        mSkinnedPosition[i]=transformPoint(skin,mPosition[i]);
        mSkinnedNormal[i] = transformVector(skin, mNormal[i]);
    }

    mPosAttrib->Set(mSkinnedPosition);
    mNormAttrib->Set(mSkinnedNormal);
}
```

The code for skinning with matrices looks a little different, but it's still the same skinning algorithm. Instead of transforming each vertex four times and scaling the results, the matrices are scaled and added together. The result is a single skin matrix.

Even though the vertex is only transformed once, four new matrix multiplications are introduced. The number of required operations is about the same, so why implement matrix palette skinning? When you implement GPU skinning, it's easy to use GLSL's built-in matrices.

In this section, you implemented a `Mesh` class. The Mesh class uses the following vertex format:

- The position (`vec3`)
- The normal (`vec3`)
- The texture coordinates (`vec2`)
- The influences (`ivec4`)
- The weights (`vec4`)

With this definition, you can render a skinned mesh. In the following section, you will learn how to load a mesh from a glTF file.

glTF – loading meshes

Now that you have a functional `Mesh` class, you can, in theory, skin the mesh on the CPU. However, there is one problem—you can't actually load a mesh from a glTF file yet. Let's address this next.

Start by creating a new helper function, `MeshFromAttributes`. This is only a helper function, so there is no need to expose it to the header file. glTF stores a mesh as a collection of primitives and each primitive is a collection of attributes. These attributes contain the same information as our attribute class, such as positions, normals, weights, and so on.

The `MeshFromAttribute` helper function takes a mesh and a `cgltf_attribute` function, along with some additional data required for parsing. The attribute contains one of our mesh components, such as the position, normal, UV coordinate, weights, or influences. This attribute provides the appropriate mesh data.

All values are read in as floating-point numbers, but the joint influences that affect the vertex are stored as integers. Don't cast the float to an int directly; there is a chance that due to a precision issue, the cast will return the wrong number. Instead, convert the float into an integer by adding 0.5 then casting. That way, the integer truncation always brings it to the correct number.

gLTF stores the indices that affect a joint relative to the joints array of the skin that is being parsed, not the node hierarchy. The `joints` array, in turn, is a pointer to a node. You can this node pointer and use the `GetNodeIndex` function to convert it into an index in the node hierarchy.

Follow these steps to implement mesh loading from a glTF file:

1. Implement the `MeshFromAttribute` function in the `GLTFHelpers` namespace. Start the implementation by figuring out how many attributes the current component has:

```cpp
// In the GLTFHelpers namespace
void GLTFHelpers::MeshFromAttribute(Mesh& outMesh,
                  cgltf_attribute& attribute,
                  cgltf_skin* skin, cgltf_node* nodes,
                  unsigned int nodeCount) {
    cgltf_attribute_type attribType = attribute.type;
    cgltf_accessor& accessor = *attribute.data;

    unsigned int componentCount = 0;
    if (accessor.type == cgltf_type_vec2) {
        componentCount = 2;
    }
    else if (accessor.type == cgltf_type_vec3) {
        componentCount = 3;
    }
    else if (accessor.type == cgltf_type_vec4) {
        componentCount = 4;
    }
```

2. Parse the data out of the provided accessor using the `GetScalarValues` helper
   function. Create references to the position, normal, texture coordinate, influences,
   and weights vectors of the mesh; the `MeshFromAttribute` function will write to
   these references:

```
std::vector<float> values;
GetScalarValues(values, componentCount, accessor);
unsigned int acessorCount = accessor.count;

std::vector<vec3>& positions = outMesh.GetPosition();
std::vector<vec3>& normals = outMesh.GetNormal();
std::vector<vec2>& texCoords = outMesh.GetTexCoord();
std::vector<ivec4>& influences =
                        outMesh.GetInfluences();
std::vector<vec4>& weights = outMesh.GetWeights();
```

3. Loop through all the values in the current accessor and assign them to the
   appropriate vector based on the accessor type. The position, texture coordinates,
   and weights components can all be found by reading the data from the values vector
   and assigning them directly to the appropriate vector in the mesh:

```
for (unsigned int i = 0; i < acessorCount; ++i) {
    int index = i * componentCount;
    switch (attribType) {
    case cgltf_attribute_type_position:
        positions.push_back(vec3(values[index + 0],
                                 values[index + 1],
                                 values[index + 2]));
        break;
    case cgltf_attribute_type_texcoord:
        texCoords.push_back(vec2(values[index + 0],
                                 values[index + 1]));
        break;
    case cgltf_attribute_type_weights:
        weights.push_back(vec4(values[index + 0],
                               values[index + 1],
                               values[index + 2],
                               values[index + 3]));
        break;
```

4. After reading in the normal, check its squared length. If the normal is invalid, return a valid vector and consider logging an error. If the normal is valid, normalize it before pushing it into the normals vector:

```
case cgltf_attribute_type_normal:
{
    vec3 normal = vec3(values[index + 0],
                       values[index + 1],
                       values[index + 2]);
    if (lenSq(normal) < 0.000001f) {
        normal = vec3(0, 1, 0);
    }
    normals.push_back(normalized(normal));
}
break;
```

5. Read in the joints that influence the current vertex. These joints are stored as floating-point numbers. Convert them into integers:

```
case cgltf_attribute_type_joints:
{
    // These indices are skin relative.  This
    // function has no information about the
    // skin that is being parsed. Add +0.5f to
    // round, since we can't read integers
    ivec4 joints(
        (int)(values[index + 0] + 0.5f),
        (int)(values[index + 1] + 0.5f),
        (int)(values[index + 2] + 0.5f),
        (int)(values[index + 3] + 0.5f)
    );
```

6. Use the GetNodeIndex helper function to convert the joint indices so that they go from being relative to the joints array to being relative to the skeleton hierarchy:

```
    joints.x = GetNodeIndex(
               skin->joints[joints.x],
               nodes, nodeCount);
    joints.y = GetNodeIndex(
               skin->joints[joints.y],
               nodes, nodeCount);
    joints.z = GetNodeIndex(
               skin->joints[joints.z],
               nodes, nodeCount);
    joints.w = GetNodeIndex(
```

```
                       skin->joints[joints.w],
                   nodes, nodeCount);
```

7. Make sure that even the invalid nodes have a value of 0. Any negative joint indices
will break the skinning implementation:

```
                joints.x = std::max(0, joints.x);
                joints.y = std::max(0, joints.y);
                joints.z = std::max(0, joints.z);
                joints.w = std::max(0, joints.w);

            influences.push_back(joints);
        }
        break;
        }
    }
}// End of MeshFromAttribute function
```

A **mesh** in gLTF is made up of **primitives**. A primitive contains attributes such as
positions and normals. Every primitive in glTF is expressed as a mesh in the framework
you've created so far since it doesn't have a concept of sub-meshes.

With the `MeshFromAttribute` function now finished, implement the `LoadMeshes`
function next. This is the function used to load the actual mesh data; it needs to be
declared in `GLTFLoader.h` and implemented in `GLTFLoader.cpp`. Follow these
steps to implement the `LoadMeshes` function:

1. To implement the `LoadMeshes` function, first, loop through all of the nodes
in the glTF file. Only process nodes that have both a mesh and a skin; any other
nodes should be skipped:

```
std::vector<Mesh> LoadMeshes(cgltf_data* data) {
    std::vector<Mesh> result;
    cgltf_node* nodes = data->nodes;
    unsigned int nodeCount = data->nodes_count;

    for (unsigned int i = 0; i < nodeCount; ++i) {
        cgltf_node* node = &nodes[i];
        if (node->mesh == 0 || node->skin == 0) {
            continue;
        }
```

2. Loop through all the primitives in the glTF file. Create a new mesh for each primitive. Loop through all the attributes in the primitive and populate the mesh data by calling the `MeshFromAttribute` helper function:

```
int numPrims = node->mesh->primitives_count;
for (int j = 0; j < numPrims; ++j) {
    result.push_back(Mesh());
    Mesh& mesh = result[result.size() - 1];

    cgltf_primitive* primitive =
            &node->mesh->primitives[j];

    unsigned int ac=primitive->attributes_count;
    for (unsigned int k = 0; k < ac; ++k) {
        cgltf_attribute* attribute =
                &primitive->attributes[k];
        GLTFHelpers::MeshFromAttribute(mesh,
                *attribute, node->skin,
                nodes, nodeCount);
    }
}
```

3. Check whether the primitive contains indices. If it does, the index buffer of the mesh needs to be filled out as well:

```
if (primitive->indices != 0) {
    int ic = primitive->indices->count;
    std::vector<unsigned int>& indices =
                        mesh.GetIndices();
    indices.resize(ic);

    for (unsigned int k = 0; k < ic; ++k) {
        indices[k]=cgltf_accessor_read_index(
                primitive->indices, k);
    }
}
```

4. The mesh is complete. Call the `UpdateOpenGLBuffers` function to make sure the mesh can be rendered and return the resulting vector of meshes:

```
                mesh.UpdateOpenGLBuffers();
        }
    }

    return result;
} // End of the LoadMeshes function
```

Since glTF stores an entire scene, not just a mesh, it supports multiple meshes—each one is made up of primitives, which are the actual triangles. Primitives in glTF can be thought of as sub-meshes. The glTF loader presented here assumes that a file contains a single model only. In the next section, you will learn how to move mesh skinning from the CPU to the GPU using shaders.

Implementing GPU skinning

You created some basic shaders in *Chapter 6, Building an Abstract Renderer and OpenGL*—the `static.vert` shader and the `lit.frag` shader. The `static.vert` shader can be used to display a static, unskinned mesh, which is loaded with the `LoadMeshes` function. The `static.vert` shader can even display a CPU skinned mesh.

Create a new file, `skinned.vert`. Follow these steps to implement a vertex shader that can perform matrix palette skinning. The code is very similar to the one used for `static.vert`; the differences are highlighted:

1. Each vertex gets two new components—the joint indices that affect the vertex and the weight of each joint. These new components can be stored in `ivec4` and `vec4`:

```
#version 330 core

uniform mat4 model;
uniform mat4 view;
uniform mat4 projection;

in vec3 position;
in vec3 normal;
in vec2 texCoord;
in vec4 weights;
in ivec4 joints;
```

2. Next, add two matrix arrays to the shader—each array is `120` in length. This length is arbitrary; the shader only needs as many new uniform matrices as the skinned mesh has joints. You could configure this automatically by generating a new shader string in code every time a skeleton with a new number of bones is loaded:

```
uniform mat4 pose[120];
uniform mat4 invBindPose[120];

out vec3 norm;
out vec3 fragPos;
out vec2 uv;
```

3. When the main function of the shader runs, calculate a skin matrix. The skin matrix is generated the same way as the CPU skinning-example skin matrix. It uses the same logic, just in a shader executing on the GPU:

```
void main() {
    mat4 skin = (pose[joints.x] * invBindPose[joints.x])
                    * weights.x;
        skin+= (pose[joints.y] * invBindPose[joints.y])
                    * weights.y;
        skin+= (pose[joints.z] * invBindPose[joints.z])
                    * weights.z;
        skin+= (pose[joints.w] * invBindPose[joints.w])
                    * weights.w;
```

4. The mesh should deform before it is placed in the world. Multiply the vertex position and normal by the skin matrix before applying the model matrix. All the relevant code is highlighted here:

```
    gl_Position= projection * view * model *
                    skin * vec4(position,1.0);

    fragPos = vec3(model * skin * vec4(position, 1.0));
    norm = vec3(model * skin * vec4(normal, 0.0f));
    uv = texCoord;
}
```

To add skinning support to the vertex shader, you add two new attributes to each vertex that represent up to four joints that can affect the vertex. By using the joint and weight attributes, a skin matrix is constructed. To skin the mesh, multiply the vertex or normal by the skin matrix before applying the rest of the vertex transformation pipeline.

Summary

In this chapter, you learned the difference between a bind pose and a rest pose. You also created a `Skeleton` class that contains them both. You learned about the general concept of skinning—both rigid (one bone per vertex) and smooth (multiple bones per vertex) skinning.

In this chapter, we implemented a primitive mesh class and we covered the process of skinning a mesh on both the CPU and GPU, as well as loading a bind pose out of a glTF file that does not store bind pose data.

You can now apply the skills you learned. With the skinning code complete, you can display fully animated models. The models can be loaded from glTF files, which is an open file format specification.

In the downloadable samples for this book, `Chapter10/Sample01` contains a sample that draws the rest pose, bind pose, and current animated pose. `Chapter10/Sample02` demonstrates how to use both GPU and CPU skinning.

In the next chapter, you will learn how to optimize various aspects of the animation pipeline. This includes the pose generation and skinning and caching transform parent lookups steps.

11
Optimizing the Animation Pipeline

By now, you have written an entire animation system that can load a standard file format, gLTF, and perform skinning on either the CPU or GPU. The animation system performs well enough for most simple animations.

In this chapter, you will explore the ways to optimize the animation system to make it faster and less resource-intensive. This involves exploring alternative ways to perform skinning, improving the speed of sample animation clips, and revisiting how matrix palettes are generated.

Each of these topics is explored on its own, and you can choose to implement as few or as many of these optimizations as you wish. All of them are simple and can be used to replace a less optimal version of the pipeline with ease.

The following topics will be covered in this chapter:

- Pre-generating the skin matrix
- Storing the skin pallette in a texture
- Faster sampling
- The Pose palette generation
- Exploring `Pose::GetGlobalTransform`

Pre-generating the skin matrix

One of the bigger problems with **Vertex Shader Skinning** is the number of uniforms that the system takes up. One mat4 object takes up four uniform slots and the skinned vertex shader currently has two matrix arrays that have 120 elements each. That comes to a total of 960 uniform slots, which is excessive.

What happens with those two matrix arrays in the vertex shader? They get multiplied together, as follows:

```
mat4 skin=(pose[joints.x]*invBindPose[joints.x])*weights.x;
   skin += (pose[joints.y]*invBindPose[joints.y])*weights.y;
   skin += (pose[joints.z]*invBindPose[joints.z])*weights.z;
   skin += (pose[joints.w]*invBindPose[joints.w])*weights.w;
```

One easy optimization here is to combine the pose * invBindPose multiplication so that the shader only needs one array. This does mean that some of the skinning process is moved back to the CPU, but this change clears up 480 uniform slots.

Generating the skin matrix

Generating the skin matrix doesn't need an API call—it's simple. Generate a matrix palette from the current animated pose using the GetMatrixPalette function of the Pose class. Then, multiply each matrix in the palette by the inverse bind pose matrix of the same index.

It's the responsibility of the code that displays the mesh to calculate these matrices. For example, a simple update loop might look like this:

```
void Sample::Update(float deltaTime) {
    mPlaybackTime = mAnimClip.Sample(mAnimatedPose,
                        mPlaybackTime + deltaTime);

    mAnimatedPose.GetMatrixPalette(mPosePalette);
    vector<mat4>& invBindPose = mSkeleton.GetInvBindPose();

    for (int i = 0; i < mPosePalette.size(); ++i) {
        mPosePalette[i] = mPosePalette[i] * invBindPose[i];
    }

    if (mDoCPUSkinning) {
        mMesh.CPUSkin(mPosePalette);
    }
}
```

In the preceding code sample, an animation clip was sampled into a pose. The pose was converted into a vector of matrices. Each matrix in that vector was then multiplied by the inverse bind pose matrix of the same index. The resulting vector of matrices is the combined skin matrix.

If the mesh is CPU skinned, this is a good place to call the CPUSkin function. This function needs to be re-implemented to work with a combined skin matrix. If the mesh is GPU skinned, the shader needs to be edited so that it only uses one matrix array, and the rendering code needs to be updated to only pass one uniform array.

In the following section, you will explore how to re-implement the CPUSkin function so that it works with the combined skin matrix. This will speed up the CPU skinning process a little bit.

CPU skinning

You need a new skinning method that respects the pre-multiplied skin matrix. This function takes a reference to a vector of matrices. Each position is transformed by the combined skin matrix of all four of the bones that affect it. Those four results are then scaled and added together.

Add the following CPU skinning function to Mesh.cpp. Don't forget to add the function declaration to Mesh.h:

1. Start implementing the CPUSkin function by making sure the mesh is valid. A valid mesh has at least one vertex. Make sure that the mSkinnedPosition and mSkinnedNormal vectors are large enough to hold all the vertices:

```
void Mesh::CPUSkin(std::vector<mat4>& animatedPose) {
    unsigned int numVerts = mPosition.size();
    if (numVerts == 0) {
        return;
    }
    mSkinnedPosition.resize(numVerts);
    mSkinnedNormal.resize(numVerts);
```

2. Next, loop through every vertex in the mesh:

```
    for (unsigned int i = 0; i < numVerts; ++i) {
        ivec4& j = mInfluences[i];
        vec4& w = mWeights[i];
```

3. Transform each vertex by the animated pose four times—once for each joint that influences the vertex. To find the skinned vertex, scale each of the transformed vertices by the appropriate weight and add together the results:

```
vec3 p0 = transformPoint(animatedPose[j.x],
                         mPosition[i]);
vec3 p1 = transformPoint(animatedPose[j.y],
                         mPosition[i]);
vec3 p2 = transformPoint(animatedPose[j.z],
                         mPosition[i]);
vec3 p3 = transformPoint(animatedPose[j.w],
                         mPosition[i]);
mSkinnedPosition[i] = p0 * w.x + p1 * w.y +
                      p2 * w.z + p3 * w.w;
```

4. Find the skinned normal of the vertex in the same way:

```
vec3 n0 = transformVector(animatedPose[j.x],
                          mNormal[i]);
vec3 n1 = transformVector(animatedPose[j.y],
                          mNormal[i]);
vec3 n2 = transformVector(animatedPose[j.z],
                          mNormal[i]);
vec3 n3 = transformVector(animatedPose[j.w],
                          mNormal[i]);
mSkinnedNormal[i] = n0 * w.x + n1 * w.y +
                    n2 * w.z + n3 * w.w;
}
```

5. Finish off the function by uploading the skinned vertex positions and the skinned vertex normals to the position and normal attributes:

```
mPosAttrib->Set(mSkinnedPosition);
mNormAttrib->Set(mSkinnedNormal);
}
```

The core skinning algorithm remains the same; the only thing that changes is how the transformed position is generated. Instead of having to combine the animated pose and the inverse bind pose, this function can now just use the already-combined matrix.

In the next section, you will explore how to move this skinning function into a vertex shader. Combining the animated and inverse bind poses is still done on the CPU, but skinning the actual vertices can be implemented in a vertex shader.

GPU skinning

Implementing pre-multiplied skin-matrix skinning in a vertex shader is simple. Replace the input uniforms for the pose and inverse bind pose with the new pre-multiplied skin pose. Generate the skin matrix using this new uniform array. That's all there is to it—the rest of the skinning pipeline remains unchanged.

Create a new file, `preskinned.vert`, to implement the new pre-skinned vertex shader in. Copy the contents of `skinned.vert` into this new file. Follow these steps to modify the new shader:

1. The old skinned vertex shader has uniforms for pose and inverse bind pose. Both uniforms are arrays of matrices. Remove these uniforms:

   ```
   uniform mat4 pose[120];
   uniform mat4 invBindPose[120];
   ```

2. Replace them with the new `animated` uniform. This is a single array of matrices and each element in the array contains the `animated` pose and the inverse bind pose matrices multiplied together:

   ```
   uniform mat4 animated[120];
   ```

3. Next, find where the skin matrix is generated. The code for generating the skin matrix looks like this:

   ```
   mat4 skin = (pose[joints.x] * invBindPose[joints.x]) *
               weights.x;
        skin += (pose[joints.y] * invBindPose[joints.y]) *
               weights.y;
        skin += (pose[joints.z] * invBindPose[joints.z]) *
               weights.z;
        skin += (pose[joints.w] * invBindPose[joints.w]) *
               weights.w;
   ```

4. Replace this with the new `animated` uniform. For each joint that affects the vertex, scale the `animated` uniform matrix by the appropriate weight and sum the results:

   ```
   mat4 skin = animated[joints.x] * weights.x +
               animated[joints.y] * weights.y +
               animated[joints.z] * weights.z +
               animated[joints.w] * weights.w;
   ```

The rest of the shader stays the same. The only thing you need to update is the uniforms that the shader takes and how the skin matrix is generated. When rendering, the animated matrix can be set as follows:

```
// mPosePalette Generated in the Update method!
int animated = mSkinnedShader->GetUniform("animated")
Uniform<mat4>::Set(animated, mPosePalette);
```

You may have noticed that the CPU skinning implementation and the GPU skinning implementation are different. The CPU implementation transforms the vertex four times, then scales and sums the results. The GPU implementation scales and sums the matrices and only transforms the vertex once. Both implementations are valid and they both produce the same results.

In the following section, you will explore how to avoid using uniform matrix arrays for skinning.

Storing the skin palette in a texture

Pre-generating the skin matrix cuts the number of uniform slots that the skinned shader needs in half, but it's possible to reduce the number of uniform slots needed to just one. This can be done by encoding the pre-generated skin matrix in a texture and reading that texture in the vertex shader instead of in a uniform array.

So far in this book, you have only dealt with the RGB24 and RGBA32 textures. In these formats, the three or four components of a pixel are encoded using 8 bits per component. This can only hold 256 unique values. These textures do not provide the amount of precision needed to store floating-point numbers.

There is another texture format that can be useful here—a FLOAT32 texture. With this texture format, each component of a vector gets a full 32-bit floating-point number to back it, giving you full precision. This texture can be sampled with a special sampler function that doesn't normalize the data. The FLOAT32 texture can be treated as a buffer that the CPU can write to and the GPU can read from.

The benefit of this method is that the number of required uniform slots becomes just one—the uniform slot that is needed is the sampler for the FLOAT32 texture. The downside is speed. Having to sample a texture for every vertex is more expensive than a quick uniform array lookup. Remember, each of these sample lookups needs to return several 32-bit floating-point numbers. That is a lot of data to transfer.

We will not cover the implementation of a texture to store the skin matrices here, as there is a large section dedicated to that topic in *Chapter 15*, *Rendering Large Crowds with Instancing*, which includes the full code implementation.

Faster sampling

The current animation-clip sampling code performs well, so long as each animation lasts under 1 second. With multiple minute-long animation clips, such as a cutscene, the animation system's performance starts to suffer. Why does the performance worsen with longer animations? The culprit is the following bit of code in the `Track::FrameIndex` function:

```
for (int i = (int)size - 1; i >= 0; --i) {
    if (time >= mFrames[i].mTime) {
        return i;
    }
}
```

The presented loop goes through every frame in the track. If an animation has a lot of frames, the performance starts to get worse. Remember, this bit of code is executed for each animated component of each animated bone in an animation clip.

This function currently does a linear search, but it can be optimized with a more efficient search. Since time only ever increases, performing a binary search is a natural optimization to use here. However, binary search isn't the best optimization. It's possible to turn this loop into a constant lookup.

Sampled animations have a uniform cost to play back, regardless of length. They time every frame at a known sampling interval, and finding the correct frame index is just a matter of normalizing the provided time and moving it into the sampled interval range. Unfortunately, sampling an animation such as this takes up a lot of memory.

What if you still sampled the animation track at given intervals, but instead of containing a full pose, each interval points to the keyframes that are to its left and right? With this approach, the additional memory overhead is minimal and finding the correct frame is constant.

Optimizing the Track class

There are two ways to handle optimizing the `Track` class. You can either create a new class that has most of the `Track` class's functionality and maintains a lookup table for known sample times or extend the `Track` class. This section takes the latter approach—we will extend the `Track` class.

The `FastTrack` subclass contains a vector of unsigned integers. The `Track` class is sampled at uniform time intervals. For each time interval, the frame on the left of the play head (the frame right before time) is recorded into this vector.

All new code is added to the existing `Track.h` and `Track.cpp` files. Follow these steps to implement the `FastTrack` class:

1. Find the `FrameIndex` member function of the `Track` class and mark it as `virtual`. This change allows the new subclass to re-implement the `FrameIndex` function. The updated declaration should look like this:

    ```cpp
    template<typename T, int N>
    class Track {
    // ...
            virtual int FrameIndex(float time, bool looping);
    // ...
    ```

2. Create a new class, `FastTrack`, that inherits from `Track`. The `FastTrack` class contains a vector of unsigned integers—the overloaded `FrameIndex` function and a function to populate the vector of unsigned integers:

    ```cpp
    template<typename T, int N>
    class FastTrack : public Track<T, N> {
    protected:
        std::vector<unsigned int> mSampledFrames;
        virtual int FrameIndex(float time, bool looping);
    public:
        void UpdateIndexLookupTable();
    };
    ```

3. To make the `FastTrack` class easier to work with, use typedef to create aliases for scalar, vector and quaternion types:

    ```cpp
    typedef FastTrack<float, 1> FastScalarTrack;
    typedef FastTrack<vec3, 3> FastVectorTrack;
    typedef FastTrack<quat, 4> FastQuaternionTrack;
    ```

4. In the .cpp file, add a template declaration for the scalar, vector, and quaternion fast tracks:

    ```cpp
    template FastTrack<float, 1>;
    template FastTrack<vec3, 3>;
    template FastTrack<quat, 4>;
    ```

Since the `FastTrack` class is a subclass of `Track`, the existing APIs all work unchanged. The performance gain from implementing track sampling this way is greater when the animation in question has more frames. In the next section, you will learn how to build the index lookup table.

Implementing UpdateIndexLookupTable

The `UpdateIndexLookupTable` function is responsible for populating the `mSampledFrames` vector. This function needs to sample the animation at fixed time intervals and record the frame before the animation time for each interval.

How many samples should the `FastTrack` class contain? This question is very context-dependent as different games have different requirements. For the context of this book, 60 samples per second should be enough:

1. Start implementing the `UpdateIndexLookupTable` function by making sure that the track is valid. A valid track will have at least two frames:

```
template<typename T, int N>
void FastTrack<T, N>::UpdateIndexLookupTable() {
    int numFrames = (int)this->mFrames.size();
    if (numFrames <= 1) {
        return;
    }
}
```

2. Next, find the number of samples that are needed. Since the class has 60 samples for every second of animation, multiply the duration by 60:

```
    float duration = this->GetEndTime() -
                        this->GetStartTime();
    unsigned int numSamples = duration * 60.0f;
    mSampledFrames.resize(numSamples);
```

3. For each sample, find the time of the sample along the track. To find the time, multiply the normalized iterator by the animation duration and add the start time of the animation to it:

```
    for (unsigned int i = 0; i < numSamples; ++i) {
        float t = (float)i / (float)(numSamples - 1);
        float time = t*duration+this->GetStartTime();
```

4. Finally, it's time to find the frame index for each given time. Find the frame that comes before the sampling time for this iteration and record it in the `mSampledFrames` vector. If the sampled frame is the last frame, return the index right before the last index. Remember, the `FrameIndex` function should never return the last frame:

```
            unsigned int frameIndex = 0;
            for (int j = numFrames - 1; j >= 0; --j) {
                if (time >= this->mFrames[j].mTime) {
                    frameIndex = (unsigned int)j;
                    if ((int)frameIndex >= numFrames - 2) {
                        frameIndex = numFrames - 2;
                    }
                    break;
                }
            }
            mSampledFrames[i] = frameIndex;
        }
    }
```

The `UpdateIndexLookupTable` function is intended to be called at load time. It could be optimized to be faster by remembering the last used index of the inner `j` loop since, on each `i` iteration, the frame index only increases. In the next section, you will learn how to implement `FrameIndex` to use the `mSampledFrames` vector.

Implementing FrameIndex

The `FrameIndex` function is responsible for finding the frame right before a given time. The optimized `FastTrack` class uses a lookup array instead of looping through every frame of the track. All input times have a very similar performance cost. Follow these steps to override the `FrameIndex` function in the `FastTrack` class:

1. Start implementing the `FrameIndex` function by making sure that the track is valid. A valid track must have at least two or more frames:

```
template<typename T, int N>
int FastTrack<T,N>::FrameIndex(float time,bool loop){
    std::vector<Frame<N>>& frames = this->mFrames;
    unsigned int size = (unsigned int)frames.size();
    if (size <= 1) {
        return -1;
    }
}
```

2. Next, make sure the requested sample time falls between the start and end times of the track. If the track is looping, use `fmodf` to keep it in a valid range:

```
if (loop) {
    float startTime = this->mFrames[0].mTime;
    float endTime = this->mFrames[size - 1].mTime;
    float duration = endTime - startTime;

    time = fmodf(time - startTime,
                 endTime - startTime);
    if (time < 0.0f) {
        time += endTime - startTime;
    }
    time = time + startTime;
}
```

3. If the track is not looping, clamp to the first or next to last frame:

```
else {
    if (time <= frames[0].mTime) {
        return 0;
    }
    if (time >= frames[size - 2].mTime) {
        return (int)size - 2;
    }
}
```

4. Find the normalized sample time and frame index. The frame index is the normalized sample time scaled by the number of samples. If the index is invalid, return -1; otherwise, return the frame that the index points to:

```
float duration = this->GetEndTime() -
                 this->GetStartTime();
float t = time / duration;
unsigned int numSamples = (duration * 60.0f);
unsigned int index = (t * (float)numSamples);
if (index >= mSampledFrames.size()) {
    return -1;
}
return (int)mSampledFrames[index];
}
```

The `FrameIndex` function is almost always called with a valid time since it's a protected helper function. This means the time it takes to find the index of a frame is uniform, regardless of the number of frames in the track. In the next section, you will learn how to convert an unoptimized `Track` class into an optimized `FastTrack` class.

Converting tracks

Now that `FastTrack` exists, how do you create it? You could either create a new load function that loads a `FastTrack` class instead of `Track`. Alternatively, you could create a function that converts an existing `Track` class into a `FastTrack` class. This chapter takes the latter approach. Follow these steps to create a function that converts the `Track` objects into the `FastTrack` objects:

1. Declare the `OptimizeTrack` function in `FastTrack.h`. The function is templated. It takes the same template types as `Track`:

```
template<typename T, int N>
FastTrack<T, N> OptimizeTrack(Track<T, N>& input);
```

2. Declare the template specializations of the `OptimizeTrack` function for all three types that track to `FastTrack.cpp`. This means declaring specializations that work with the scalar, vector 3, and quaternion tracks:

```
template FastTrack<float, 1>
OptimizeTrack(Track<float, 1>& input);
template FastTrack<vec3, 3>
OptimizeTrack(Track<vec3, 3>& input);
template FastTrack<quat, 4>
OptimizeTrack(Track<quat, 4>& input);
```

3. To implement the `OptimizeTrack` function, resize the resulting track so that it is the same size as the input track and match the interpolation. The overloaded `[]` operator function can be used to copy the per-frame data:

```
template<typename T, int N>
FastTrack<T, N> OptimizeTrack(Track<T, N>& input) {
    FastTrack<T, N> result;
    result.SetInterpolation(input.GetInterpolation());
    unsigned int size = input.Size();
    result.Resize(size);
    for (unsigned int i = 0; i < size; ++i) {
        result[i] = input[i];
    }
    result.UpdateIndexLookupTable();
```

```
        return result;
    }
```

It's not enough to just optimize the `Track` class into `FastTrack`. The `TransformTrack` class needs to change as well. It needs to contain the new, optimized `FastTrack` class. In the next section, you will change the `TransformTrack` class so that it is templated and can contain either `Track` or `FastTrack`.

Creating FastTransformTrack

Higher-level structures that use the `Track` class, such as `TransformTrack`, need to accommodate for the new `FastTrack` subclass. The `FastTrack` class has the same signature as the `Track` class. Because the signature of the class is the same, it's easy to template the `TransformTrack` class so that it can use either of these classes.

In this section, you will rename the `TransformTrack` class to `TTransformTrack` and template the class. Then, you will `typedef` template specializations as `TransformTrack` and `FastTransformTrack`. This way, the `TransformTrack` class stays the same and the optimized transform track uses all the same code:

1. Change the name of the `TransformTrack` class to `TTransformTrack` and template the class. The template takes two arguments—the type of vector track and the type of quaternion track to use. Update the `mPosition`, `mRotation`, and `mScale` tracks to use the new templated types:

```
template <typename VTRACK, typename QTRACK>
class TTransformTrack {
protected:
    unsigned int mId;
    VTRACK mPosition;
    QTRACK mRotation;
    VTRACK mScale;
public:
    TTransformTrack();
    unsigned int GetId();
    void SetId(unsigned int id);
    VTRACK& GetPositionTrack();
    QTRACK& GetRotationTrack();
    VTRACK& GetScaleTrack();
    float GetStartTime();
    float GetEndTime();
    bool IsValid();
    Transform Sample(const Transform& r,float t,bool l);
};
```

2. Typedef this class into `TransformTrack`, with `VectorTrack` and `QuaternionTrack` for arguments. Typedef it again into `FastTransformTrack`, with `FastVectorTrack` and `FastQuaternionTrack` as template arguments:

```
typedef TTransformTrack<VectorTrack,
    QuaternionTrack> TransformTrack;
typedef TTransformTrack<FastVectorTrack,
    FastQuaternionTrack> FastTransformTrack;
```

3. Declare the optimization function that converts `TransformTrack` into `FastTransformTrack`:

```
FastTransformTrack OptimizeTransformTrack(
                   TransformTrack& input);
```

4. Add template specifications for both `typedef` functions in `TransformTrack.cpp`:

```
template TTransformTrack<VectorTrack, QuaternionTrack>;
template TTransformTrack<FastVectorTrack,
                   FastQuaternionTrack>;
```

5. Implement the `OptimizeTransformTrack` function. Copy the track ID, then copy the individual tracks by value:

```
FastTransformTrack OptimizeTransformTrack(
                   TransformTrack& input) {
    FastTransformTrack result;

    result.SetId(input.GetId());
    result.GetPositionTrack() = OptimizeTrack<vec3, 3> (
                             input.GetPositionTrack());
    result.GetRotationTrack() = OptimizeTrack<quat, 4>(
                             input.GetRotationTrack());
    result.GetScaleTrack()    = OptimizeTrack<vec3, 3> (
                             input.GetScaleTrack());

    return result;
}
```

Because `OptimizeTransformTrack` copies the actual track data by value, it can be a little slow. This function is intended to be called during initialization. In the next section, you will template the `Clip` class, similar to how you did with the `Transform` class, to create `FastClip`.

Creating FastClip

The user of this animation system interacts with the `Clip` objects. To accommodate the new `FastTrack` class, the `Clip` class is similarly templated and split into `Clip` and `FastClip`. You will implement a function to convert the `Clip` objects into the `FastClip` objects. Follow these steps to template the `Clip` class:

1. Change the name of the `Clip` class to `TClip` and template the class. The template only takes one type—the type of transform track that the `TClip` class contains. Change the type of `mTracks` and the return type of `[] operator` so that it is the template type:

```
template <typename TRACK>
class TClip {
protected:
    std::vector<TRACK> mTracks;
    std::string mName;
    float mStartTime;
    float mEndTime;
    bool mLooping;
public:
    TClip();
    TRACK& operator[](unsigned int index);
// ...
```

2. Typedef `TClip` with a `TransformTrack` type as `Clip`. Typedef `TClip` with a `FastTransformTrack` type as `FastClip`. This way, the `Clip` class doesn't change and the `FastClip` class can reuse all the existing code:

```
typedef TClip<TransformTrack> Clip;
typedef TClip<FastTransformTrack> FastClip;
```

3. Declare a function to convert a `Clip` object into a `FastClip` object:

```
FastClip OptimizeClip(Clip& input);
```

4. Declare template specializations of these typedefed classes in `Clip.cpp`:

```
template TClip<TransformTrack>;
template TClip<FastTransformTrack>;
```

5. To implement the `OptimizeClip` function, copy the name and looping value of the input clip. For each joint in the clip, call the `OptimizeTransformTrack` function on its track. Don't forget to calculate the duration of the new `FastClip` object before returning a copy of it:

```
FastClip OptimizeClip(Clip& input) {
    FastClip result;
    result.SetName(input.GetName());
    result.SetLooping(input.GetLooping());
    unsigned int size = input.Size();
    for (unsigned int i = 0; i < size; ++i) {
        unsigned int joint = input.GetIdAtIndex(i);
        result[joint] =
                OptimizeTransformTrack(input[joint]);
    }
    result.RecalculateDuration();
    return result;
}
```

As with the rest of the conversion functions, `OptimizeClip` is only intended to be called at initialization time. In the following section, you will explore how to optimize the `Pose` palette generation.

The Pose palette generation

The final optimization you should think about is the process of generating a matrix palette from `Pose`. If you look at the `Pose` class, the following bit of code converts a pose into a linear array of matrices:

```
void Pose::GetMatrixPalette(std::vector<mat4>& out) {
    unsigned int size = Size();
    if (out.size() != size) {
        out.resize(size);
    }

    for (unsigned int i = 0; i < size; ++i) {
        Transform t = GetGlobalTransform(i);
        out[i] = transformToMat4(t);
```

```
        }
    }
```

By itself, this function isn't too bad, but the `GetGlobalTransform` function loops through every joint all the way up the specified joints transform chain until the root joint. This means the function wastes a considerable amount of time finding matrices for transforms that it has already found the matrices for during a previous iteration.

To fix this, you need to make sure that the order of the joints in the `Pose` class is ascending. That is, all the parent joints must have a lower index than their child joints in the `mJoints` array.

Once this order is set, you can iterate through all the joints and know that the parent matrix of the joint at the current index has already been found. This is because all the parent elements have a lower index than their children. To combine the local matrix of this joint with the global matrix of its parent joint, you just have to multiply the previously found world matrix and local matrix together.

There is no guarantee that the input data can be trusted to have the joints listed in this specific order. To fix this, you need to write some code to re-arrange the joints of a `Pose` class. In the next section, you will learn how to improve the `GetMatrixPalette` function so that it uses the optimized method if it can and falls back to the unoptimized method if it can't.

Changing the GetMatrixPalette function

In this section, you will modify the `GetMatrixPalette` function to pre-cache global matrices if the parent index of the current joint is lower than the joint. If this assumption is ever broken, the function needs to fall back into the slower calculation mode.

There will be two loops in the `GetMatrixPalette` function. The first loop finds and stores the global matrix of a transform. If the joint parent has a smaller index than the joint, the optimized method is used. If the joint's parent isn't smaller, the first loop breaks out and gives the second loop a chance to run.

In this second loop, each joint falls back to calling the slow `GetWorldTransform` function to find its world transforms. This loop is the fallback code used if the optimized loop fails. If the optimized loop executes all the way, this second loop isn't executed:

```
void Pose::GetMatrixPalette(std::vector<mat4>& out) {
    int size = (int)Size();
    if ((int)out.size() != size) { out.resize(size); }

    int i = 0;
```

```
    for (; i < size; ++i) {
        int parent = mParents[i];
        if (parent > i) { break; }

        mat4 global = transformToMat4(mJoints[i]);
        if (parent >= 0) {
            global = out[parent] * global;
        }
        out[i] = global;
    }

    for (; i < size; ++i) {
        Transform t = GetGlobalTransform(i);
        out[i] = transformToMat4(t);
    }
}
```

This change adds very minimal overhead to the GetMatrixPalette function but quickly makes up for that. It makes the matrix palette calculations run fast, if possible, but still execute if not possible. In the following section, you will learn how to re-arrange the joints of a loaded model to make the GetMatrixPalette function always take the fast path.

Reordering joints

Not all models will be well formatted; because of this, they won't all be able to take advantage of the optimized GetMatrixPalette function. In this section, you will learn how to re-arrange the bones of a model so that it can take advantage of the optimized GetMatrixPalette function.

Create a new file, RearrangeBones.h. Use a dictionary whose keyvalue pairs are bone indices to remapped bone indices. The RearrangeSkeleton function generates this dictionary and rearranges the bind, inverse bind, and rest poses in the skeleton.

Once the RearrangeSkeleton function has generated BoneMap, you can use it to process any meshes or animation clips that affect the current skeleton. Follow these steps to re-order the joints so that a skeleton can always take advantage of the optimized GetMatrixPalette path:

1. Add the following function declarations to the RearrangeBones.h file:

    ```
    typedef std::map<int, int> BoneMap;

    BoneMap RearrangeSkeleton(Skeleton& skeleton);
    ```

```
void RearrangeMesh(Mesh& mesh, BoneMap& boneMap);
void RearrangeClip(Clip& clip, BoneMap& boneMap);
void RearrangeFastclip(FastClip& clip, BoneMap& boneMap);
```

2. Begin implementing the `RearrangeSkeleton` function in a new file,
   `ReearrangeBones.cpp`. First, create references to the rest and bind poses, then
   make sure that the skeleton that you are re-arranging isn't empty. If it is empty, just
   return an empty dictionary:

```
BoneMap RearrangeSkeleton(Skeleton& skeleton) {
    Pose& restPose = skeleton.GetRestPose();
    Pose& bindPose = skeleton.GetBindPose();
    unsigned int size = restPose.Size();
    if (size == 0) { return BoneMap(); }
```

3. Next, create a two-dimensional integer array (a vector of vectors of integers). Each
   element of the outer vector represents one bone and the indices of this vector and
   the `mJoints` array in the bind or rest poses are parallel. The inner vector represents
   all the children that the joint at the index of the outer vector contains. Loop through
   every joint in the rest pose:

```
std::vector<std::vector<int>> hierarchy(size);
std::list<int> process;
for (unsigned int i = 0; i < size; ++i) {
    int parent = restPose.GetParent(i);
```

4. If a joint has a parent, add the index of the joint to the parent's vector of children
   nodes. If a node is a root node (so it has no parent), add it directly to the process
   list. This list will be used later to traverse the map depth:

```
    if (parent >= 0) {
        hierarchy[parent].push_back((int)i);
    }
    else {
        process.push_back((int)i);
    }
}
```

5. To figure out how to re-order bones, you need to keep two maps—one that maps from the old configuration to the new one and one that maps from the new configuration back to the old one:

```
BoneMap mapForward;
BoneMap mapBackward;
```

6. For each element, if it contains children, add the children to the process list. This way, all the joints are processed and the joints higher up in the transform hierarchy are processed first:

```
int index = 0;
while (process.size() > 0) {
    int current = *process.begin();
    process.pop_front();
    std::vector<int>& children = hierarchy[current];

    unsigned int numChildren = children.size();
    for (unsigned int i = 0; i < numChildren; ++i) {
        process.push_back(children[i]);
    }
```

7. Set the current index of the forward map to the index of the joint that is being processed. The current index of the forward map is an atomic counter. Do the same thing for the backward map, but switch the key-value pair around. Don't forget to add the null node (-1) to both maps:

```
    mapForward[index] = current;
    mapBackward[current] = index;
    index += 1;
}

mapForward[-1] = -1;
mapBackward[-1] = -1;
```

8. Now that the maps are filled in, you need to build new rest and bind poses whose bones are in the correct order. Loop through every joint in the original rest and bind poses and copy their local transforms to the new poses. Do the same thing for the joint names:

```
Pose newRestPose(size);
Pose newBindPose(size);
std::vector<std::string> newNames(size);
```

```
        for (unsigned int i = 0; i < size; ++i) {
            int thisBone = mapForward[i];
            newRestPose.SetLocalTransform(i,
                    restPose.GetLocalTransform(thisBone));
            newBindPose.SetLocalTransform(i,
                    bindPose.GetLocalTransform(thisBone));
            newNames[i] = skeleton.GetJointName(thisBone);
```

9. Finding the new parent joint ID for each joint requires two mapping steps. First, map the current index to the bone in the original skeleton. This returns the parent of the original skeleton. Map this parent index back to the new skeleton. This is why there are two dictionaries, to make this mapping fast:

```
        int parent = mapBackward[bindPose.GetParent(
                                        thisBone)];
            newRestPose.SetParent(i, parent);
            newBindPose.SetParent(i, parent);
        }
```

10. Once the new rest and bind poses are found and the joint names have been re-arranged accordingly, write this data back to the skeleton by calling the public Set method. The Set method of the skeleton also calculates the inverse bind pose matrix palette:

```
        skeleton.Set(newRestPose, newBindPose, newNames);
        return mapBackward;
    } // End of RearrangeSkeleton function
```

The RearrangeSkeleton function re-arranges the bones in a skeleton so that the skeleton can take advantage of the optimized version of GetMatrixPalette. Rearranging the skeleton is not enough. Since the joint indices moved, any clips or meshes that reference this skeleton are now broken. In the next section, you will implement helper functions to re-arrange the joints in a clip.

Reordering clips

To rearrange an animation clip, loop through all the tracks in the clip. For each track, find the joint ID, then convert that joint ID using the (backward) bone map that was returned by the RearrangeSkeleton function. Write the modified joint ID back into the tack:

```
void RearrangeClip(Clip& clip, BoneMap& boneMap) {
    unsigned int size = clip.Size();
```

```
        for (unsigned int i = 0; i < size; ++i) {
            int joint = (int)clip.GetIdAtIndex(i);
            unsigned int newJoint = (unsigned int)boneMap[joint];
            clip.SetIdAtIndex(i, newJoint);
        }
    }
```

If you have implemented the `FastClip` optimization from earlier in this chapter, the `RearrangeClip` function should still work since it is a subclass of `Clip`. In the next section, you will learn how to re-arrange the joints in a mesh, which will be the last step needed to use this optimization.

Reordering meshes

To rearrange the joints that affect the skinning of a mesh, loop through every vertex of the mesh and remap all four of the joint indices stored in the influences attribute of that vertex. The weights of the joint don't need to be edited since the joint itself didn't change; only its index in the array changed.

Changing the mesh in this way only edits the CPU copy of the mesh. Call `UpdateOpenGLBuffers` to upload the new attribute to the GPU as well:

```
void RearrangeMesh(Mesh& mesh, BoneMap& boneMap) {
    std::vector<ivec4>& influences = mesh.GetInfluences();
    unsigned int size = (unsigned int)influences.size();

    for (unsigned int i = 0; i < size; ++i) {
        influences[i].x = boneMap[influences[i].x];
        influences[i].y = boneMap[influences[i].y];
        influences[i].z = boneMap[influences[i].z];
        influences[i].w = boneMap[influences[i].w];
    }

    mesh.UpdateOpenGLBuffers();
}
```

With the `RearrangeMesh` function implemented, you can load a skeleton, then call the `RearrangeSkeleton` function and store the bone map it returns. Using this bone map, you can also fix any meshes or animation clips that reference the skeleton with the `RearrangeClip` and `RearrangeMesh` functions. After an asset is processed in this way, `GetMatrixPalette` always takes the optimized path. In the next section, you will explore caching transforms in a hierarchy.

Exploring Pose::GetGlobalTransform

One of the things that makes the `GetGlobalTransform` function of the `Pose` class is that it always calculates the world transform. Consider a situation where you request the world transform of a node, then immediately after, the world transform of its parent node. The original request calculates and uses the world transform of the parent node, but as soon as the next request is made, that same transform is calculated again.

The solution to this is to add two new arrays to the `Pose` class. One is a vector of world space transforms and the other contains dirty flags. Any time a joint's local transform is set, the dirty flag of the joint needs to be set to `true`.

When a world transform is requested, the dirty flag of the transform and all its parents is checked. If there is a dirty transform in that chain, the world transform is re-calculated. If the dirty flag is not set, the cached world transform is returned.

You will not implement this optimization in this chapter. This optimization adds a significant amount of memory to each instance of the `Pose` class. Except for cases of inverse kinematics, the `GetGlobalTransform` function is rarely used. For skinning, the `GetMatrixPalette` function is used to retrieve world space matrices and that function is already optimized.

Summary

In this chapter, you explored how to optimize an animation system for several scenarios. These optimizations reduce the number of uniforms that a vertex skinning shader requires, speeding up the sampling of animations with many keyframes and generating the matrix palette of a pose faster.

Keep in mind that there is no one-size-fits-all solution. If all the animations in a game have a few keyframes, the added overhead of optimizing animation sampling with a lookup table might not be worth the additional memory. However, changing the sampling function to use a binary search might be worth it. Similar pros and cons exist for each optimization strategy; you must pick what makes sense for your particular use case.

When looking at the sample code for this chapter, `Chapter11/Sample00` contains the code for this chapter in its entirety. `Chapter11/Sample01` shows how to use pre-skinned meshes, `Chapter11/Sample02` shows how to use the `FastTrack` class for faster sampling, and `Chapter11/Sample03` shows how to rearrange bones for faster palette generation.

In the next chapter, you will explore how to blend animations to switch between two animations smoothly. The chapter will also explore the blending techniques for modifying existing animations by additive blending.

12
Blending between Animations

The transition from one animation to another can be jarring. Imagine if a character is in the middle of a punch and the player decides that they want to start running. If the animation just switches from the jump clip to the run clip, the transitions will be hard and unnatural.

Animation blending can fix this by generating intermediate frames that are an average of both animations. This fade is usually short—a quarter of a second or less. The smooth animated transition generated by this short blend provides a much better looking experience.

This chapter explores how to implement animation blending and additive animation blending and how to set up a crossfade controller to manage a blend queue. The following topics will be covered:

- Pose blending
- Crossfading animations
- Additive blending

Pose blending

Animation blending is a linear blend between two poses in the local space of each joint. Think of it as a `lerp` or `mix` function but applied to an entire pose. This technique does not blend animation clips; rather, it blends the poses that these clips have been sampled into.

When blending two poses, the entire pose does not need to be blended. Assume there are two animations—a run cycle and an attack. If the player presses the attack button, the top half of the attack pose is blended in over a short period of time, maintains a weight of 1 throughout the animation, and is then blended out near the end of the animation.

This is an example of using pose blending to create a running attack animation without having to animate the legs of the attack animation. The attack animation could be blended on top of a walk cycle for a walking animation. Animation blending can be used to transition smoothly between animations or to combine multiple animations into a new one.

In the following section, you will declare a `Blend` function for the `Pose` class. This `Blend` function will linearly interpolate between two poses, similar to how a vector `lerp` works. The function needs two poses and an interpolation value, commonly represented as `t`, which has a range of 0 to 1

Declaring the Blend function

The `Blend` function takes two poses—a mix value and a root node—as arguments. When the mix value is 0, the `Blend` function returns the first pose, and when it is 1, it returns the second pose. For any values between 0 and 1, the poses are blended. The root node decides which node (and its children) of the second animation should be blended into the first animation.

To accommodate specifying a root bone to start blending from, there needs to be a way to check whether one node is in the hierarchy of another node. The `IsInHierarchy` function takes a `Pose` class, a node that is the root node, and a node that is the search node. If the search node is a descendant of the root node, the function returns `true`:

```
bool IsInHierarchy(Pose& pose, unsigned int root,
                   unsigned int search);
void Blend(Pose& output, Pose& a, Pose& b, float t, int root);
```

When blending two poses, it is assumed that the poses are similar. Similar poses have the same number of joints, and each joint has the same parent index between the poses. In the following section, you will implement the `Blend` function.

Implementing the Blend function

For blending to work, it must happen in local space, which is convenient for blending between two poses. Loop through all the joints in the input poses and interpolate between the local transforms of the joint in both poses that are being blended. For the position and scale, use the vector `lerp` function, and for the rotation, use the quaternion `nlerp` function.

To support an animation root, check whether the current transform is a descendant of the blend root. If it is, carry out the blend. If it is not, skip the blend and keep the transform values of the first input pose. Follow these steps to implement the hierarchy check and `Blend` functions:

1. To check whether one joint is the descendant of another, follow the descendant joint all the way up the hierarchy until the root node. If any of the nodes encountered in this hierarchy are the node that you are checking against, return `true`:

    ```
    bool IsInHierarchy(Pose& pose, unsigned int parent,
                       unsigned int search) {
        if (search == parent) {
            return true;
        }
        int p = pose.GetParent(search);

        while (p >= 0) {
            if (p == (int)parent) {
                return true;
            }
            p = pose.GetParent(p);
        }

        return false;
    }
    ```

2. To blend two poses together, loop through the joints of each pose. If the current joint is not in the blend root's hierarchy, don't blend it. Otherwise, blend the `Transform` objects using the `mix` function you wrote in *Chapter 5, Implementing Transforms*. The `mix` function takes quaternion neighborhooding into account:

    ```
    void Blend(Pose& output, Pose& a, Pose& b,
               float t, int root) {
        unsigned int numJoints = output.Size();
        for (unsigned int i = 0; i < numJoints; ++i) {
            if (root >= 0) {
    ```

```
        if (!IsInHierarchy(output, root, i)) {
            continue;
        }
    }

    output.SetLocalTransform(i, mix(
        a.GetLocalTransform(i),
        b.GetLocalTransform(i), t)
    );
  }
}
```

If two animations are blended using the whole hierarchy, the root argument to `Blend` will be negative. With a negative joint for the blend root, the `Blend` function skips the `IsInHierarchy` check. In the following section, you will explore how to fade between two animations for a smooth transition.

Crossfading animations

The most common use case for blending animations is crossfading between two animations. A **crossfade** is a fast blend from one animation to another. The goal of the crossfade is to hide the transition between two animations.

Once a crossfade is done, the active animation needs to be replaced by the animation that you are fading to. If you are fading to multiple animations, they are all evaluated. The ones that end the soonest are removed first. Animations that are requested are added to a list, and animations that have faded out are removed from the list.

In the following section, you will build a `CrossFadeController` class that takes care of the crossfade logic. This class provides a simple intuitive API that makes fading between animations simple with just one function call.

Creating helper classes

When fading an animation into an already-sampled pose, you need to know what the animation being faded is, it's current playtime, the length of the fade durations, and the current time of the fade. These values are used to perform the actual blend and contain data about the state of the blend.

Create a new file and name it `CrossFadeTarget.h` to implement the
`CrossFadeTarget` helper class in. This helper class contains the variables described
previously. The default constructor should set the value of everything to `0`. A convenience
constructor that takes a clip pointer, pose reference, and duration is also provided:

```
struct CrossFadeTarget {
   Pose mPose;
   Clip* mClip;
   float mTime;
   float mDuration;
   float mElapsed;

   inline CrossFadeTarget()
           : mClip(0), mTime(0.0f),
             mDuration(0.0f), mElapsed(0.0f) { }
   inline CrossFadeTarget(Clip* target,Pose& pose,float dur)
           : mClip(target), mTime(target->GetStartTime()),
             mPose(pose), mDuration(dur), mElapsed(0.0f) { }
};
```

The `mPose`, `mClip`, and `mTime` variables of the `CrossFadeTarget` helper class are
used in every frame to sample the animation that is being faded to. The `mDuration` and
`mElapsed` variables are used to control how much the animation should be faded in.

In the next section, you will implement a class that controls animation playback and
fading.

Declaring the cross-fade controller

Keeping track of the currently playing clip and managing the fading is the job of a new
`CrossFadeController` class. Create a new file, `CrossFadeController.h`,
to declare the new class in. This class needs to contain a skeleton, a pose, the current
playback time, and an animation clip. It also needs a vector of the `CrossFadeTarget`
objects that control the animation blending.

Both the `CrossFadeController` and `CrossFadeTarget` classes contain pointers
to animation clips, but they don't own these pointers. Because neither class owns the
memory for the pointers, the generated constructor, copy constructor, assignment
operator, and destructor should be fine to use.

The `CrossFadecontroller` class needs functions to set the current skeleton, retrieve the current pose, and retrieve the current clip. The current animation can be set with the `Play` function. New animations can be blended in using the `FadeTo` function. Since the `CrossFadeController` class manages animation playback, it needs an `Update` function to sample the animation clips:

```cpp
class CrossFadeController {
protected:
    std::vector<CrossFadeTarget> mTargets;
    Clip* mClip;
    float mTime;
    Pose mPose;
    Skeleton mSkeleton;
    bool mWasSkeletonSet;
public:
    CrossFadeController();
    CrossFadeController(Skeleton& skeleton);
    void SetSkeleton(Skeleton& skeleton);
    void Play(Clip* target);
    void FadeTo(Clip* target, float fadeTime);
    void Update(float dt);
    Pose& GetCurrentPose();
    Clip* GetcurrentClip();
};
```

The entire `mTargets` list is evaluated with every frame. Each animation is evaluated and blended into the currently playing animation.

In the following section, you will implement the `CrossFadeController` class.

Implementing the cross-fade controller

Create a new file, `CrossFadeController.cpp`. `CrossFadeController` is implemented in this new file. Follow these steps to implement `CrossFadeController`:

1. In the default constructor, set a default value of 0 for the current clip and time and mark the skeleton as not set. There is a convenience constructor that takes a skeleton reference. The convenience constructor should call the `SetSkeleton` function:

```cpp
CrossFadeController::CrossFadeController() {
    mClip = 0;
    mTime = 0.0f;
    mWasSkeletonSet = false;
```

```
    }

CrossFadeController::CrossFadeController(Skeleton&
skeleton) {
    mClip = 0;
    mTime = 0.0f;
    SetSkeleton(skeleton);
}
```

2. Implement the `SetSkeleton` function, which copies the provided skeleton into `CrossFadeController`. It marks the class as having its skeleton set and copies the rest pose into the internal pose of the crossfade controller:

```
void CrossFadeController::SetSkeleton(
                           Skeleton& skeleton) {
    mSkeleton = skeleton;
    mPose = mSkeleton.GetRestPose();
    mWasSkeletonSet = true;
}
```

3. Implement the `Play` function. This function should clear any active crossfades. It should set the clip and playback time, but it also needs to reset the current pose to the rest pose of the skeleton:

```
void CrossFadeController::Play(Clip* target) {
    mTargets.clear();
    mClip = target;
    mPose = mSkeleton.GetRestPose();
    mTime = target->GetStartTime();
}
```

4. Implement the `FadeTo` function, which should check whether the requested fade target is valid. A fade target is only valid if it is not the first or last item in the fade list. Assuming these conditions are met, the `FadeTo` function adds the provided animation clip and duration to the fade list:

```
void CrossFadeController::FadeTo(Clip* target,
                                 float fadeTime) {
    if (mClip == 0) {
        Play(target);
        return;
    }

    if (mTargets.size() >= 1) {
```

```
        Clip* clip=mTargets[mTargets.size()-1].mClip;
        if (clip == target) {
            return;
        }
    }
    else {
        if (mClip == target) {
            return;
        }
    }

    mTargets.push_back(CrossFadeTarget(target,
            mSkeleton.GetRestPose(), fadeTime));
}
```

5. Implement the Update function to play the active animation and blend in any other animations that are in the fade list:

```
void CrossFadeController::Update(float dt) {
    if (mClip == 0 || !mWasSkeletonSet) {
        return;
    }
```

6. Set the current animation as the target animation and remove the fade object if an animation has finished fading. Only one target is removed per frame. If you want to remove all the faded-out targets, change the loop to go backward:

```
    unsigned int numTargets = mTargets.size();
    for (unsigned int i = 0; i < numTargets; ++i) {
        float duration = mTargets[i].mDuration;
        if (mTargets[i].mElapsed >= duration) {
            mClip = mTargets[i].mClip;
            mTime = mTargets[i].mTime;
            mPose = mTargets[i].mPose;
            mTargets.erase(mTargets.begin() + i);
            break;
        }
    }
```

7. Blend the fade list with the current animation. The current animation and all the animations in the fade list will need to be sampled:

```
    numTargets = mTargets.size();
    mPose = mSkeleton.GetRestPose();
    mTime = mClip->Sample(mPose, mTime + dt);
```

```
        for (unsigned int i = 0; i < numTargets; ++i) {
            CrossFadeTarget& target = mTargets[i];
            target.mTime = target.mClip->Sample(
                        target.mPose, target.mTime + dt);

            target.mElapsed += dt;
            float t = target.mElapsed / target.mDuration;
            if (t > 1.0f) { t = 1.0f; }
            Blend(mPose, mPose, target.mPose, t, -1);
        }
    }
```

8. Finish the `CrossFadeController` class implementation with the
    `GetCurrentPose` and `GetCurrentclip` helper functions. These
    are simple getter functions:

```
    Pose& CrossFadeController::GetCurrentPose() {
        return mPose;
    }

    Clip* CrossFadeController::GetcurrentClip() {
        return mClip;
    }
```

Instead of manually controlling what animation is playing, you can now create
an instance of `CrossFadeController` to control animation playback. The
`CrossFadeController` class automatically fades to new animations when you start
playing them. In the next section, you will explore additive animation blending.

Additive blending

Additive animations are used to modify an animation by adding in extra joint movements.
A common example is leaning left. If there is a leaning-left animation that simply bends
the character's spine, it can be added to a walking animation to create a leaning-left-while-
walking animation, a running animation, or any other kind of animation.

Not all animations are a good fit for additive animations. Additive animations are usually
specifically made. I have added a `Lean_Left` animation to the `Woman.gltf` file
provided with the sample code for this chapter. This animation is made to be additive.
It only bends one of the spine joints.

Additive animations typically don't play according to time, but rather, according to some other input. Think of leaning left as an example—it should be controlled by the user's joystick. The closer the joystick is to the left, the further in the animation the lean should go. It's common to sync the playback of additive animations to something other than time.

Declaring additive animations

The functions for additive blending are declared in `Blending.h`. The first function, `MakeAditivePose`, samples the additive clip at time 0 into an output pose. This output pose is the reference that is used to add two poses together.

The `Add` function performs the additive blending process between two poses. The additive blending formula is *result pose = input pose + (additive pose – additive base pose)*. The first two arguments, which are the output pose and the input pose, can point to the same pose. To apply an additive pose, both the additive pose and a reference for the additive pose are needed:

```
Pose MakeAdditivePose(Skeleton& skeleton, Clip& clip);
void Add(Pose& output, Pose& inPose, Pose& addPose,
        Pose& additiveBasePose, int blendroot);
```

The `MadeAdditivePose` helper function generates the additive base pose that the `Add` function takes for its fourth argument. The function is intended to be called during initialization time. In the next section, you will implement these functions.

Implementing additive animations

Implement the `MakeAdditivePose` function in `Blending.cpp`. This function is only intended to be called during load time. It should sample the provided clip at the start time of the clip. The result of that sample is the additive base pose:

```
Pose MakeAdditivePose(Skeleton& skeleton, Clip& clip) {
    Pose result = skeleton.GetRestPose();
    clip.Sample(result, clip.GetStartTime());
    return result;
}
```

The formula for additive blending is *result pose = input pose + (additive pose – additive base pose)*. The subtraction of the additive base pose only applies the delta of the additive animation between the first and current frames of the animation. Because of this, you can only animate one bone, say, one of the spine bones, and achieve an effect that makes the character lean left.

To implement additive blending, loop through every joint of the pose. As with regular animation blending, there is a `blendroot` parameter that needs to be considered. Follow the provided formula using the local transform of each joint:

```
void Add(Pose& output, Pose& inPose, Pose& addPose,
         Pose& basePose, int blendroot) {
   unsigned int numJoints = addPose.Size();
   for (int i = 0; i < numJoints; ++i) {
      Transform input = inPose.GetLocalTransform(i);
      Transform additive = addPose.GetLocalTransform(i);
      Transform additiveBase=basePose.GetLocalTransform(i);

      if (blendroot >= 0 &&
          !IsInHierarchy(addPose, blendroot, i)) {
        continue;
      }

      // outPose = inPose + (addPose - basePose)
      Transform result(input.position +
          (additive.position - additiveBase.position),
           normalized(input.rotation *
           (inverse(additiveBase.rotation) *
           additive.rotation)),
           input.scale + (additive.scale -
           additiveBase.scale)
      );
      output.SetLocalTransform(i, result);
   }
}
```

> **Important information**
>
> Quaternions don't have a subtraction operator. To remove the rotation of quaternion A from quaternion B, multiply B by the inverse of A. The inverse of a quaternion applies the opposite of a rotation, which is why a quaternion multiplied by its inverse results in the identity.

Additive animations are most often used to create new animation variants—for example, mixing a walking animation with a crouching pose to create a crouched walk. All animations can be additively blended with the crouched pose to create crouching versions of the animations programmatically.

Summary

In this chapter, you learned how to blend multiple animations. Blended animations can blend the whole hierarchy or just a subset. You also built a system to manage the fading between animations when a new animation plays. We also covered additive animations, which can be used to create a new motion when given the joint angles to interpolate between.

There are four samples included in the downloadable materials for this chapter. Sample00 is all the code up to this point in the book. Sample01 demonstrates how to use the Blend function by blending between a walk and a run animation on a timer. Sample02 demonstrates the use of the cross-fade controller by crossfading to random animations and Sample03 demonstrates how to use additive animation blending.

In the next chapter, you will learn about inverse kinematics. Inverse kinematics allows you to figure out how the limb of a character should be bent according to where its ends are. Think about pinning the foot of a character onto uneven terrain.

13
Implementing Inverse Kinematics

Inverse Kinematics (**IK**) is the process of solving how a set of joints should be oriented to reach a specified point in world space. For example, you could specify a point for a character to touch. By using IK, you can figure out how to rotate the character's shoulder, elbow, and wrist in a way that the character's finger is always touching a specific point.

There are two algorithms commonly used for IK, that is, CCD and FABRIK. Both will be covered in this chapter. By the end of this chapter, you should be able to do the following:

- Understand how CCD IK works
- Implement a CCD solver
- Understand how FABRIK works
- Implement a FABRIK solver
- Implement ball-and-socket constraints
- Implement hinge constraints
- Understand where and how IK solvers fit into an animation pipeline

Creating a CCD solver

In this section, you will learn about and implement the CCD IK algorithm. **CCD** stands for **Cyclic Coordinate Descent**. This algorithm can be used to pose a chain of joints in a way that the last joint on the chain comes as close as possible to touching a target. You will be able to use CCD to create limb and other IK systems where a chain needs to be solved using a target point.

There are three important concepts for CCD. First, there is the **goal**, the point in space you are trying to touch. Next is the **IK chain**, which is a list of all of the joints that will need to rotate to reach the goal. Finally, there is the **end effector**, which is the last joint in the chain (the one that needs to touch the goal).

With a goal, chain, and end effector, the CCD algorithm in pseudocode looks like this:

```
// Loop through all joints in the chain in reverse,
// starting with the joint before the end effecor
foreach joint in ikchain.reverse() {
    // Find a vector from current joint to end effector
    jointToEffector = effector.position - joint.position
    // Find a vector from the current joint to the goal
    jointToGoal = goal.position - joint.position
    // Rotate the joint so the joint to effector vector
    // matches the orientation of the joint to goal vector
    joint.rotation = fromToRotation(jointToEffector,
                        jointToGoal) * joint.rotation
}
```

The CCD algorithm looks simple but how does it work? Start with the joint right before the effector. Rotating the effector would have no effect on the chain. Find a vector from the joint before the effector to the target, and then a vector from the joint to the effector. Rotate the joint in question so that the two vectors line up. Repeat for each joint until the base joint:

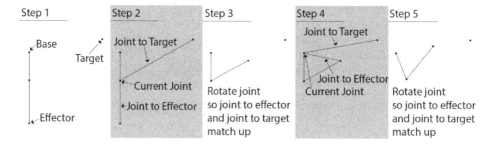

Figure 13.1: Visualizing the CCD algorithm

Looking at *Figure 13.1*, the end effector does not touch the target. Why not? CCD is an iterative algorithm and the preceding steps describe one iteration. Multiple iterations per frame are needed to achieve convergence. In the following sections, we will learn how to declare the CCD solver, which will lead us to the implementation of the `CCDSolver` class.

Declaring the CCD solver

In this section, you will declare the CCD solver. This will give you a chance to familiarize yourself with the API and understand how the class works at a high level before diving into the implementation.

Create a new file, `CCDSolver.h`, that the `CCDSolver` class will be declared in this file. The `CCDSolver` class should contain a vector of transforms that make up the IK chain. Assume that the IK chain has a parent-child relationship where every index is the child of the index before it, making 0 our root node. As such, every transform in the IK chain is declared in local space. Follow these steps to declare the CCD IK solver:

1. Begin by declaring the `CCDSolver` class with three variables: a list of transforms to form the IK chain, the number of iterations to perform, and some small delta that can be used to control how close the target has to be to the goal before the chain is considered solved. Declare the default constructor as well:

    ```
    class CCDSolver {
    protected:
        std::vector<Transform> mIKChain;
        unsigned int mNumSteps;
        float mThreshold;
    public:
        CCDSolver();
    ```

2. Implement getter and setter functions for the size of the IK chain, the number of steps, and the threshold values. Declare which `[] operator` is to be used to get and set local joint transform. Declare the `GetGlobalTransform` function, which will return the global transform of a joint:

    ```
    unsigned int Size();
    void Resize(unsigned int newSize);

    Transform& operator[](unsigned int index);
    Transform GetGlobalTransform(unsigned int index);
    ```

```
    unsigned int GetNumSteps();
    void SetNumSteps(unsigned int numSteps);

    float GetThreshold();
    void SetThreshold(float value);
```

3. Declare the `Solve` function, which will be called to solve the IK chain. A transform is provided, but only the position component of the transform is ever used. The `Solve` function returns `true` if the chain was solved, otherwise, it returns `false`:

```
    bool Solve(const Transform& target);
};
```

The `mNumSteps` variable is used to make sure the solver doesn't fall into an infinite loop. There is no guarantee that the end effector will ever reach the goal. Limiting the number of iterations helps to avoid a potential infinite loop. In the following section, you will start to implement the CCD solver.

Implementing the CCD solver

Create a new file, `CCDSolver.cpp`, in which to implement the CCD solver. Follow these steps to implement the CCD solver:

1. Define the default constructor to assign values to the number of steps and the threshold. Use a small threshold such as `0.0001f`. Use `15` for the default number of steps:

```
CCDSolver::CCDSolver() {
    mNumSteps = 15;
    mThreshold = 0.00001f;
}
```

2. Implement the `Size` and `Resize` functions, which control the size of the IK chain, and `[] operator` contains the value of each joint in the chain:

```
unsigned int CCDSolver::Size() {
    return mIKChain.size();
}

void CCDSolver::Resize(unsigned int newSize) {
    mIKChain.resize(newSize);
}

Transform& CCDSolver::operator[](unsigned int index) {
```

```
        return mIKChain[index];
    }
```

3. Implement getter and setter functions for the number of steps and the threshold that the solver contains:

```
unsigned int CCDSolver::GetNumSteps() {
    return mNumSteps;
}

void CCDSolver::SetNumSteps(unsigned int numSteps) {
    mNumSteps = numSteps;
}

float CCDSolver::GetThreshold() {
    return mThreshold;
}

void CCDSolver::SetThreshold(float value) {
    mThreshold = value;
}
```

4. Implement the GetGlobalTransform function, which probably looks familiar. It concatenates the transform of the specified joint with the transform of all of its parent joints and returns the global transform of the specified joint:

```
Transform CCDSolver::GetGlobalTransform(unsigned int x) {
    unsigned int size = (unsigned int)mIKChain.size();
    Transform world = mIKChain[x];
    for (int i = (int) x - 1; i >= 0; --i) {
        world = combine(mIKChain[i], world);
    }
    return world;
}
```

5. Implement the `Solve` function by making sure the size of the chain is valid and storing local variables for the index of the last element and the vector of the target position:

```
bool CCDSolver::Solve(const Transform& target) {
    unsigned int size = Size();
    if (size == 0) { return false; }
    unsigned int last = size - 1;
    float thresholdSq = mThreshold * mThreshold;
    vec3 goal = target.position;
```

6. Loop from 0 to `mNumSteps` to perform the correct number of iterations. On every iteration, get the position of the end effector and check whether it's close enough to the goal. If it is close enough, return early:

```
for (unsigned int i = 0; i < mNumSteps; ++i) {
    vec3 effector = GetGlobalTransform(last).
position;
        if (lenSq(goal - effector) < thresholdSq) {
            return true;
        }
```

7. In each iteration, loop through the entire IK chain. Start the iteration at `size - 2`; since `size - 1` is the last element, rotating the last element has no effect on any bones:

```
for (int j = (int)size - 2; j >= 0; --j) {
```

8. For each joint in the IK chain, get the world transform of the joint. Find a vector from the position of the joint to the position of the end effector. Find another vector from the position of the current joint to the position of the goal:

```
effector=GetGlobalTransform(last).position;

        Transform world = GetGlobalTransform(j);
        vec3 position = world.position;
        quat rotation = world.rotation;

        vec3 toEffector = effector - position;
        vec3 toGoal = goal - position;
```

9. Next, find a quaternion that rotates from the position to effector vector to the position to goal vector. There is an edge case in which the vector pointing to the effector or to the goal could be a zero vector:

```
quat effectorToGoal;
if (lenSq(toGoal) > 0.00001f) {
    effectorToGoal = fromTo(toEffector,
                             toGoal);
}
```

10. Use this vector to rotate the joint into the correct orientation in the world space. Rotate the world space orientation of the joint by the inverse of the joint's previous world rotation to move the quaternion back into the joint space:

```
quat worldRotated =rotation *
                    effectorToGoal;
quat localRotate = worldRotated *
                   inverse(rotation);
mIKChain[j].rotation = localRotate *
                       mIKChain[j].rotation;
```

11. As the joint moves, check how close the end effector moved to the goal at each iteration. If it's close enough, return early from the function, with a value of `true`:

```
effector=GetGlobalTransform(last).position;
if (lenSq(goal - effector) < thresholdSq) {
    return true;
}
        }
    }
```

12. If the goal wasn't reached, the IK chain can't be solved, at least not in the number of iterations specified. Simply return `false` to signal that the function failed to reach its target:

```
    return false;
} // End CCDSolver::Solve function
```

This CCD solver can be used to solve a single chain that has one origin and one end effector. There are more advanced ways of handling IK chains where a single chain could have multiple end effectors. However, those are much less common due to the additional implementation complexity. In the next section, you will start to explore a different IK algorithm, FABRIK.

Creating a FABRIK solver

FABRIK (Forward And Backward Reaching Inverse Kinematics) has a more natural, humanoid looking convergence. Like CCD, FABRIK works with an IK chain that has a base, end effector, and target to reach for. Unlike CCD, FABRIK works with positions, not rotations. The FABRIK algorithm is easier to understand since it can be implemented using only vectors.

In many ways, FABRIK can be used as a drop-in replacement for CCD. Both algorithms address the same problem, but they take different approaches to address it. FABRIK tends to converge faster and look better for humanoid animation, so you will probably use it as the solver for character limbs.

Working with positions instead of rotations will not work well when it comes to humanoid rigs, which need to be animated by rotating joints. This can be solved by adding a pre- and post-process step to the algorithm. The pre-process step will convert all transforms in the IK chain into world space position vectors. The post-process step will convert those vectors into rotation data.

The FABRIK algorithm has two parts. First, iterate backward from the end effector to the base. When iterating backward, move the effector to the target. Next, move every bone so they are relative to the effector; this will keep the chain intact. Next, move the base back to its original position and move every bone relative to the base so the chain stays intact.

In pseudocode, the FABRIK algorithm looks like this:

```
void Iterate(const Transform& goal) {
    startPosition = chain[0]
    // Iterate backwards
    chain[size - 1] = goal.position;
    for (i = size - 2; i >= 0; --i) {
        current = chain[i]
        next = chain[i + 1]
        direction = normalize(current - next)
        offset = direction * length[i + 1]
        chain[i] = next + offset
    }

    // Iterate forwards
    chain[0] = startPosition
    for (i  = 1; i < size; ++i) {
        current = chain[i]
        prev = chain[i - 1]
        direction = normalize(current - prev)
        offset = direction * length[i]
```

```
        chain[i] = prev + offset
    }
}
```

To visualize FABRIK, set the end effector to where the target is. Find a vector from the end effector to the last joint. Move the last joint to be along this vector, maintaining its distance to the end effector. Repeat for each joint until the base is reached. This will move the base joint out of position.

To do the forward iteration, put the base back to where it should be. Find a vector to the next joint. Place the next joint on this vector, maintaining its distance to the base. Repeat this all of the way down the chain:

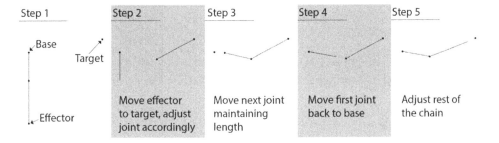

Figure 13.2: Visualizing the FABRIK algorithm

Both FABRIK and CCD will try to solve an IK chain, but they converge on the goal differently. CCD tends to curl, while FABRIK tends to stretch. FABRIK usually generates more natural results for humanoid animation. In the following section, you will start to declare the FABRIKSolver class, followed by the implementation of the class.

Declaring the FABRIK solver

The FABRIK solver will need more memory to run since it has to convert local joint transformations into global positions. The algorithm can be broken down into several steps that can all be implemented as protected helper functions.

Create a new file, FABRIKSolver.h. This file will be used to declare the FABRIKSolver class. Follow these steps to declare the FABRIKSolver class:

1. Begin by declaring the FABRIKSolver class, which needs to keep track of the IK chain, the maximum number of steps, and some distance threshold. Declare a vector of world space positions and a vector of joint lengths. These vectors are needed because the FABRIK algorithm does not take rotations into account:

```
class FABRIKSolver {
protected:
    std::vector<Transform> mIKChain;
    unsigned int mNumSteps;
    float mThreshold;
    std::vector<vec3> mWorldChain;
    std::vector<float> mLengths;
```

2. Declare helper functions to copy the IK chain into the world position vector, to iterate forward, to iterate backward, and to copy the final world positions back into the IK chain:

```
protected:
    void IKChainToWorld();
    void IterateForward(const vec3& goal);
    void IterateBackward(const vec3& base);
    void WorldToIKChain();
```

3. Declare a default constructor, getter and setter functions for the size of the chain, the number of iterations to solve the chain, and the epsilon value of how far the end joint needs to be from the target:

```
public:
    FABRIKSolver();

    unsigned int Size();
    void Resize(unsigned int newSize);

    unsigned int GetNumSteps();
    void SetNumSteps(unsigned int numSteps);

    float GetThreshold();
    void SetThreshold(float value);
```

4. Declare getter and setter functions for the local transforms stored in the IK chain. Declare a function to retrieve the global transform of a joint. Finally, declare the `Solve` function, which solves the IK chain when given a target:

```
Transform GetLocalTransform(unsigned int index);
void SetLocalTransform(unsigned int index,
                                const Transform& t);
Transform GetGlobalTransform(unsigned int index);

bool Solve(const Transform& target);
};
```

The FABRIK algorithm is a little more complicated to implement than the CCD algorithm was, but the steps are easier to break down into functions. In the following section, you will start to implement the functions of the `FABRIKSolver` class.

Implementing the FABRIK solver

The FABRIK algorithm works on world space positions. This means, for each iteration, the IK chain will need to convert local joint transformations into world positions and store the result. After the chain is solved, the world positions vector will need to be converted back into relative offsets and stored back in the IK chain.

Create a new file, `FABRIKSolver.cpp`; the `FABRIKSolver` class will be implemented in this file. Follow these steps to implement the `FABRIKSolver` class:

1. Implement the constructor of the `FABRIKSolver` class. It needs to set the number of steps and the threshold to default values:

```
FABRIKSolver::FABRIKSolver() {
    mNumSteps = 15;
    mThreshold = 0.00001f;
}
```

2. Implement the trivial getter and setter functions for the number of steps and the threshold values:

```
unsigned int FABRIKSolver::GetNumSteps() {
    return mNumSteps;
}

void FABRIKSolver::SetNumSteps(unsigned int numSteps) {
    mNumSteps = numSteps;
}
```

```
float FABRIKSolver::GetThreshold() {
    return mThreshold;
}

void FABRIKSolver::SetThreshold(float value) {
    mThreshold = value;
}
```

3. Implement a getter and setter function for the size of the chain. The setter function needs to set the size of the chain, the world chain, and the lengths' vector:

```
unsigned int FABRIKSolver::Size() {
    return mIKChain.size();
}

void FABRIKSolver::Resize(unsigned int newSize) {
    mIKChain.resize(newSize);
    mWorldChain.resize(newSize);
    mLengths.resize(newSize);
}
```

4. Implement methods for getting and setting the local transform of an element in the IK chain:

```
Transform FABRIKSolver::GetLocalTransform(
                        unsigned int index) {
    return mIKChain[index];
}

void FABRIKSolver::SetLocalTransform(unsigned int index,
                        const Transform& t) {
    mIKChain[index] = t;
}
```

5. Implement the getter function to retrieve the global transform and concatenate all of the transforms to the root:

```
Transform FABRIKSolver::GetGlobalTransform(
                        unsigned int index) {
    unsigned int size = (unsigned int)mIKChain.size();
    Transform world = mIKChain[index];
    for (int i = (int)index - 1; i >= 0; --i) {
        world = combine(mIKChain[i], world);
    }
```

```
        return world;
    }
```

6. Implement the `IKChainToWorld` function, which will copy the IK chain into the world transform vector and record the segment lengths. The lengths array stores the distance of a joint from its parent. This means that the root joint will always contain the length 0. For non-root joints, the distance at the `i` index is the distance between the joints `i` and `i-1`:

```
void FABRIKSolver::IKChainToWorld() {
    unsigned int size = Size();
    for (unsigned int i = 0; i < size; ++i) {
        Transform world = GetGlobalTransform(i);
        mWorldChain[i] = world.position;

        if (i >= 1) {
            vec3 prev = mWorldChain[i - 1];
            mLengths[i] = len(world.position - prev);
        }
    }
    if (size > 0) {
        mLengths[0] = 0.0f;
    }
}
```

7. Implement the `WorldToIKChain` function next, which will convert the world position IK chain back into local space transforms. Loop through all of the joints. For each joint, find the world space transform of the current joint and the next one. Cache the world space position and rotation of the current joint:

```
void FABRIKSolver::WorldToIKChain() {
    unsigned int size = Size();
    if (size == 0) { return; }

    for (unsigned int i = 0; i < size - 1; ++i) {
        Transform world = GetGlobalTransform(i);
        Transform next = GetGlobalTransform(i + 1);
        vec3 position = world.position;
        quat rotation = world.rotation;
```

8. Create a vector that points from the current joint to the next one. This is the rotation between the current node and the next node:

```
vec3 toNext = next.position - position;
toNext = inverse(rotation) * toNext;
```

9. Construct a vector that points from the world space IK chain of the next joint to the current position. This is the rotation between the current node and the desired position of the next node:

```
vec3 toDesired = mWorldChain[i + 1] - position;
toDesired = inverse(rotation) * toDesired;
```

10. Align these two vectors by using the fromTo quaternion function. Apply the final delta rotation to the current joint's IK chain rotation:

```
        quat delta = fromTo(toNext, toDesired);
        mIKChain[i].rotation = delta *
                                mIKChain[i].rotation;

    }
}
```

11. Next, implement the IterateBackward function, which sets the last element in the chain to be at the goal. This breaks the IK chain. Adjust all other joints using the stored distanced so that the chain remains intact. After this function executes, the end effector is always at the goal and the initial joint is probably no longer at the base:

```
void FABRIKSolver::IterateBackward(const vec3& goal) {
    int size = (int)Size();
    if (size > 0) {
        mWorldChain[size - 1] = goal;
    }

    for (int i = size - 2; i >= 0; --i) {
        vec3 direction = normalized(mWorldChain[i] -
                                mWorldChain[i + 1]);
        vec3 offset = direction * mLengths[i + 1];
        mWorldChain[i] = mWorldChain[i + 1] + offset;
    }
}
```

12. Implement the `IterateForward` function. This function rearranges the IK chain so that the first link starts at the origin of the chain. This function needs to set the initial joint to be at the base, and it iterates through all other joints, adjusting them to keep the IK chain intact. After this function executes, the end effector might be at the goal if the chain is solvable and has sufficient iterations:

```
void FABRIKSolver::IterateForward(const vec3& base) {
    unsigned int size = Size();
    if (size > 0) {
        mWorldChain[0] = base;
    }

    for (int i = 1; i < size; ++i) {
        vec3 direction = normalized(mWorldChain[i] -
                                    mWorldChain[i - 1]);
        vec3 offset = direction * mLengths[i];
        mWorldChain[i] = mWorldChain[i - 1] + offset;
    }
}
```

13. Start to implement the `Solve` function by copying the IK chain into the world positions vector and fill out the lengths vector. This can be done with the `IKChainToWorld` helper function. Cache the base and goal positions:

```
bool FABRIKSolver::Solve(const Transform& target) {
    unsigned int size = Size();
    if (size == 0) { return false; }
    unsigned int last = size - 1;
    float thresholdSq = mThreshold * mThreshold;

    IKChainToWorld();
    vec3 goal = target.position;
    vec3 base = mWorldChain[0];
```

14. Iterate from `0` to `mNumSteps`. For each iteration, check whether the goal and end effector are close enough for the chain to be solved. If they are, copy the world positions back into the chain with the `WorldToIKChain` helper function and return early. If they are not close enough, do the iteration by calling the `IterateBackward` and `IterateForward` methods:

```
for (unsigned int i = 0; i < mNumSteps; ++i) {
    vec3 effector = mWorldChain[last];
    if (lenSq(goal - effector) < thresholdSq) {
        WorldToIKChain();
```

```
                return true;
        }

        IterateBackward(goal);
        IterateForward(base);
}
```

15. After the iteration loop, copy the world positions vector back into the IK chain regardless of whether the solver was able to solve the chain. Check one last time whether the end effector has reached its goal, and return the appropriate Boolean:

```
WorldToIKChain();
vec3 effector = GetGlobalTransform(last).position;
if (lenSq(goal - effector) < thresholdSq) {
    return true;
}

return false;
}
```

The FABRIK algorithm is popular because it tends to converge on the end goal fast, the results look good for humanoid characters, and the algorithm is easy to implement. In the next section, you will learn how to add constraints to either the FABRIK or CCD solver.

Implementing constraints

Both CCD and FABRIK solvers produce good results, but neither produces predictable results. In this section, you will learn what constraints are, where the IK solver constraints can be applied, and how to apply constraints. This will let you build much more realistic IK solvers.

Consider an IK chain that is supposed to represent a leg. You would want to make sure that the motion of each joint is predictable, for example, the knee should probably not bend forward.

This is where constraints are useful. The knee joint is a hinge; if a hinge constraint is applied, the leg IK chain will look more realistic. Using constraints, you can set rules for each joint in an IK chain.

The following steps will show you where to apply constraints in both the CCD and FABRIK solvers:

1. Constraints can be applied to both CCD and FABRIK solvers, and they must be applied after each iteration. For CCD, this means inserting a bit of code here:

```
bool CCDSolver::Solve(const vec3& goal) {
    // Local variables and size check
    for (unsigned int i = 0; i < mNumSteps; ++i) {
        // Check if we've reached the goal
        for (int j = (int)size - 2; j >= 0; --j) {
            // Iteration logic
            // -> APPLY CONSTRAINTS HERE!
            effector = GetGlobalTransform(last).position;
            if (lenSq(goal - effector) < thresholdSq) {
                return true;
            }
        }
    }
    // Last goal check
}
```

2. Applying constraints to the FABRIK solver is more complex. The constraint is applied to each iteration, and the IK chain needs to be converted between the world position chain and IK chain on every iteration. Apply constraints every iteration after copying the data to the transform chain:

```
bool FABRIKSolver::Solve(const vec3& goal) {
    // Local variables and size check
    IKChainToWorld();
    vec3 base = mWorldChain[0];

    for (unsigned int i = 0; i < mNumSteps; ++i) {
        // Check if we've reached the goal
        IterateBackward(goal);
        IterateForward(base);
        WorldToIKChain();//NEW, NEEDED FOR CONSTRAINTS
        // -> APPLY CONSTRAINTS HERE!
        IKChainToWorld();//NEW, NEEDED FOR CONSTRAINTS
    }
    // Last goal check
}
```

The reason that the `Solve` function is virtual is so you can extend each of the `IKChain` classes into specific types of chains such as `LegIKChain` or `ArmIKChain` and add the constraint code to the solve method directly. In the following sections, you will explore common types of constraints.

Ball-and-socket constraint

Bal- and-socket joints work like a shoulder joint. The joint can rotate on all three axes, but there is an angle constraint preventing it from rotating freely. *Figure 13.3* shows what a ball-and-socket constraint looks like visually:

Figure 13.3: A ball-and-socket constraint visualized

To build a ball-and-socket constraint, you need to know the rotation of both the current joint and its parent. You can construct forward vectors from these quaternions and check the angle of the forward vectors. If the angle is greater than a provided limit, the rotation needs to be adjusted.

To limit the rotation, find the rotation axis. The cross product between the two forward directions is perpendicular to both; this is the rotation axis. Create a quaternion that brings the angle limit along this axis into the local space of the current joint and set that quaternion to be the rotation of the joint:

```
void ApplyBallSocketConstraint(int i, float limit) {
    quat parentRot = i == 0 ? mOffset.rotation :
                    GetWorldTransform(i - 1).rotation;
    quat thisRot = GetWorldTransform(i).rotation;

    vec3 parentDir = parentRot * vec3(0, 0, 1);
    vec3 thisDir = thisRot * vec3(0, 0, 1);
    float angle = ::angle(parentDir, thisDir);

    if (angle > limit * QUAT_DEG2RAD) {
        vec3 correction = cross(parentDir, thisDir);
```

```
        quat worldSpaceRotation = parentRot *
            angleAxis(limit * QUAT_DEG2RAD, correction);
        mChain[i].rotation = worldSpaceRotation *
                              inverse(parentRot);
    }
}
```

The ball-and-socket constraint is usually applied to the hip or shoulder joints of a character. These also tend to be the root joints for the limb IK chains. In the next section, you will explore another type of constraint, that is, the hinge constraint.

Hinge constraint

The hinge constraint is like an elbow or a knee. It only allows for rotation on one specific axis. *Figure 13.4* demonstrates what a hinge joint looks like visually:

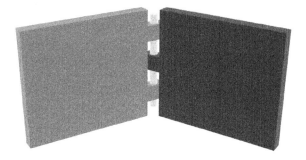

Figure 13.4: A hinge constraint visualized

To implement a hinge constraint, you need to know the world space rotation of the current joint and the parent joint. Multiply the axis normal by both rotation quaternions and find a quaternion between the two; this is the amount you need to rotate to constrain the joint to an axis. Bring this rotation back into the joint space and apply the rotation:

```
void ApplyHingeSocketConstraint(int i, vec3 axis) {
    Transform joint = GetWorldTransform(i);
    Transform parent = GetWorldTransform(i - 1);

    vec3 currentHinge = joint.rotation * axis;
    vec3 desiredHinge = parent.rotation * axis;

    mChain[i].rotation = mChain[i].rotation *
                         fromToRotation(currentHinge,
                                        desiredHinge);
}
```

Hinge constraints are often used for elbow or knee joints. In the following section, you will explore how to use IK to align a character's feet to the ground.

Using IK to align a character's feet to the ground

In this section, you will learn how IK can be used to modify an animation so it looks more correct. Specifically, you will learn how to use IK to stop a character's feet from going through the ground when walking over uneven surfaces.

Now that you can solve IK chains using CCD or FABRIK, let's explore how these solvers can be used. There are two common uses for IK, that is, to position hands or to position feet. In this section, you will explore what it takes to clamp a character's foot to the ground as the character is walking.

To solve foot clamping, you could check the last global position of the foot against the current global position. If the foot motion hits anything on the way, pin the foot to the ground. Even the most trivial solutions have edge cases: what happens if the up motion is too far away? At what point in the animation cycle can we interpolate between pinned and non-pinned positions?

To make implementation easier, the ground clamping strategy for this chapter will remain simple. First, check whether the foot is colliding with anything above it, clipping through the terrain, for example. To do this, cast a ray from the hip of the character to the ankle.

If the ray hits anything, the hit point will be the goal of the leg IK chain. If the ray does not hit anything, the current position of the character's ankle will be the goal of the leg IK chain. Next, do the same ray cast, but do not stop at the ankle of the character; just keep going.

If this ray hits anything, the hit point is a future IK goal. If the ray does not hit anything, set the future IK goal to the current IK goal. Now there are two goals, one that's in free motion and one that's pinned to the ground.

If you use the current goal, the feet of the character might snap to the ground abruptly. If you use the future goal, the character won't walk—it will just drag its feet on the ground. Instead, you have to interpolate between the two goals by some value.

The interpolation value should come from the animation itself. When the character's foot is down, the current goal should be used; when it's up, the future goal should be used. As the character's foot is being placed up or down, the goal position should `lerp`.

With the IK goal known, the IK solver can figure out how to bend the character's leg. Once the leg joints are in world space, we adjust the head of the foot to always be on the terrain following some similar steps as you did to solve the legs.

In the following sections, you will explore each of the steps described here in more detail. However, there is a bit of a catch. Most of the values that are needed are specific to the model that is being used for rendering; a different character will need values tuned differently.

Finding the foot goals

Cast a ray straight down from a bit below the hip of the character to a bit below the ankle. This ray cast should go straight down, following the position of the ankle. However, how far under the hit the ray should start and how far below the ankle it should go are model-specific:

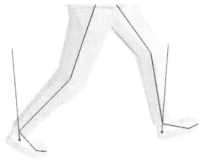

Figure 13.5: Ray cast to find the foot goal

Record the result of this ray cast regardless of how far away the hit point is. This point will be treated as the IK goal, which is always clamped to the ground. Check whether the ray has hit anything between its origin and the bottom of the ankle. If it did, that will be the ankle goal. If it did not, the ankle goal will be the position of the ankle.

It is important to keep in mind that the character's ankle is being positioned, not the bottom of its foot. Therefore, the goal point needs to be moved up by the distance of the ankle to the floor:

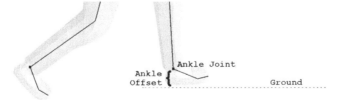

Figure 13.6: Offset to position the character's ankle

These foot goals will control how the IK system overrides the animation. When walking, and if the foot motion is not obstructed, the IK system should not be noticeable. In the next section, you will learn how to control the interpolation of the foot between the animated and the pinned goal points.

Interpolating the foot goals

To interpolate between the current and future IK goals, you will need some knowledge of the animation clip that is currently playing. Specifically, you need to know what phase the leg is in; is it grounded, being lifted, suspended, or being placed? A common way to encode this information is with a scalar curve.

The idea is to create two scalar curves, one for the left and one for the right leg. These curves correspond to the stride of the current step. For example, when the left foot is off the ground, the value of the left scalar curve needs to be 0. If the left foot is on the ground, the value of the left curve needs to be 1. The curve looks like this:

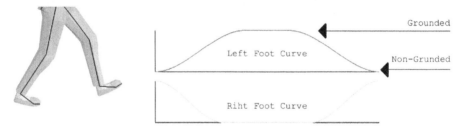

Figure 13.7: Walk cycle stride expressed as scalar curves

Sample these curves based on the current normalized playback time. The resulting value will be between 0 and 1. Use this 0 to 1 value as the blend weight when blending the non-IK adjusted animation and the IK adjusted animation together. This curve is usually authored by eye using a curve editor. The curve is specific to the animation that is currently playing.

In the next section, you will explore how to adjust the vertical placement of the IK character to avoid hyperextending limbs.

Vertical character placement

Next, the character needs to be positioned vertically so that it looks good. If the character is placed too far up, it would end up with the legs in a hyperextended state. Too low, and the IK system will bend the legs too much:

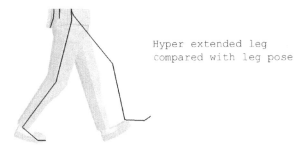

Figure 13.8: IK hyperextension compared to sampled animation

How the character is positioned is relative to how it was modeled. If the character was modeled assuming (0, 0, 0) is the center point on the ground, you can place it right on the surface below, and sink it into the surface just a bit.

The character needs to be sunk into the surface a little bit to allow the IK system to do some work and avoid hyperextension. This raises the question: what is the surface that the character's feet need to be aligned with? The alignment position can come from a collision/physics system, or in a simpler example, just a ray cast going straight down from the character.

Collision surfaces and visual surfaces are not the same. Consider a staircase: the collision geometry is usually a ramp. The display geometry is what looks like an actual staircase. In a situation like this, the character's position should be relative to the collision geometry, but the IK goals should be positioned in relation to the visual geometry.

What if there is only one geometry used for both collisions and visuals? In this scenario, place the character to either of the clamped IK goals, whichever one is lower. This will ensure that the ground is always reachable without hyperextension.

IK pass

It's time to solve the leg IK chain. Before doing this, copy joints from the animated pose into the IK solver. For each leg, copy the global transform of the hip joint into the root of the IK solver. Copy the local transform of the knee into joint 1, and the local transform of the ankle into joint 2. Then, run the IK solver. The solver will place the character's feet at the goal points, which are clamped to the ground.

Foot alignment

The clamped foot animation is smooth at this point, and the feet will no longer clip inside the ground. But only the leg of the character looks correct, not the feet. Take a look at the foot of a character on a non-flat surface—there is still a decent amount of clipping happening:

Figure 13.9: The leg is clamped to the ground, but the foot is oriented wrong

To solve this, create a toe ray. The toe ray will be positioned at the ankle joint of the character, and some distance along the forward axis of the character. This will ensure that the toe target is always looking forward, even if, in the animation, the toe is pointing down. Adjust the vertical position of the toe ray to shoot from above the knee to a little below the toe:

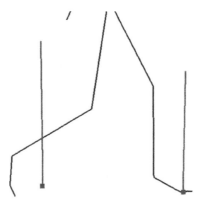

Figure 13.10: To cast the offset forward, even if the toe points down

Position the toe similar to how the leg was positioned. Find a goal that is the position of the current toe, clamped to the ground. Interpolate between the ground clamped goal and the active animation goal by the current normalized time of the animation.

This toe goal will be used to rotate the foot. Find a vector from the ankle to the current toe position. Find a vector from the ankle to the goal toe position. Create a quaternion that rotates between these two vectors. Rotate the ankle by this quaternion.

In this section, you learned how to find foot goals, interpolate between them, and use those goals and the IK system to align a character's feet to the ground. Ground alignment is just one of the use cases for IK solvers. Similar systems can be used with arms to grab things or the whole body to create a ragdoll system.

Summary

In this chapter, you implemented CCD and FABRIK IK solvers. Both solvers can solve an IK chain, but they converge differently. Which algorithm works better is very much context-dependent.

You also learned how constraints can be used to limit the range of motion for a specific joint. With the right constraints in place, an IK system modifies the current animation so that it interacts with the environment. You explored how to achieve this in the feet grounding section of this chapter.

In the downloadable content for this book, there are 4 samples for this chapter. `Sample00` contains the code up to this point. `Sample01` demonstrates how a CCD solver can be used, and `Sample02` demonstrates how a FABRIK solver can be used. `Sample03` demonstrates foot clamping and ground alignment for a character walking along a path.

In the next chapter, you will learn how dual quaternions can be used for skinning. Dual quaternion skinning better maintains the volume of a mesh than linear blended skinning when the mesh is bent or rotated.

Further reading

Other than FABRIK and CCD, IK chains are sometimes solved analytically or with Jacobian matrices:

- For more info on analytical IK solvers, check out `http://theorangeduck.com/page/simple-two-joint`.

- A complete Jacobian solver implementation is covered in *Game Programming Gems 4*.

14
Using Dual Quaternions for Skinning

The current skinning implementation blends between skin weights linearly, and this is called **Linear Blended Skinning (LBS)** or, sometimes, **Linear Skin Blending**. Linearly blending the skin does not preserve the volume of a model, which introduces skinning artifacts. An easy way to visualize this artifact is to twist one end of a rectangle by 180 degrees, as shown in the following screenshot:

Linear Skin Blending   Dual Quaternion
                                        Skin Blending

Figure 14.1: Comparing linear blended and dual quaternion skinning

An alternate to Linear Skin Blending is **Dual Quaternion Skin Blending**. When dual quaternions are used, the volume of the model is maintained. In this chapter, you will implement dual quaternion mesh skinning. By the end of this chapter, you should be able to use dual quaternions to skin an animated character. The following topics are covered in this chapter:

- Introducing dual quaternions
- Implementing dual quaternions
- Skinning with dual quaternions
- Understanding how to use dual quaternion skinning

Introducing dual quaternions

A dual quaternion combines linear and rotational transformations together into one variable. This single variable can be interpolated, transformed, and concatenated. A dual quaternion can be represented with two quaternions or eight floating-point numbers.

Dual numbers are like complex numbers. A complex number has a real part and an imaginary part, and a dual number has a real part and a dual part. Assuming ε is the dual operator, a dual number can be represented as $x = real + \varepsilon dual$, where $\varepsilon^2 = 0$ and $\varepsilon \neq 0$.

Operations on dual numbers are done as imaginary numbers, where the dual components and real components must be acted on separately. For example, dual quaternion addition can be expressed in the following way:

$$(real_a + \varepsilon dual_a) + (real_b + \varepsilon dual_b) = (real_a + real_b) + \varepsilon(dual_a + dual_b)$$

Notice how the real and dual parts are added independently.

> **Important note**
>
> If you are interested in the more formal mathematics behind dual quaternions, check out *A Beginner's Guide to Dual-Quaternions* by Ben Kenwright, at `https://cs.gmu.edu/~jmlien/teaching/cs451/uploads/Main/dual-quaternion.pdf`.

Dual quaternions are just an extension of dual numbers. The real and dual parts are represented by quaternions instead of scalar values, and most of the mathematical operations just work. In the next section, you will begin to implement dual quaternions in code.

Implementing dual quaternions

In this section, you will implement dual quaternions in code. By the end of this section, you will have implemented a dual quaternion struct, along with all the mathematical functions needed for using dual quaternions to skin a mesh.

Dual quaternions need to be implemented as structures, similar to transforms or matrices. Create two new files, `DualQuaternion.h` and `DualQuaternion.cpp`. You will implement the math relevant to dual quaternions in these files.

Start by declaring a `DualQuaternion` structure. This structure will allow you to access the data in the dual quaternion struct as two quaternions or a floating-point array of eight numbers. The constructor should set the dual quaternion to identity. The identity dual quaternion has an identity quaternion in its real part and a zero quaternion in its dual part, as illustrated in the following code block:

```
struct DualQuaternion {
    union {
        struct {
            quat real;
            quat dual;
        };
        float v[8];
    };
    inline DualQuaternion() : real(0, 0, 0, 1), dual(0, 0, 0,
0) { }
    inline DualQuaternion(const quat& r, const quat& d) :
        real(r), dual(d) { }
};
```

The real part of a dual quaternion holds rotation data, and the dual part holds position data. Dual quaternions do not handle scaling. In the following section, you will declare and implement common dual quaternion operations such as addition and multiplication.

In the *Implementing dual quaternion operations* subsection, you will implement trivial dual quaternion operators such as addition, scaling, multiplication, and comparison operators. In the *Measuring, normalizing, and inverting dual quaternions* section, you will learn how to implement the dot product for a dual quaternion, how to measure the dual quaternion, and how to invert it. In the *Converting transforms and dual quaternions* section, you will learn how to convert between the `DualQuaternion` and `Transform` structs. Finally, in the *Transforming vectors and points* section, you will learn how to transform vectors and points with dual quaternions, as transforms or matrices would.

Implementing dual quaternion operations

You will need to define some mathematical operators to work with dual quaternions. These functions are addition, scalar multiplication, dual quaternion multiplication, and equality comparison operators.

Two dual quaternions are combined through multiplication. Unlike matrices and quaternions, dual quaternions multiply left to right. Follow these steps to implement the dual quaternion operations:

1. Declare the addition, scalar multiplication, dual quaternion multiplication, and equality comparison operators in `DualQuaternion.h`, like this:

```
DualQuaternion operator+(const DualQuaternion &l,
                         const DualQuaternion &r);
DualQuaternion operator*(const DualQuaternion &dq,
                         float f);
// Multiplication order is left to right
// This is the OPPOSITE of matrices and quaternions
DualQuaternion operator*(const DualQuaternion &l,
                         const DualQuaternion &r);
bool operator==(const DualQuaternion &l,
                const DualQuaternion &r);
bool operator!=(const DualQuaternion &l,
                const DualQuaternion &r);
```

2. Implement the addition, scalar multiplication, and comparison functions. They are all component-wise operations. Perform component-wise operations separately on the real and dual components of the dual quaternion, as follows:

```
DualQuaternion operator+(const DualQuaternion &l,
                         const DualQuaternion &r) {
   return DualQuaternion(l.real+r.real,l.dual+r.dual);
}

DualQuaternion operator*(const DualQuaternion &dq,
                         float f) {
   return DualQuaternion(dq.real * f, dq.dual * f);
}

bool operator==(const DualQuaternion &l,
                const DualQuaternion &r) {
   return l.real == r.real && l.dual == r.dual;
}
```

```
bool operator!=(const DualQuaternion &l,
                const DualQuaternion &r) {
    return l.real != r.real || l.dual != r.dual;
}
```

3. Start implementing dual quaternion multiplication by first making sure both dual quaternions are normalized, as follows:

```
// Remember, multiplication order is left to right.
// This is the opposite of matrix and quaternion
// multiplication order
DualQuaternion operator*(const DualQuaternion &l, const
DualQuaternion &r) {
    DualQuaternion lhs = normalized(l);
    DualQuaternion rhs = normalized(r);
```

4. Combine the real parts of both the normalized quaternions together. The dual parts are more involved because ε^2 must equal 0. Satisfy this requirement by multiplying the dual and real sides of both quaternions and adding the results, like this:

```
    return DualQuaternion(lhs.real * rhs.real,
                          lhs.real * rhs.dual +
                          lhs.dual * rhs.real);
}
```

For the most part, the common dual quaternion operators are intuitive, but the multiplication order of dual quaternions being against convention makes them a little hard to deal with. In the next section, you will learn about the dot product and normal implementations for dual quaternions.

Measuring, normalizing, and inverting dual quaternions

The dot product measures how similar two dual quaternions are. The rules for the dual quaternion dot product are the same as the vector and quaternion dot products. The result of the dot product is a scalar value that has the following properties:

- It is positive if the dual quaternions point in the same direction.
- It is negative if the dual quaternions point in opposite directions.
- It is zero if the dual quaternions are perpendicular.

Non-unit dual quaternions can introduce an unwanted skew into the transformation represented by a dual quaternion. To normalize a dual quaternion, both the real part and dual part will need to be divided by the length of the real part.

Normalizing a dual quaternion is like normalizing a regular quaternion, operating mainly on the real part. First, find the length of the real part of the dual quaternion, then divide both the real and dual parts by the length. This normalizes both the real and dual parts to the length of the real part.

Since the dot product only considers direction, the imaginary part of the dual quaternion is not used. Find the dot product of the real parts of both dual quaternions. The dual quaternion `conjugate` operation is an extension of quaternion conjugates, to find the conjugate of both real and dual parts respectively.

Follow these steps to implement the `dot product`, `invert`, and `normalize` functions:

1. Declare the dual quaternion dot product, conjugate and normalization functions in `DualQuaternion.h`, as follows:

    ```
    float dot(const DualQuaternion& l,
              const DualQuaternion& r);
    DualQuaternion conjugate(const DualQuaternion& dq);
    DualQuaternion normalized(const DualQuaternion& dq);
    void normalize(DualQuaternion& dq);
    ```

2. Implement the dot product by finding the quaternion dot product of the real parts of both dual quaternions and returning their result, like this:

    ```
    float dot(const DualQuaternion& l,
              const DualQuaternion& r) {
        return dot(l.real, r.real);
    }
    ```

3. Implement the `conjugate` function by taking the quaternion conjugate of the real and dual parts separately, like this:

    ```
    DualQuaternion conjugate(const DualQuaternion& dq) {
        return DualQuaternion(conjugate(dq.real),
                              conjugate(dq.dual));
    }
    ```

4. Implement the `normalized` function by finding the length of the real part and scaling both the dual and real parts by the inverse of the length, as follows:

```
DualQuaternion normalized(const DualQuaternion& dq) {
    float magSq = dot(dq.real, dq.real);
    if (magSq  < 0.000001f) {
        return DualQuaternion();
    }
    float invMag = 1.0f / sqrtf(magSq);

    return DualQuaternion(dq.real * invMag,
                          dq.dual * invMag);
}
```

5. Implement a `normalize` function. Unlike `normalized`, the `normalize` function takes a dual quaternion reference and normalizes it in place, like this:

```
void normalize(DualQuaternion& dq) {
    float magSq = dot(dq.real, dq.real);
    if (magSq  < 0.000001f) {
        return;
    }
    float invMag = 1.0f / sqrtf(magSq);

    dq.real = dq.real * invMag;
    dq.dual = dq.dual * invMag;
}
```

If a dual quaternion changes over time, it might become non-normalized due to a floating-point error. If the length of the real part of the dual quaternion is not 1, the dual quaternion needs to be normalized. Instead of checking the length against one, which would involve a square root operation, you should check if the square length is 1, and this way, the operation is much faster. In the following section, you will learn how to convert between transforms and dual quaternions.

Converting transforms and dual quaternions

Dual quaternions hold similar data to transforms, without the scale component. It's possible to convert between the two, but the scale will be lost.

When converting a transform to a dual quaternion, the real part of a dual quaternion maps to the rotation of a transform. To calculate the dual part, create a pure quaternion from the translation vector of the transform. Then, multiply this pure quaternion by the rotation of the transform. The result needs to be halved—divide it by two or multiply it by 0.5.

When converting a dual quaternion to a transform, the transform rotation still maps the real part of the dual quaternion. To find the position, multiply the dual part by two and combine the result with the inverse of the transform's rotation. This yields a pure quaternion. The vector part of this pure quaternion is the new position.

Follow these steps to implement the code to convert between `Transform` and `DualQuaternion` objects:

1. Declare functions to convert a dual quaternion to a transform and a transform to a dual quaternion in `DualQuaternion.h`, as follows:

```
DualQuaternion transformToDualQuat(const Transform& t);
Transform dualQuatToTransform(const DualQuaternion& dq);
```

2. Implement the `transformToDualQuat` function. The resulting dual quaternion does not need to be normalized. The code for this can be seen in the following snippet:

```
DualQuaternion transformToDualQuat(const Transform& t) {
    quat d(t.position.x, t.position.y, t.position.z, 0);

    quat qr = t.rotation;
    quat qd = qr * d * 0.5f;

    return DualQuaternion(qr, qd);
}
```

3. Implement the `dualQuatToTransform` function. The input dual quaternion is assumed to already be normalized. The code for this can be seen in the following snippet:

```
Transform dualQuatToTransform(const DualQuaternion& dq) {
    Transform result;

    result.rotation = dq.real;

    quat d = conjugate(dq.real) * (dq.dual * 2.0f);
    result.position = vec3(d.x, d.y, d.z);
```

```
        return result;
    }
```

Dual quaternions can be converted to and from matrices as well; however, that operation is generally not used. Dual quaternions are used to replace matrices in the skinning pipeline, so the matrix conversion isn't necessary. In the following section, you will explore how a dual quaternion can transform a vector or a point.

Transforming vectors and points

Dual quaternions contain rigid transformation data. This means that dual quaternions can be used to transform vectors and points. To transform a point by a dual quaternion, break the dual quaternion down into rotation and position components, then transform the vector the same way a transform would, but without scale.

Follow these steps to declare and implement `transform` functions for both vectors and points using dual quaternions:

1. Declare the `transformVector` and `transformPoint` functions in `DualQuaternion.h`, like this:

    ```
    vec3 transformVector(const DualQuaternion& dq,
                         const vec3& v);
    vec3 transformPoint(const DualQuaternion& dq,
                        const vec3& v);
    ```

2. Rotating a vector by a dual quaternion is trivial. Since the real part of the dual quaternion contains the rotation, multiply the vector by the real part of the dual quaternion, as follows:

    ```
    vec3 transformVector(const DualQuaternion& dq,
                         const vec3& v) {
        return dq.real * v;
    }
    ```

3. To transform a point by a dual quaternion, convert the dual quaternion to rotation and translation components. Then, apply the following translation and rotation components to the vector: `rotation * vector + translation`. This formula works the same way as a transform moving the point, but without a scale component. The code for this can be seen in the following snippet:

    ```
    vec3 transformPoint(const DualQuaternion& dq,
                        const vec3& v) {
    ```

```
        quat d = conjugate(dq.real) * (dq.dual * 2.0f);
        vec3 t = vec3(d.x, d.y, d.z);

        return dq.real * v + t;
}
```

The dual quaternion class can now be used in place of the `Transform` class. Dual quaternions can be arranged in a hierarchy and combined using multiplication, and with these new functions, a dual quaternion can transform a point or a vector directly.

In this section, you implemented dual quaternions in code. All the functions that you will need to work with dual quaternions are implemented as well. In the next section, you will learn how to do mesh skinning using dual quaternions.

Skinning with dual quaternions

In this section, you will learn how to modify the skinning algorithm so that it works with dual quaternions instead of matrices. Specifically, you will replace the skin matrix with a skin dual quaternion that will transform both the vertex position and normal position.

The problem dual quaternions solve is the linear blending of matrices, which is currently implemented in a vertex shader. Specifically, this is the bit of code that introduces the skinning artifacts:

```
mat4 skin;
skin  = (pose[joints.x] * invBindPose[joints.x]) * weights.x;
skin += (pose[joints.y] * invBindPose[joints.y]) * weights.y;
skin += (pose[joints.z] * invBindPose[joints.z]) * weights.z;
skin += (pose[joints.w] * invBindPose[joints.w]) * weights.w;
```

There are three stages in the animation pipeline where it makes sense to replace matrices with dual quaternions. Each of these will have the same result. The three places where this should be implemented are listed here, as follows:

1. Convert the matrices to dual quaternions in the vertex shader.

2. Convert the matrices of the current pose to dual quaternions, then pass dual quaternions to the vertex shader.

3. Convert each transform of the current pose to a dual quaternion, then accumulate the world transform as a dual quaternion.

In this chapter, you will implement the third option and add a `GetDualQuaternionPalette` function to the `Pose` class. You will also add an overload for the `GetInvBindPose` function of the `Skeleton` class. In the following section, you will begin to modify the `Skeleton` class to support dual quaternion skinned animation.

Modifying the pose class

The `Pose` class needs two new functions—one to retrieve the world dual quaternion of a specified joint (that is, `GetGlobalDualQuaternion`), and one to convert the pose to a dual quaternion palette. Follow these steps to declare and implement these functions:

1. Add declarations for the `GetDualQuaternionPalette` and `GetGlobalDualQuaternion` functions to the `Pose` class in `Pose.h`, as follows:

```
class Pose {
// Existing functions and interface
public: // NEW
void GetDualQuaternionPalette(vector<DualQuaternion>& o);
DualQuaternion GetGlobalDualQuaternion(unsigned int i);
};
```

2. Implement the `GetGlobalDualQuaternion` function to return the world space dual quaternion of a joint, as follows:

```
DualQuaternion Pose::GetGlobalDualQuaternion(
                        unsigned int index) {
    DualQuaternion result = transformToDualQuat(
                            mJoints[index]);
    for (int p = mParents[index]; p >= 0;
        p = mParents[p]) {
        DualQuaternion parent = transformToDualQuat(
                            mJoints[p]);
        // Remember, multiplication is in reverse!
        result = result * parent;
    }
    return result;
}
```

3. Implement the `GetDualQuaternionPalette` function, which should loop through all the joints stored in the current pose and store their world space dual quaternions in the output vector, as follows:

```
void Pose::GetDualQuaternionPalette(
        vector<DualQuaternion>& out) {
    unsigned int size = Size();
    if (out.size() != size) {
        out.resize(size);
    }

    for (unsigned int i = 0; i < size; ++i) {
        out[i] = GetGlobalDualQuaternion(i);
    }
}
```

The dual quaternion conversion happens in joint local space, and because of this, you didn't need to add any additional data to the `Pose` class and were able to add two new functions instead. In the next section, you will modify the `Skeleton` class to provide the inverse bind pose as dual quaternions.

Modifying the skeleton class

In order to skin a mesh using dual quaternions, the inverse bind pose of the mesh will need to be expressed using dual quaternions as well. In this section, you will add an overload to the `GetInvBindPose` function that will fill out a reference to a vector of dual quaternion objects. Follow these steps to implement the new `GetInvBindPose` function:

1. Declare an additional `GetInvBindPose` function in the `Skeleton` class that will take a reference to a vector of dual quaternions as an argument. When the function is finished, it will have filled out the vector with inverse bind pose dual quaternions. The code for this can be seen in the following snippet:

```
class Skeleton {
// Existing functions and interface
public: // GetInvBindPose is new
    void GetInvBindPose(vector<DualQuaternion>& pose);
};
```

2. Implement the `GetInvBindPose` function override in `Skeleton.cpp`. Resize the input vector to be as large as the bind pose. For each joint, get the global dual quaternion representation of the joint. Finally, store the conjugate of each world space dual quaternion in the output vector. The code for this can be seen in the following snippet:

```
void Skeleton::GetInvBindPose(std::vector<DualQuaternion>&
    outInvBndPose) {
    unsigned int size = mBindPose.Size();
    outInvBndPose.resize(size);

    for (unsigned int i = 0; i < size; ++i) {
        DualQuaternion world =
            mBindPose.GetGlobalDualQuaternion(i);
        outInvBndPose[i] = conjugate(world);
    }
}
```

You can now convert both an animated pose and the inverse bind pose of a skeleton into arrays of dual quaternions. But in order to use these dual quaternions in a shader, they need to be passed to that shader somehow. In the following section, you will implement a new dual quaternion uniform type to do this.

Creating new uniform types

In order to use dual quaternions as a replacement for matrices, there needs to be a way to use them as shader uniforms. A dual quaternion can be treated as a 2x4 matrix, which can be set with the `glUniformMatrix2x4fv` function.

Declare a template specialization for the `Uniform` class using a `DualQuaternion`. The `Set` function needs to be implemented. It should use the `glUniformMatrix2x4fv` function to upload the dual quaternion array as a 2x4 matrix. Implement the new `Set` function, as shown in the following code snippet:

```
template Uniform<DualQuaternion>;

template<>
void Uniform<DualQuaternion>::Set(unsigned int slot,
                                  DualQuaternion* inputArray,
                                  unsigned int arrayLength) {
    glUniformMatrix2x4fv(slot, arrayLength,
                         false, inputArray[0].v);
}
```

Since the `Set` function is templated, it does not need to be declared in the header file; it's just a specialized instance of the function. In the following section, you will explore how to implement a vertex shader that uses dual quaternions for skinning.

Creating a dual quaternion shader

The only thing left to do in order to support dual quaternion skinning is to implement a vertex shader. The new vertex shader will be similar to its linear-blended skinning counterpart. Instead of having two `mat4` uniform arrays for the matrix palettes, this shader will have two `mat2x4` uniform arrays for dual quaternions.

The shader will have to blend dual quaternions together. Whenever two quaternions (the real part of the dual quaternions) are blended, there is a chance that the blend happens in the wrong neighborhood and the quaternion interpolates the long way around. Neighborhooding will need to be kept in mind when blending.

Follow these steps to implement the new vertex shader:

1. Start declaring the shader with the **OpenGL Shading Language (GLSL)** version and the `model`, `view`, and `projection` uniforms, as follows:

    ```
    #version 330 core

    uniform mat4 model;
    uniform mat4 view;
    uniform mat4 projection;
    ```

2. Declare the vertex structure. The input values for a vertex are as follows: `position`, `normal`, texture coordinates, and weight and joint influences. Each vertex should have up to four weights and influences. The code for this can be seen in the following snippet:

    ```
    in vec3 position;
    in vec3 normal;
    in vec2 texCoord;
    in vec4 weights;
    in ivec4 joints;
    ```

3. Declare the output values passed to the fragment shader. These are the vertex normal, the fragment position in the world space, and the uv coordinate, as illustrated in the following code snippet:

```
out vec3 norm;
out vec3 fragPos;
out vec2 uv;
```

4. Declare the skinning uniforms. These are no longer arrays of mat4; they are now arrays of mat2x4. A mat2x4 has two columns with four rows. Subscripting a mat2x4, index 0 is the real part of our dual quaternion, and index 1 is the dual part. The code can be seen in the following snippet:

```
uniform mat2x4 pose[120];
uniform mat2x4 invBindPose[120];
```

5. Implement a quaternion multiply function. The code for this is the same as that created in *Chapter 4, Implementing Quaternions*, and can be seen in the following snippet:

```
vec4 mulQ(vec4 Q1, vec4 Q2) {
    return vec4(
        Q2.x*Q1.w + Q2.y*Q1.z - Q2.z*Q1.y + Q2.w*Q1.x,
        -Q2.x*Q1.z + Q2.y*Q1.w + Q2.z*Q1.x + Q2.w*Q1.y,
        Q2.x*Q1.y - Q2.y*Q1.x + Q2.z*Q1.w + Q2.w*Q1.z,
        -Q2.x*Q1.x - Q2.y*Q1.y - Q2.z*Q1.z + Q2.w*Q1.w
    );
}
```

6. Implement the `normalize` dual quaternion function. A dual quaternion is normalized by dividing both its real and dual parts by the magnitude of the real part. The code can be seen in the following snippet:

```
mat2x4 normalizeDq(mat2x4 dq) {
    float invMag = 1.0 / length(dq[0]);
    dq[0] *= invMag;
    dq[1] *= invMag;
    return dq;
}
```

7. Implement the dual quaternion multiplication function to combine dual quaternions, as follows:

```
mat2x4 combineDq(mat2x4 l, mat2x4 r) {
    l = normalizeDq(l);
    r = normalizeDq(r);

    vec4 real = mulQ(l[0], r[0]);
    vec4 dual = mulQ(l[0], r[1]) + mulQ(l[1], r[0]);

    return mat2x4(real, dual);
}
```

8. Implement a function to transform vectors by dual quaternions, as follows:

```
vec4 transformVector(mat2x4 dq, vec3 v) {
  vec4 real = dq[0];
  vec3 r_vector = real.xyz;
  float r_scalar = real.w;

  vec3 rotated = r_vector * 2.0f * dot(r_vector, v) +
   v * (r_scalar * r_scalar - dot(r_vector, r_vector))+
   cross(r_vector, v) * 2.0f * r_scalar;

  return vec4(rotated, 0);
}
```

9. Implement a function to transform points by dual quaternions, as follows:

```
vec4 transformPoint(mat2x4 dq, vec3 v) {
    vec4 real = dq[0];
    vec4 dual = dq[1];

    vec3 rotated = transformVector(dq, v).xyz;
    vec4 conjugate = vec4(-real.xyz, real.w);
    vec3 t = mulQ(conjugate, dual * 2.0).xyz;

    return vec4(rotated + t, 1);
}
```

10. Implement the main method of the vertex shader. Start the implementation by neighborhooding joints 1, 2, and 3 (`joints.y`, `joints.z`, `joints.w`) to joint 0 (`joints.x`), as follows:

```
void main() {
    vec4 w = weights;
    // Neighborhood all of the quaternions correctly
    if (dot(pose[joints.x][0], pose[joints.y][0]) < 0.0)
        { w.y *= -1.0; }
    if (dot(pose[joints.x][0], pose[joints.z][0]) < 0.0)
        { w.z *= -1.0; }
    if (dot(pose[joints.x][0], pose[joints.w][0]) < 0.0)
        { w.w *= -1.0; }
```

11. Combine the world space dual quaternion of each joint with the inverse bind pose dual quaternion of the same joint. Remember: dual quaternion multiplication is left to right. Store the result of each multiplication in a new variable. The code can be seen in the following snippet:

```
// Combine
mat2x4 dq0 = combineDq(invBindPose[joints.x],
                       pose[joints.x]);
mat2x4 dq1 = combineDq(invBindPose[joints.y],
                       pose[joints.y]);
mat2x4 dq2 = combineDq(invBindPose[joints.z],
                       pose[joints.z]);
mat2x4 dq3 = combineDq(invBindPose[joints.w],
                       pose[joints.w]);
```

12. Blend the four skinning dual quaternions together. Implement the blend using dual quaternion scalar multiplication and dual quaternion addition. Don't forget to normalize the skin dual quaternion. The code can be seen in the following snippet:

```
mat2x4 skinDq = w.x * dq0 + w.y * dq1 +
                w.z * dq2 + w.w * dq3;
skinDq = normalizeDq(skinDq);
```

13. Skin the vertex using the `transformPoint` function with the skin dual quaternion. Put the resulting `vec4` through the normal model-view-projection pipeline, as follows:

```
vec4 v = transformPoint(skinDq, position);
gl_Position = projection * view * model * v;
fragPos = vec3(model * v);
```

14. Transform the normal similarly. Don't forget to pass the uv coordinates to the fragment shader as well. The code can be seen in the following snippet:

```
vec4 n = transformVector(skinDq, normal);
norm = vec3(model * n);
uv = texCoord;
}
```

Any animation that animates scale will not work with this method. This dual quaternion implementation does not have scaling support. It is possible to hack scaling support on top of dual quaternions, but the work involved outweighs its benefits in terms of performance.

In this section, you learned how to implement skinning with dual quaternions. This includes modifying pose data and the Skeleton class, creating new uniforms, and building a new shader. In the following section, you will explore how to use the dual quaternion code written up to this point.

Understanding how to use dual quaternion skinning

This section will explore how you can take the dual quaternion skinning code that you have written so far and implement it in an existing application. This code is meant to be for reference only; you do not have to follow along with it.

Using the dual quaternion-skinned shader is trivial; it would be easy to switch between skinning methods at runtime. The following steps demonstrate how the dual quaternion shader or a linear-skinned shader could be used to animate the same model.

Keep track of both the dual quaternion pose palette and inverse bind pose palette, as well as the linear blend pose palette and inverse bind pose palette. Have a look at the following code:

```
// For dual quaternion skinning
std::vector<DualQuaternion> mDqPosePalette;
std::vector<DualQuaternion> mDqInvBindPalette;

// For linear blend skinning
std::vector<mat4> mLbPosePalette;
std::vector<mat4> mLbInvBindPalette;
```

When the application initializes, cache the inverse bind pose both as a vector of matrices and a vector of dual quaternions, as follows:

```
mCurrentPose = mSkeleton.GetRestPose();

mCurrentPose.GetDualQuaternionPalette(mDqPosePalette);
mSkeleton.GetInvBindPose(mDqInvBindPalette);

mCurrentPose.GetMatrixPalette(mLbPosePalette);
mLbInvBindPalette = mSkeleton.GetInvBindPose();
```

When an animation is sampled, convert the resulting pose palette to both dual quaternion and linear blend versions, as follows:

```
mPlayTime = mClips[mClip].Sample(mCurrentPose,
                                 mPlayTime + dt);
mCurrentPose.GetDualQuaternionPalette(mDqPosePalette);
mCurrentPose.GetMatrixPalette(mLbPosePalette);
```

When the animation is being rendered, make sure that the correct uniforms are used, as follows:

```
if (mSkinningMethod == SkinningMethod::DualQuaternion) {
    Uniform<DualQuaternion>::Set(
            shader->GetUniform("pose"), mDqPosePalette);
    Uniform<DualQuaternion>::Set(
    shader->GetUniform("invBindPose"), mDqInvBindPalette);
}
else {
    Uniform<mat4>::Set(shader->GetUniform("pose"),
                       mLbPosePalette);
    Uniform<mat4>::Set(shader->GetUniform("invBindPose"),
                       mLbInvBindPalette);
}
```

In this sample, switching between the linear blended skinning and the dual quaternion skinning shaders is as simple as changing the value of the mSkinningMethod variable. This works because the only difference between the two shaders is the pose palette uniforms.

Summary

In this chapter, you learned the math behind dual quaternions and implemented a dual quaternion class. You discovered some of the skinning artifacts that can result from linear blend skinning and how dual quaternions can be used to avoid these artifacts. The dual quaternion skinning shader you implemented in this chapter can be used to replace the linear blend skinning shader.

If you look under `Chapter14` in the downloadable materials for this book, there are two samples. `Sample00` contains all the code up to this point. `Sample01` renders the same twisting cube model twice. The first cube is rendered with a linear blend skinning shader. The second one is rendered with a dual quaternion shader.

In the next chapter, you will explore how indexed drawing can be used to animate large crowds. This is interesting because it involves moving pose generation to the **graphics processing unit** (**GPU**) and performing the entire skinned animation pipeline in a vertex shader.

15
Rendering Instanced Crowds

This final chapter explores how to render large crowds using instancing. Crowd rendering is an interesting topic because it moves pose generation (sampling) and blending onto the GPU, making the entire animation pipeline run in a vertex shader.

To move pose generation to the vertex shader, animation information needs to be encoded in a texture. The focus of this chapter will be encoding animation data into textures and using that texture to create an animated pose.

Without instancing, drawing a large crowd would mean making lots of draw calls, which would hurt the frame rate. Using instancing, one mesh can be drawn many times. If there is only one draw call, the animated poses for each character in the crowd will need to be generated differently.

In this chapter, you will explore moving animation sampling into the vertex shader in order to draw large crowds. The following topics will be covered in this chapter:

- Storing arbitrary data in textures
- Retrieving arbitrary data from textures
- Baking animations into a texture

- Sampling animation textures in a vertex shader
- Optimizing the crowd system

Storing data in textures

Sampling animations is not a trivial task. There are a lot of loops and functions, which makes animation sampling on the GPU a difficult problem. One way to address this problem is to simplify it.

Instead of sampling an animation in real-time, it could be sampled at set time intervals. The process of sampling an animation at set intervals and writing the resulting data to a file is called baking.

Once the animation data is baked, the shader no longer has to sample an actual animation clip. Instead, it can look up the nearest sampled pose based on time. So, where does this animation data get baked to? Animation can be baked into textures. Textures can be used as data buffers, and there is already an easy way to read texture data in shaders.

Normally, the storage type and information in a texture is abstracted away by the sampling function in the shader. For example, the `texture2D` function in GLSL takes normalized uv coordinates as an argument and returns a four-component vector with values ranging from 0 to 1.

But none of that information is what's in the texture. When a texture is created with `glTexImage2D`, it takes an internal texture format (GL_RGBA), a source format (usually GL_RGBA again), and a data type (usually GL_UNSIGNED_BYTE). These parameters are used to convert whatever the underlying data type is into the normalized values that `texture2D` returns.

There are two problems with this when it comes to storing arbitrary data in textures. The first is the granularity of the data. In the case of GL_RGBA, each sampled floating-point component only has 256 unique values. Second, what if a value needs to be stored that is not normalized to the 0 to 1 range?

This is where floating-point textures come in. You can create a four-component floating-point texture that has a GL_RGBA32F format. This texture will be much larger than other textures because each pixel will store four full 32-bit floating-point numbers.

A floating-point texture can store arbitrary data. In the following section, you will learn how to retrieve the arbitrary data from a floating-point texture. After that, you will explore how a shader can read data from a floating-point texture.

Reading data from textures

This section explores how animation data stored in textures can be retrieved in a shader. In this section, you will learn how to sample the texture and what sampler states should be used when sampling the texture.

Once the data is in the right format, sampling it becomes the next challenge. The `glTexImage2D` function expects normalized `uv` coordinates and returns a normalized value. On the other hand, the `texelFetch` function can be used to sample a texture using pixel coordinates and return the raw data at those coordinates.

The `texelFetch` glsl takes three arguments: a sampler, an `ivec2`, and an integer. `ivec2` is the *x* and *y* coordinates of the pixel being sampled, in pixel space. The last integer is the mip level to use, which, for this chapter, will always be `0`.

A mipmap is a chain of progressively lower resolution versions of the same image. When a mip level is scaled down, data is lost. This data loss alters the contents of the animation. Avoid generating mips for animation textures.

Because the data needs to be read in exactly the same way it was written out, any interpolation would ruin the animation data as well. Make sure that animation textures are sampled using nearest neighbor sampling.

Using `texelFetch` instead of `glTexImage2D` to sample a texture should return the correct data. Textures can be sampled in either the vertex or the fragment shader. In the next section, you will explore what animation data should be stored in these floating-point textures.

Encoding animation data

Now that you know how to read and write data to a texture, the next question is, what data needs to be written in the texture? You will be encoding animation data into textures. Each animation clip will be sampled at set intervals. The resulting poses from all those samples will be stored in a texture.

To encode this data, the *x* axis of the texture will represent time. The *y* axis of the texture will represent a bone in the skeleton being animated. Each bone will take up three rows: one for the position, one for the rotation, and one for the scale.

The animation clip will be sampled at set intervals to make sure that there are as many samples as the texture is wide. For example, for a *256x256* animation texture, the animation clip will need to be sampled 256 times.

When sampling the animation clip to encode it into a texture, for each sample, you will find the world space transform of each bone and write it into the texture. The *y* coordinate is going to be `joint_index * 3 + component`, where the valid components are `position = 0`, `rotation = 1`, and `scale = 3`.

Once these values have been written to the texture, upload the texture to the GPU and use it. In the next section, you will explore how a shader evaluates this animation texture.

Exploring per-instance data

When rendering a large crowd, each actor in the crowd has certain properties. In this section, you will explore what that per-instance data is and how to pass it to the shader. This will greatly reduce the amount of data that is uploaded to the GPU as uniform arrays every frame.

Moving the skinning pipeline to a vertex shader does not completely remove needing to pass crowd-related uniform to the shader. Every actor in a crowd will need some data uploaded to the GPU. The per-instance data is much smaller than what would be uploaded if pose palette matrices were being used.

Each actor in the crowd will need a position, rotation, and scale to build a model matrix. Actors will need to know the current frame to sample and the time between the current and next frames to blend.

The total size of each actor's instance data is 11 floats and 2 integers. That's only 52 bytes per instance. Per-instance data will always be passed using uniform arrays. The size of each array is the number of actors the crowd contains. Each element of the array represents a unique actor.

The shader will be responsible for building the appropriate matrices out of the per-instance data and the animation texture. Blending between the current and next frame is optional; the blend will not be 100% correct, but it should still look good.

In the next section, you will implement an `AnimationTexture` class, which will let you work with animated textures in code.

Creating an animation texture

In this section, you will implement all the code needed to work with floating-point textures in a `AnimTexture` class. Each `AnimTexture` object will contain a 32-bit floating point RGBA texture. There will be two copies of this data: one on the CPU and one uploaded to the GPU.

The CPU buffer is kept around to easily modify the contents of the texture in bulk before saving it to disk, or uploading it to OpenGL. It keeps the API simple at the cost of some additional memory.

There is no standard 32-bit texture format, so saving and writing to disk will simply dump the binary contents of the `AnimTexture` class to disk. In the next section, you will begin to implement the `AnimTexture` class. This class will provide an easy-to-use interface for implementing 32-bit floating-point textures.

Declaring the AnimTexture class

Animation textures are assumed to always be square; the width and height don't need to be tracked separately. It should be enough to use a single size variable. The `AnimTexture` class will always have two copies of the texture in memory at a time, one on the CPU and one on the GPU.

Create a new file called `AnimTexture.h` and declare the `AnimTexture` class in this file. Follow these steps to declare the `AnimTexture` class:

1. Declare the `AnimTexture` class. It has three member variables: a floating-point array, an integer for the size of the texture, and a handle to the OpenGL texture object:

    ```
    class AnimTexture {
    protected:
        float* mData;
        unsigned int mSize;
        unsigned int mHandle;
    ```

2. Declare `AnimTexture` with a default constructor, copy constructor, assignment operator, and destructor:

    ```
    public:
        AnimTexture();
        AnimTexture(const AnimTexture&);
        AnimTexture& operator=(const AnimTexture&);
        ~AnimTexture();
    ```

3. Declare functions in order to save `AnimTexture` to disk and to load it up again:

    ```
        void Load(const char* path);
        void Save(const char* path);
    ```

4. Declare a function to upload the data from the `mData` variable to an OpenGL texture:

```
void UploadTextureDataToGPU();
```

5. Declare getters and setter functions for the CPU side data that `AnimTexture` contains:

```
unsigned int Size();
void Resize(unsigned int newSize);
float* GetData();
```

6. Declare `GetTexel`, which takes the *x* and *y* coordinates and returns a `vec4`, as well as a `SetTexel` function to set `vec3` or `quat` objects. These functions will write to the texture's data:

```
void SetTexel(unsigned int x, unsigned int y,
              const vec3& v);
void SetTexel(unsigned int x, unsigned int y,
              const quat& q);
vec4 GetTexel(unsigned int x, unsigned int y);
```

7. Declare functions to bind and unbind the texture for rendering. This will be done the same way as the `Set` and `Unset` functions of the `Texture` class:

```
void Set(unsigned int uniform, unsigned int texture);
void UnSet(unsigned int textureIndex);
unsigned int GetHandle();
};
```

The `AnimTexture` class is a convenient way to work with floating-point textures. The `get` and `SetTexel` methods can read and write to the texture using an intuitive API. In the next section, you will begin to implement the `AnimTexture` class.

Implementing the AnimTexture class

In this section, you will implement the `AnimTexture` class, which contains OpenGL code for working with floating-point textures and provides an easy-to-use API. If you want to use a graphics API other than OpenGL, this class will need to be rewritten using that API.

When an `AnimTexture` is saved to disk, the entire `mData` array is written to the file as a large binary blob. This large texture data takes up quite a bit of memory; for example, a *512x512* texture takes up about 4 MB. Texture compression is not a good fit, since the animation data needs to be precise.

The `SetTexel` functions are the main way we will be writing data to the animation texture. These functions take *x* and *y* coordinates, as well as a `vec3` or quaternion value. The function needs to figure out the right index into the `mData` array based on the given *x* and *y* coordinates, then set the pixel values accordingly.

Create a new file called `AnimTexture.cpp`. Implement the `AnimTexture` class in this new file. Now, follow these steps to implement the `AnimTexture` class:

1. Implement the default constructor. It should set data and size to zero and generate a new OpenGL shader handle:

```
AnimTexture::AnimTexture() {
    mData = 0;
    mSize = 0;
    glGenTextures(1, &mHandle);
}
```

2. Implement the copy constructor. It should do the same thing that the default constructor does and use the assignment operator to copy the actual texture data:

```
AnimTexture::AnimTexture(const AnimTexture& other) {
    mData = 0;
    mSize = 0;
    glGenTextures(1, &mHandle);
    *this = other;
}
```

3. Implement the assignment operator. It only needs to copy the CPU side data; the OpenGL handle can be left alone:

```
AnimTexture& AnimTexture::operator=(
                        const AnimTexture& other) {
    if (this == &other) {
        return *this;
    }

    mSize = other.mSize;
    if (mData != 0) {
        delete[] mData;
    }
```

```
        mData = 0;
        if (mSize != 0) {
            mData = new float[mSize * mSize * 4];
            memcpy(mData, other.mData,
                sizeof(float) * (mSize * mSize * 4));
        }
        return *this;
    }
```

4. Implement the destructor of the `AnimTexture` class. It should delete the internal floating-point array and free the OpenGL handle that the class is holding onto:

```
AnimTexture::~AnimTexture() {
    if (mData != 0) {
        delete[] mData;
    }
    glDeleteTextures(1, &mHandle);
}
```

5. Implement the `Save` function. It should write the size of `AnimTexture` to the file and write the contents of `mData` as a large binary blob:

```
void AnimTexture::Save(const char* path) {
    std::ofstream file;
    file.open(path, std::ios::out | std::ios::binary);
    if (!file.is_open()) {
        cout << "Couldn't open " << path << "\n";
    }

    file << mSize;
    if (mSize != 0) {
        file.write((char*)mData,
            sizeof(float) * (mSize * mSize * 4));
    }
    file.close();
}
```

6. Implement the `Load` function to load serialized animation data back into memory:

```
void AnimTexture::Load(const char* path) {
    std::ifstream file;
    file.open(path, std::ios::in | std::ios::binary);
    if (!file.is_open()) {
        cout << "Couldn't open " << path << "\n";
    }
```

```
    file >> mSize;
    mData = new float[mSize * mSize * 4];
    file.read((char*)mData,
        sizeof(float) * (mSize * mSize * 4));
    file.close();
    UploadTextureDataToGPU();
}
```

7. Implement the `UploadDataToGPU` function. Its implementation is very similar to `Texture::Load` but uses `GL_RGBA32F` instead of `GL_FLOAT`:

```
void AnimTexture::UploadTextureDataToGPU() {
    glBindTexture(GL_TEXTURE_2D, mHandle);

    glTexImage2D(GL_TEXTURE_2D, 0, GL_RGBA32F, mSize,
                    mSize, 0, GL_RGBA, GL_FLOAT, mData);

    glTexParameteri(GL_TEXTURE_2D, GL_TEXTURE_WRAP_S,
                    GL_CLAMP_TO_EDGE);
    glTexParameteri(GL_TEXTURE_2D, GL_TEXTURE_WRAP_T,
                    GL_CLAMP_TO_EDGE);

    glTexParameteri(GL_TEXTURE_2D,
                    GL_TEXTURE_MIN_FILTER, GL_LINEAR);
    glTexParameteri(GL_TEXTURE_2D,
                    GL_TEXTURE_MAG_FILTER, GL_LINEAR);

    glBindTexture(GL_TEXTURE_2D, 0);
}
```

8. Implement the size, OpenGL handle, and floating-point data getter functions:

```
unsigned int AnimTexture::Size() {
    return mSize;
}

unsigned int AnimTexture::GetHandle() {
    return mHandle;
}

float* AnimTexture::GetData() {
    return mData;
}
```

9. Implement the `resize` function, which should set the size of the `mData` array. The argument this function takes is the width or height of the animation texture:

```
void AnimTexture::Resize(unsigned int newSize) {
    if (mData != 0) {
        delete[] mData;
    }
    mSize = newSize;
    mData = new float[mSize * mSize * 4];
}
```

10. Implement the `Set` function. It works similar to `Texture::Set`:

```
void AnimTexture::Set(unsigned int uniformIndex, unsigned
int textureIndex) {
    glActiveTexture(GL_TEXTURE0 + textureIndex);
    glBindTexture(GL_TEXTURE_2D, mHandle);
    glUniform1i(uniformIndex, textureIndex);
}
```

11. Implement the `UnSet` function. It works similar to `Texture::UnSet`:

```
void AnimTexture::UnSet(unsigned int textureIndex) {
    glActiveTexture(GL_TEXTURE0 + textureIndex);
    glBindTexture(GL_TEXTURE_2D, 0);
    glActiveTexture(GL_TEXTURE0);
}
```

12. Implement the `SetTexel` function, which takes a vector, 3, as an argument. This function should set the unused A component of the pixel to 0:

```
void AnimTexture::SetTexel(unsigned int x,
                unsigned int y, const vec3& v) {
    unsigned int index = (y * mSize * 4) + (x * 4);

    mData[index + 0] = v.x;
    mData[index + 1] = v.y;
    mData[index + 2] = v.z;
    mData[index + 3] = 0.0f;
}
```

13. Implement the `SetTexel` function, which takes a quaternion as an argument:

```
void AnimTexture::SetTexel(unsigned int x,
                 unsigned int y, const quat& q) {
    unsigned int index = (y * mSize * 4) + (x * 4);

    mData[index + 0] = q.x;
    mData[index + 1] = q.y;
    mData[index + 2] = q.z;
    mData[index + 3] = q.w;
}
```

14. Implement the `GetTexel` function. This function will always return a `vec4`, which contains every component of the pixel:

```
vec4 AnimTexture::GetTexel(unsigned int x,
                    unsigned int y) {
    unsigned int index = (y * mSize * 4) + (x * 4);

    return vec4(
        mData[index + 0],
        mData[index + 1],
        mData[index + 2],
        mData[index + 3]
    );
}
```

In this section, you learned how to create a 32-bit floating-point texture and manage the data inside it. The `AnimTexture` class should let you work with floating-point textures using an intuitive API, without you having to worry about any OpenGL functions. In the next section, you will create a function that will sample an animation clip and write the resulting animation data to a texture.

Animation baker

In this section, you will learn how to take an animation clip and encode it into an animation texture. This process is called baking.

Texture baking is implemented using a helper function that bakes the animation into a texture. This `Bake` function will sample the animation at set intervals and write the skeleton hierarchy for each sample into a floating-point texture.

For arguments, the `Bake` function needs a skeleton, an animation clip, and a reference to an `AnimTexture` to write to. The skeleton is important as it provides the rest pose, which will be used for any joint that isn't present in the animation clip. Every joint of the skeleton will get baked into the texture. Let's get started:

1. Create a new file called `AnimBaker.h` and add the declaration of the `BakeAnimationToTexture` function to it:

```
void BakeAnimationToTexture(Skeleton& skel, Clip& clip,
                            AnimTexture& outTex);
```

2. Create a new file called `AnimBaker.cpp`. Begin implementing the `BakeAnimationToTexture` function in this file:

```
void BakeAnimationToTexture(Skeleton& skel, Clip& clip,
                            AnimTexture& tex) {
    Pose& bindPose = skel.GetBindPose();
```

3. To bake an animation into a texture, first, create a pose that the animation will be sampled into. Then, loop across the x dimension of the texture, which is time:

```
Pose pose = bindPose;
unsigned int texWidth = tex.Size();
for (unsigned int x = 0; x < texWidth; ++x) {
```

4. For each iteration, find the normalized value of the iterator (`iterator index / (size - 1)`). Multiply the normalized time by the duration of the clip, then add the start time of the clip. Sample the clip at this time for the current pixel:

```
float t = (float)x / (float)(texWidth - 1);
float start = clip.GetStartTime();
float time = start + clip.GetDuration() * t;
clip.Sample(pose, time);
```

5. Once the clip has been sampled, loop through all the joints in the bind pose. Find the global transform of the current joint and write the data into the texture using `SetTexel`:

```
for (unsigned int y = 0;y<pose.Size()*3;y+=3) {
    Transform node=pose.GetGlobalTransform(y/3);
    tex.SetTexel(x, y + 0, node.position);
    tex.SetTexel(x, y + 1, node.rotation);
    tex.SetTexel(x, y + 2, node.scale);
}
```

6. Before the `Bake` function returns, call the `UploadTextureDataToGPU` function
    on the provided animation texture. This will make the texture usable immediately
    after it has been baked:

    ```
        } // End of x loop
        tex.UploadTextureDataToGPU();
    }
    ```

At a high level, the animation texture is used as a timeline where the *x* axis is time and
the *y* axis is the transform of an animated joint at that time. In the next section, you
will create the crowd shader. The crowd shader uses the date baked into a texture by
`BakeAnimationToTexture` to sample an animation's current pose.

Creating a crowd shader

To render a crowd, you will need to create a new shader. The crowd shader will have
projection and view uniforms, but no model uniform. This is because all actors are drawn
with the same projection and view matrices but require a unique model matrix. Instead
of model matrices, the shader will have three uniform arrays: one for position, one for
rotation, and one for scale.

The value that will be placed into these arrays will be an instance index – the index of
the current mesh being rendered. Each vertex gets a copy of its mesh instance through
a built-in `glsl` variable, `gl_InstanceID`. Each vertex will construct a model matrix
using the position, rotation, and scale uniform arrays.

The inverse bind pose is like a matrix uniform array with regular skinning, but the
animated pose is not. To find the animated pose, the shader will have to sample the
animation texture. Since each vertex is skinned to four vertices, the animated pose
has to be found four times for every vertex.

Create a new file called `crowd.vert`. The crowd shader will be implemented in this file.
Follow these steps to implement the crowd shader:

1. Begin implementing the shader by defining two constants: one for the maximum
    number of bones and one for the maximum number of supported instances:

    ```
    #version 330 core

    #define MAX_BONES 60
    #define MAX_INSTANCES 80
    ```

2. Declare the uniforms that are shared by all actors in the crowd. This includes the view and projection matrices, inverse bind pose palette, and animation texture:

```
uniform mat4 view;
uniform mat4 projection;
uniform mat4 invBindPose[MAX_BONES];
uniform sampler2D animTex;
```

3. Declare the uniforms that are unique to each actor in the crowd. This includes the transformation of the actor, the current and next frame, and the blend time:

```
uniform vec3 model_pos[MAX_INSTANCES];
uniform vec4 model_rot[MAX_INSTANCES];
uniform vec3 model_scl[MAX_INSTANCES];
uniform ivec2 frames[MAX_INSTANCES];
uniform float time[MAX_INSTANCES];
```

4. Declare the vertex structure. Per-vertex data is the same as for any skinned mesh:

```
in vec3 position;
in vec3 normal;
in vec2 texCoord;
in vec4 weights;
in ivec4 joints;
```

5. Declare the output values for the crowd shader:

```
out vec3 norm;
out vec3 fragPos;
out vec2 uv;
```

6. Implement a function that multiplies a vector and a quaternion. This function will have the same implementation as the transformVector function you built in *Chapter 4, Implementing Quaternions*, except it's running in a shader:

```
vec3 QMulV(vec4 q, vec3 v) {
    return q.xyz * 2.0f * dot(q.xyz, v) +
           v * (q.w * q.w - dot(q.xyz, q.xyz)) +
           cross(q.xyz, v) * 2.0f * q.w;
}
```

7. Implement the `GetModel` function. Given an instance index, this function should sample the animation texture and return a *4x4* transformation matrix:

```
mat4 GetModel(int instance) {
    vec3 position = model_pos[instance];
    vec4 rotation = model_rot[instance];
    vec3 scale = model_scl[instance];

    vec3 xBasis = QMulV(rotation, vec3(scale.x, 0, 0));
    vec3 yBasis = QMulV(rotation, vec3(0, scale.y, 0));
    vec3 zBasis = QMulV(rotation, vec3(0, 0, scale.z));

    return mat4(
        xBasis.x, xBasis.y, xBasis.z, 0.0,
        yBasis.x, yBasis.y, yBasis.z, 0.0,
        zBasis.x, zBasis.y, zBasis.z, 0.0,
        position.x, position.y, position.z, 1.0
    );
}
```

8. Implement the `GetPose` function with a joint and an instance where this function should return the animated world matrix of the joint. Begin the implementation by finding the x and y positions to sample the animation texture with:

```
mat4 GetPose(int joint, int instance) {
    int x_now = frames[instance].x;
    int x_next = frames[instance].y;
    int y_pos = joint * 3;
```

9. Sample the current frame's position, rotation, and scale from the animation texture:

```
        vec4 pos0 = texelFetch(animTex, ivec2(x_now,
                               (y_pos + 0)), 0);
        vec4 rot0 = texelFetch(animTex, ivec2(x_now,
                               (y_pos + 1)), 0);
        vec4 scl0 = texelFetch(animTex, ivec2(x_now,
                               (y_pos + 2)), 0);
```

10. Sample the next frame's position, rotation, and scale from the animation texture:

```
vec4 pos1 = texelFetch(animTex, ivec2(x_next,
                       (y_pos + 0)), 0);
vec4 rot1 = texelFetch(animTex, ivec2(x_next,
                       (y_pos + 1)), 0);
vec4 scl1 = texelFetch(animTex, ivec2(x_next,
                       (y_pos + 2)), 0);
```

11. Interpolate between the transforms of both frames:

```
if (dot(rot0, rot1) < 0.0) { rot1 *= -1.0; }
vec4 position = mix(pos0, pos1, time[instance]);
vec4 rotation = normalize(mix(rot0,
                          rot1, time[instance]));
vec4 scale = mix(scl0, scl1, time[instance]);
```

12. Use the interpolated position, rotation, and scale to return a 4x4 matrix:

```
vec3 xBasis = QMulV(rotation, vec3(scale.x, 0, 0));
vec3 yBasis = QMulV(rotation, vec3(0, scale.y, 0));
vec3 zBasis = QMulV(rotation, vec3(0, 0, scale.z));

return mat4(
    xBasis.x, xBasis.y, xBasis.z, 0.0,
    yBasis.x, yBasis.y, yBasis.z, 0.0,
    zBasis.x, zBasis.y, zBasis.z, 0.0,
    position.x, position.y, position.z, 1.0
);
}
```

13. Begin implementing the main function of the shader by finding all four of the animated pose matrices, as well as the model matrix for the current actor in the crowd. Use `gl_InstanceID` to get the ID of the currently drawn actor:

```
void main() {
    mat4 pose0 = GetPose(joints.x, gl_InstanceID);
    mat4 pose1 = GetPose(joints.y, gl_InstanceID);
    mat4 pose2 = GetPose(joints.z, gl_InstanceID);
    mat4 pose3 = GetPose(joints.w, gl_InstanceID);
    mat4 model = GetModel(gl_InstanceID);
```

14. Continue implementing the main function by finding the `skin` matrix for the vertex:

```
mat4 skin = (pose0*invBindPose[joints.x])*weights.x;
skin += (pose1 * invBindPose[joints.y]) * weights.y;
skin += (pose2 * invBindPose[joints.z]) * weights.z;
skin += (pose3 * invBindPose[joints.w]) * weights.w;
```

15. Finish implementing the main function by putting the position and normal through the skinned vertex's transformation pipeline:

```
gl_Position = projection * view * model *
              skin * vec4(position, 1.0);
fragPos = vec3(model * skin * vec4(position, 1.0));
norm = vec3(model * skin * vec4(normal, 0.0f));
uv = texCoord;
}
```

In this section, you implemented the crowd shader. This vertex shader uses an animation texture to construct the animated pose of each vertex being rendered. It moves the pose generation part of the skinning pipeline to the GPU. The shader is meant to render instanced meshes; it uses `gl_InstanceID` to determine which instance is currently being rendered.

This shader is a good place to start, but there is always room for improvement. The shader is currently using a lot of uniform indices. Some lower-end machines might not provide enough uniforms. Several optimization strategies will be covered near the end of this chapter. In the next section, you will implement a `Crowd` class to help manage all the data that the Crowd shader needs.

Creating the Crowd utility class

In this section, you will be building the `Crowd` class. This is a utility class that will render large crowds with an easy-to-use API. The `Crowd` class encapsulates the state of a crowd.

The `Crowd` class must maintain the instance data of each actor in the class. To accommodate this, you will need to declare a maximum number of actors. Then, all the actor-specific information can be stored in arrays of structures where the index is the actor ID.

Actor-specific data includes the actor's world transform, as well as data related to its animation playback. The animation data is what frames are being interpolated, the interpolation value, and the key times for the current and next frames.

Create a new file called `Crowd.h`. The `Crowd` class will be declared in this file. Follow these steps to declare the `Crowd` class:

1. Define the maximum number of crowd actors as 80:

```
#define CROWD_MAX_ACTORS 80
```

2. Start declaring the `Crowd` class by creating vectors for all instance data. This includes data for each actor's transformation, animation frame, and time, as well as frame interpolation information:

```
struct Crowd {
protected:
    std::vector<vec3> mPositions;
    std::vector<quat> mRotations;
    std::vector<vec3> mScales;
    std::vector<ivec2> mFrames;
    std::vector<float> mTimes;
    std::vector<float> mCurrentPlayTimes;
    std::vector<float> mNextPlayTimes;
```

3. Declare the `AdjustTime`, `UpdatePlaybackTimes`, `UpdateFrameIndices`, and `UpdateInterpolationTimes` functions. The `AdjustTime` function is similar to `Clip::AdjustTimeToFitRange`; it makes sure that a given time is valid:

```
protected:
    float AdjustTime(float t, float start,
                float end, bool looping);
    void UpdatePlaybackTimes(float dt, bool looping,
                float start, float end);
    void UpdateFrameIndices(float start,
                float duration, unsigned int texWidth);
    void UpdateInterpolationTimes(float start,
                float duration, unsigned int texWidth);
```

4. Declare getter and setter functions for the size of the crowd and for the `Transform` property of each actor:

```
public:
    unsigned int Size();
    void Resize(unsigned int size);
    Transform GetActor(unsigned int index);
    void SetActor(unsigned int index,
                  const Transform& t);
```

5. Finally, declare the `Update` and `SetUniforms` functions. These are the functions that will advance the current animation and update the per-instance shader uniforms:

```
    void Update(float deltaTime, Clip& mClip,
                unsigned int texWidth);
    void SetUniforms(Shader* shader);
};
```

The `Crowd` class provides an intuitive interface for managing the per-instance information of every actor in a crowd. In the next section, you will begin to implement the `Crowd` class.

Implementing the Crowd class

The `Crowd` class provides a convenient way for you to manage all the actors in a crowd. Most of the complexity of this class is in calculating the correct playback information. This work is done in the `Update` function. The `Update` function uses three helper functions, that is, `UpdatePlaybackTimes`, `UpdateFrameIndices`, and `UpdateInterpolateionTimes`, to work.

The current animation playback time for each actor in the crowd will be stored in the `mCurrentPlayTimes` vector. The `mNextPlayTimes` vector is the estimated next time in the animation, which allows the two sampled frames to interpolate. The `UpdatePlaybackTimes` function will be updating both these vectors.

It's important to guess the playback time of the next frame because the sample rate of the animation texture is unknown. If an animation is encoded at 240 FPS and is played back at 60 FPS, for example, then the next frame is going to be four samples away.

The `mFrames` vector contains two component integer vectors. The first component is the u texture coordinate of the current animation frame. The second component is the v texture coordinate of the animation frame that would be shown in the next frame. The v texture coordinate is the joint index.

The UpdateFrameIndex function is responsible for updating this vector. To find the x coordinate of the current frame, normalize the frame time and then multiply the normalized frame time by the size of the texture. You can normalize a frame's time by subtracting the start time from the frame time and dividing the result by the duration of the clip.

The shader will need to interpolate between the current animated pose and the next animated pose. To do this, it needs to know the current normalized time between the frames of the two poses. This is stored in the mTimes variable.

The mTimes variable is updated by the UpdateInterpolationTimes function. This function finds the duration of the current frame, then normalizes the playback time relative to the current frame to that duration.

To update the Crowd class, you have to call the UpdatePlaybackTimes, UpdateFrameIndices, and UpdateInterpolateionTimes functions, in that order. After this is done, the Crowd class can set its uniform values with the SetUniforms function.

Create a new file called Crowd.cpp. The Crowd class will be implemented in this file. Follow these steps to implement the Crowd class:

1. Implement the size getter and setter functions. The setter function needs to set the size of all the vectors contained in the Crowd class:

```cpp
unsigned int Crowd::Size() {
    return mCurrentPlayTimes.size();
}

void Crowd::Resize(unsigned int size) {
    if (size > CROWD_MAX_ACTORS) {
        size = CROWD_MAX_ACTORS;
    }

    mPositions.resize(size);
    mRotations.resize(size);
    mScales.resize(size, vec3(1, 1, 1));
    mFrames.resize(size);
    mTimes.resize(size);
    mCurrentPlayTimes.resize(size);
    mNextPlayTimes.resize(size);
}
```

2. Implement the getter and setter functions for actor transformation. Position, rotation, and scale are kept in separate vectors; the actor getter and setter functions hide that implementation in favor of using `Transform` objects:

```
Transform Crowd::GetActor(unsigned int index) {
    return Transform(
        mPositions[index],
        mRotations[index],
        mScales[index] );
}

void Crowd::SetActor(unsigned int index,
                     const Transform& t) {
    mPositions[index] = t.position;
    mRotations[index] = t.rotation;
    mScales[index] = t.scale;
}
```

3. Implement the `AdjustTime` function; it's similar to the `Clip::AdjustTimeToFitRange` function:

```
float Crowd::AdjustTime(float time, float start,
                        float end, bool looping) {
    if (looping) {
        time = fmodf(time - start, end - start);
        if (time < 0.0f) {
            time += end - start;
        }
        time = time + start;
    }
    else {
        if (time < start) { time = start; }
        if (time > end) { time = end; }
    }
    return time;
}
```

4. Implement the `UpdatePlaybackTimes` helper function. This function will advance the play time for all actors by delta time:

```
void Crowd::UpdatePlaybackTimes(float deltaTime,
            bool looping, float start, float end) {
    unsigned int size = mCurrentPlayTimes.size();
    for (unsigned int i = 0; i < size; ++i) {
        float time = mCurrentPlayTimes[i] + deltaTime;
```

```
        mCurrentPlayTimes[i] = AdjustTime(time, start,
                                          end, looping);
        time = mCurrentPlayTimes[i] + deltaTime;
        mNextPlayTimes[i] = AdjustTime(time, start,
                                       end, looping);

    }
}
```

5. Implement the `UpdateFrameIndices` function. This function will convert the current play time into pixel coordinates along the animation texture's *x* axis:

```
void Crowd::UpdateFrameIndices(float start, float
duration, unsigned int texWidth) {
    unsigned int size = mCurrentPlayTimes.size();
    for (unsigned int i = 0; i < size; ++i) {
        float thisNormalizedTime =
            (mCurrentPlayTimes[i] - start) / duration;
        unsigned int thisFrame =
            thisNormalizedTime * (texWidth - 1);
        float nextNormalizedTime =
            (mNextPlayTimes[i] - start) / duration;
        unsigned int nextFrame =
            nextNormalizedTime * (texWidth - 1);
        mFrames[i].x = thisFrame;
        mFrames[i].y = nextFrame;
    }
}
```

6. Implement the `UpdateInterpolationTimes` function. This function should find the interpolation time between the current and next animated frames:

```
void Crowd::UpdateInterpolationTimes(float start,
        float duration, unsigned int texWidth) {
    unsigned int size =  mCurrentPlayTimes.size();
    for (unsigned int i = 0; i < size; ++i) {
        if (mFrames[i].x == mFrames[i].y) {
            mTimes[i] = 1.0f;
            continue;
        }
        float thisT = (float)mFrames[i].x /
                    (float)(texWidth - 1);
        float thisTime = start + duration * thisT;
        float nextT = (float)mFrames[i].y /
                    (float)(texWidth - 1);
```

```
        float nextTime = start + duration * nextT;
        if (nextTime < thisTime) {
            nextTime += duration;
        }

        float frameDuration = nextTime - thisTime;
        mTimes[i] = (mCurrentPlayTimes[i] - thisTime) /
                    frameDuration;
    }
}
```

7. Implement the `Update` method. This method relies on the
   `UpdatePlaybackTimes`, `UpdateFrameIndices`, and
   `UpdateInterpolationTimes` helper functions:

```
void Crowd::Update(float deltaTime, Clip& mClip,
                        unsigned int texWidth) {
    bool looping = mClip.GetLooping();
    float start = mClip.GetStartTime();
    float end = mClip.GetEndTime();
    float duration = mClip.GetDuration();

    UpdatePlaybackTimes(deltaTime, looping, start, end);
    UpdateFrameIndices(start, duration, texWidth);
    UpdateInterpolationTimes(start, duration, texWidth);
}
```

8. Implement the `SetUniforms` function, which passes the vectors contained in the
   `Crowd` class to the crowd shader as uniform arrays:

```
void Crowd::SetUniforms(Shader* shader) {
    Uniform<vec3>::Set(shader->GetUniform("model_pos"),
                    mPositions);
    Uniform<quat>::Set(shader->GetUniform("model_rot"),
                    mRotations);
    Uniform<vec3>::Set(shader->GetUniform("model_scl"),
                    mScales);
    Uniform<ivec2>::Set(shader->GetUniform("frames"),
                    mFrames);
    Uniform<float>::Set(shader->GetUniform("time"),
                    mTimes);
}
```

Using the Crowd class should be intuitive: create a crowd, set the playback times and model transforms of its actors, and draw the crowd. In the next section, you will explore an example of how the Crowd class can be used to draw a large crowd.

Using the Crowd class

Using the Crowd class should be intuitive, but the rendering code might not be immediately obvious. The non-instance uniforms of the crowd shader, such as the view or projection matrices, still need to be set manually. The only uniforms that the Set function of the Crowd class sets are the per-actor uniforms.

Instead of rendering with the Draw method of the Mesh class, render using the DrawInstanced method. For the number of instances argument, pass the size of the crowd. The following code snippet shows a minimal example of how a crowd can be drawn:

```
void Render(float aspect) {
    mat4 projection = perspective(60.0f, aspect, 0.01f, 100);
    mat4 view=lookAt(vec3(0,15,40), vec3(0,3,0), vec3(0,1,0));

    mCrowdShader->Bind();
    int viewUniform = mCrowdShader->GetUniform("view")
    Uniform<mat4>::Set(viewUniform, view);
    int projUniform = mCrowdShader->GetUniform("projection")
    Uniform<mat4>::Set(projUniform, projection);
    int lightUniform = mCrowdShader->GetUniform("light");
    Uniform<vec3>::Set(lightUniform, vec3(1, 1, 1));
    int invBind = mCrowdShader->GetUniform("invBindPose");
    Uniform<mat4>::Set(invBind, mSkeleton.GetInvBindPose());
    int texUniform = mCrowdShader->GetUniform("tex0");
    mDiffuseTexture->Set(texUniform, 0);
    int animTexUniform = mCrowdShader->GetUniform("animTex");
    mCrowdTexture->Set(animTexUniform, 1);
    mCrowd.SetUniforms(mCrowdShader);
    int pAttrib = mCrowdShader->GetAttribute("position");
    int nAttrib = mCrowdShader->GetAttribute("normal");
    int tAttrib = mCrowdShader->GetAttribute("texCoord");
    int wAttrib = mCrowdShader->GetAttribute("weights");
    int jAttrib = mCrowdShader->GetAttribute("joints");
    mMesh.Bind(pAttrib, nAttrib, uAttrib, wAttrib, jAttrib);
    mMesh.DrawInstanced(mCrowd.Size());
    mMesh.UnBind(pAttrib, nAttrib, uAttrib, wAttrib, jAttrib);
    mCrowdTexture->UnSet(1);
```

```
    mDiffuseTexture->UnSet(0);
    mCrowdShader->UnBind();
}
```

For the most part, the code looks similar to a regular skinned mesh. That is because the instance-specific uniforms are set by the `SetUniforms` function of the `Crowd` class. Every other uniform is set the same way as before. In the next section, you will explore how two animations can be blended in the vertex shader.

In this section, you created a `Crowd` class, which provides an easy-to-use interface so that you can set the uniforms required by the `Crowd` shader. A demonstration of how the `Crowd` class can be used to render a large crowd was also covered.

Blending animations

It is possible to blend between two animations in a vertex shader. There are two reasons why you may would want to avoid blending between animations in a vertex shader. First, doing so will double the amount of texel fetches, which will make the shader more expensive.

This explosion of texel fetches happens because you would have to retrieve two copies of the pose matrices – one for each animation – and then blend between them. The shader code for doing so might look like the following code snippet:

```
    mat4 pose0a = GetPose(animTexA, joints.x, instance);
    mat4 pose1a = GetPose(animTexA, joints.y, instance);
    mat4 pose2a = GetPose(animTexA, joints.z, instance);
    mat4 pose3a = GetPose(animTexA, joints.w, instance);

    mat4 pose0b = GetPose(animTexB, joints.x, instance);
    mat4 pose1b = GetPose(animTexB, joints.y, instance);
    mat4 pose2b = GetPose(animTexB, joints.z, instance);
    mat4 pose3b = GetPose(animTexB, joints.w, instance);

    mat4 pose0 = pose0a * (1.0 - fade) + pose0b * fade;
    mat4 pose1 = pose1a * (1.0 - fade) + pose1b * fade;
    mat4 pose2 = pose2a * (1.0 - fade) + pose2b * fade;
    mat4 pose3 = pose3a * (1.0 - fade) + pose3b * fade;
```

The other reason is that the blend isn't technically correct. The shader is doing linear blending in world space. The resulting blended skeleton will look good but won't be the same as if the joints were interpolated in local space.

If you're cross-fading between two poses, the blend is short and is only meant to hide the transition. In most cases, whether or not the transition is technically correct won't matter as much as the transition looking smooth. In the next section, you will explore using alternate texture formats.

Exploring texture formats

Animation textures are currently stored in the 32-bit floating-point texture format. This is an easy format to store animation textures in because it's the same format as the source data. This method won't work well on mobile hardware. The memory bandwidth from main memory to tiler memory is a scarce resource.

To target mobile platforms, consider changing from `GL_RGBA32F` to `GL_RGBA` with a `GL_UNSIGNED_BYTE` storage type. Switching to a standard texture format does mean losing some data. With a `GL_UNSIGNED_BYTE` storage type, each component of a color is limited to 256 unique values. These values are normalized when sampling and will be returned in a 0 to 1 range.

If any of the animation information stores values are not in the 0 to 1 range, the data will need to be normalized. The normalization scale factor will need to be passed to the shader as a uniform. If you are targeting mobile hardware, you probably only want to store rotation information anyway, which is already in the 0 to 1 range.

In the next section, you will explore how multiple animation textures can be combined into a single texture. This reduces the number of textures that need to be bound for a crowd to play multiple animations.

Combining animation textures

The act of combining many smaller textures into one larger texture is called atlasing. A large texture that contains multiple smaller textures is often called a texture atlas. The benefit of atlasing textures is needing to use fewer texture samplers.

The crowd rendering system presented in this chapter has one major drawback: while the crowd can play animations at different time offsets, they can only play the same animation. There is an easy way to work around this: atlas multiple animation textures onto one large texture.

A *1024x1024* texture, for example, can contain 16 smaller *256x256* textures. This means any member of the crowd could play 1 of 16 animations. An additional "offset" uniform has to be added to the per-instance data of the shader. This offset uniform would be an array of `MAX_INSTANCES` size.

For each character being rendered, the `GetPose` function would have to apply the offset before retrieving the animation texels. In the next section, you will explore different techniques that you can use to optimize the crowd shader by minimizing texel fetches.

Optimizing texel fetches

Even on a gaming PC, rendering over 200 crowd characters will take more than 4 milliseconds, which is a pretty long time, assuming you have a 16.6 ms frame time. So, why is crowd rendering so expensive?

Every time the `GetPose` helper function is called, the shader performs 6 texel fetches. Since each vertex is skinned to four influences, that's 24 texel fetches per vertex! Even with a low poly model, that is a lot of texel fetches. Optimizing this shader will boil down to minimizing the number of texel fetches.

The following sections present different strategies you can use to minimize the number of texel fetches per vertex.

Limiting influences

A naive way to optimize texel fetches would be to add a branch to the shader code. After all, if the weight of the matrix is 0, why bother getting the pose? This optimization could be implemented as follows:

```
mat4 pose0 = (weights.x < 0.0001)?
    mat4(1.0) : GetPose(joints.x, instance);
mat4 pose1 = (weights.y < 0.0001)?
    mat4(1.0) : GetPose(joints.y, instance);
mat4 pose2 = (weights.z < 0.0001)?
    mat4(1.0) : GetPose(joints.z, instance);
mat4 pose3 = (weights.w < 0.0001)?
    mat4(1.0) : GetPose(joints.w, instance);
```

In the best-case scenario, this might save a little bit of time. In the worst-case scenario (where every bone has exactly four influences), this will actually add an extra cost to the shader since now, every influence comes with a conditional branch.

A better way to limit texel fetches would be to limit bone influences. 3DCC tools such as Blender, 3DS Max, or Maya have export options to limit the maximum number of bone influences per vertex. You should limit the maximum number of bone influences to 1 or 2.

Generally, in a large crowd, it's hard to make out the fine details on individual actors. Because of this, lowering the bone influences to 1, effectively rigid skinning the crowd, is often doable. In the next section, you will explore how limiting the number of animated components can help reduce the number of texel fetches per vertex.

Limiting animated components

Consider an animated human character. Human joints only rotate; they never translate or scale. If you know that an animation is only animating one or two components per joint, the GetPose function can be edited to sample less data.

There is an added benefit here: the number of bones that can be encoded into an animation texture increases. If you're encoding the position, rotation, and scale, the maximum number of joints is texture size / 3. If you are encoding just one component, the number of joints that can be encoded is the size of the texture.

This optimization will make a *256x256* texture able to encode 256 rotations instead of 85 transforms. In the next section, you will explore whether interpolation between frames is needed or not.

Not interpolating

Consider the animation texture. It samples the animation in set increments to fill out every column of the texture. At 256 samples, you can encode 3.6 seconds of animation at 60 FPS.

Whether or not interpolation is needed will depend on the size of the animation texture and the length of the animation being encoded. For most in-game character animations such as run, walk, attach, or die, interpolation doesn't need frame interpolation.

With this optimization, the amount of data that's sent to the GPU is greatly reduced. The frames uniform can change from an ivec2 to an int, cutting the size of the data in half. This means that the time uniform can go away completely.

In the next section, you will explore what the combined effect of the three optimizations that you just learned about is.

Combining these optimizations

Let's explore the impact that these optimizations can have, assuming all three of the following optimizations are implemented:

- Limit the number of bone influences to 2.

- Only animate the rotation component of the transform.

- Do not interpolate between frames.

This will have reduced the number of texel fetches from 24 per vertex to just 2 per vertex. The number of joints that can be encoded into an animation texture will increase, and the amount of data that is transferred to the GPU each frame will be reduced considerably.

Summary

In this chapter, you learned how to encode animation data to textures, as well as how to interpret the data in a vertex shader. Several strategies for improving performance by changing how the animation data is encoded were also covered. This technique of writing data into a texture can be used to bake any kind of sampled data.

To bake an animation, you need to clip out into a texture. This clip was sampled at set intervals. The global position of every bone was recorded at each interval and written to a texture. In this animation texture, every joint takes up three rows: one for position, one for rotation, and one for scale.

You rendered the crowd mesh using instancing and created a shader that can read per-instance data from uniform arrays. Per instance-data for actors of the crowd, such as position, rotation, and scale, were passed to the shader as uniform arrays and interpreted using the instance ID as an index into those arrays.

Finally, you created the `Crowd` class. This utility class provides an easy-to-use interface for managing actors in a crowd. This class will automatically populate the per-instance uniform of the crowd shader. Using this class, you can easily create large, interesting crowds.

There are two samples for this chapter in the downloadable content of this book. `Sample00` is all the code we wrote in this chapter. `Sample01`, on the other hand, demonstrates how to use this code to render large crowds in practice.

Other Books You May Enjoy

If you enjoyed this book, you may be interested in these other books by Packt:

Beginning C++ Game Development, Second Edition

John Horton

ISBN: 978-1-83864-857-2

- Set up your game development project in Visual Studio 2019 and explore C++ libraries such as SFML Explore C++ OOP by building a Pong game

- Understand core game concepts such as game animation, game physics, collision detection, scorekeeping, and game sound

- Use classes, inheritance, and references to spawn and control thousands of enemies and shoot rapid-fire machine guns

- Add advanced features to your game using pointers, references, and the STL Scale and reuse your game code by learning modern game programming design patterns

Blender 3D By Example - Second Edition

Oscar Baechler, Xury Greer

ISBN: 978-1-78961-256-1

- Explore core 3D modeling tools in Blender such as extrude, bevel, and loop cut

- Understand Blender's Outliner hierarchy, collections, and modifiers

- Find solutions to common problems in modeling 3D characters and designs

- Implement lighting and probes to liven up an architectural scene using EEVEE

- Produce a final rendered image complete with lighting and post-processing effects

- Learn character concept art workflows and how to use the basics of Grease Pencil

- Learn how to use Blender's built-in texture painting tools

Leave a review - let other readers know what you think

Please share your thoughts on this book with others by leaving a review on the site that you bought it from. If you purchased the book from Amazon, please leave us an honest review on this book's Amazon page. This is vital so that other potential readers can see and use your unbiased opinion to make purchasing decisions, we can understand what our customers think about our products, and our authors can see your feedback on the title that they have worked with Packt to create. It will only take a few minutes of your time, but is valuable to other potential customers, our authors, and Packt. Thank you!

Index

Made in the USA
Coppell, TX
23 July 2020